D1633042

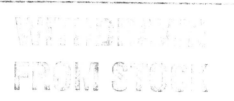
CRISIS IN THE
GLOBAL ECONOMY

SEMIOTEXT(E) ACTIVE AGENTS SERIES

Originally published as: *Crisi dell'economia globale. Mercati finanziari, lotte sociali e nuovi scenari politici.* Copyright © 2009 Ombre Corte.

Published by Semiotext(e)
2007 Wilshire Blvd., Suite 427, Los Angeles, CA 90057
www.semiotexte.com

Special thanks to John Ebert.

Cover art by Moyra Davey, *Copperhead No. 40*, 1990
Courtesy: Moyra Davey and Murray Guy Gallery.
Design by Hedi El Kholti

ISBN: 978-1-58435-087-3
Distributed by The MIT Press, Cambridge, Mass. and London, England
Printed in the United States of America

CRISIS IN THE GLOBAL ECONOMY

FINANCIAL MARKETS, SOCIAL STRUGGLES, AND NEW POLITICAL SCENARIOS

Edited by Andrea Fumagalli and Sandro Mezzadra

Translated by Jason Francis Mc Gimsey

Postface by Antonio Negri

\<e\>

Contents

Sandro Mezzadra

Introduction

1. The passion for knowledge, the impatient desire to understand the world in order to change it: certainly there is also a lot of "reason" in UniNomade, particularly in this volume that inaugurates its book series. But it is the "emotional temperature" of the discussions that animate the network that constitute its principle "added value." For four years now (the first UniNomade seminar, dedicated to "War and Democracy," was held in Padua on January 29th and 30th, 2005),[1] at least three generations of researchers and activists raised in the footsteps of the tradition of Italian *workerism*[2] periodically meet in seminars which see the participation of hundreds of people. Europe and social networking, the new forms assumed by the metropolis and governance, the "Institutions of the Common," the relations between contemporary art and activism, the metamorphoses of labor and those of the university; these are some of the themes that have been addressed over these last few years in a continuous dialogue with analogous experiences that are going on in five different continents.

Our point of departure is the awareness that we live in an era in which the very statute of knowledges is being radically modified, imposing (as the latest "Anomalous Wave" movement in Italy has demonstrated in an extraordinarily effective way) a rethinking of the relation between knowledge production and classic (academic and political) institutional spaces that had previously enjoyed a monopoly over it.[3] When knowledge—not only "technical" knowledge but "humanistic" knowledge too—becomes an immediately productive force, the critique of knowledges is nothing other than the critique of the political economy. When universities become essential nodes of metropolitan production, lingering over the defense of their "liberty" in a traditional sense isn't worth while. When the most fundamental conflicts in the development of class struggle are carried out on the terrain of knowledges, there is no party that can vindicate a primacy in the production of theory and the privileges of the "battle of ideas" are no longer reserved to "organic intellectuals."

We are schematically and problematically alluding to prodigious transformations here. We don't have any simple solutions to propose, only a sense of urgency and the conviction that it is necessary to create new spaces and new institutions within which uncharted relations between knowledge production, political practices and struggle development can be explored. UniNomade is a first step in this direction: seminar participation and project construction with hundreds of social movement activists, not as subjects "to be educated" but as full fledged protagonists, is therefore a qualifying element of the experience that we have lived over these last few years and that we will continue living, expanding and making evermore effective in the near future. A book series, which this work inaugurates is the first tool that we are adopting to extend the area of our discussion, to enter in a more direct and incisive way into public debate in order to look for interlocutors and allies.

We come, as we've said, from the great tradition of revolutionary Italian *workerism*, and our work is collocated within what is now, in the international debate, referred to with the certainly insufficient but also somewhat effective term *"post-workerism."* We nevertheless feel the need to question our own theoretic tools and to be open to discussion with other currents and with other theoretic practices that have contributed to the critical comprehension of the present in the last few years: from postcolonial studies to the most recent developments in feminism, from the reflections in new media studies to the frontiers of political philosophy, only to name a few. From a political point of view, our discussion proposal moves over 360°. We hold dear the science—and consequently the reasonableness—of subversion and don't hesitate to define ourselves, once and for all, as revolutionaries. But our theoretic and political work is not fed by empty formulas. We are interested in struggles and people that live and suffer, that build joy and cooperation in their endeavors. We would like to dialogue with these people, without asking for identification or membership cards. Only those who have nothing to say over the present quarrel about a presumed glorious heredity of the past: this is not our case.

2. The first book of the UniNomade series could only be dedicated to the global crisis in which we are living. Two seminars prepared it, the first held at the University of Bologna in the Department of Politics, Institutions and History and at the Social Center *TPO*[4] on the 12th and 13th of September 2008, and the second in Rome at the Faculty of Philosophy at the Sapienza University and at the squatted *Atelier ESC* on January 31st and February 1st of this year. But this volume doesn't merely present the papers of these two seminars: it is much more, it is the result of a collective discussion that developed over many long months and a series of other meetings held in Italy, Spain, Switzerland, Brazil and France that

involved—other than the authors of the contributions published here—innumerable social activists. A choral contemplation, therefore, only partially synthesized in the "10 Theses" that conclude this volume.

A deep conviction guided our work over these last months, under the immanent chronicle of the crisis: that which we are experiencing is a new type of crisis that is investing the whole figure of capitalism renewed from the great crisis of the '70s—beginning with the declaration of the inconvertibility of the dollar that, inaugurating in August of 1971 the regime of flexible exchange, essentially proposed to disengage the monetary system from the wage struggles of the multinational mass worker. We well know—having learned from Fernand Braudel and the theoreticians of the World System Theory—that "financialization" is not a new phenomenon. We know, for example, the importance of financial expansion that had as its epicenter the capitalist enclave of northern Italy between the end of the 14th and the beginning of the 15th century, in which "the agents of the first systemic cycle of accumulation formed and the principle characteristics of all the successive financial expansions were prefigured."[5]

However, we are convinced that in our age, independently from what we can say about our past, the thesis, central in the work of Giovanni Arrighi for example, that "systemic cycles of accumulation" are constituted by phases of "financial expansion" that are followed by phases of "material expansion" is no longer valid.[6] What seems evident, and that in particular is argued in detail in Christian Marazzi's and Andrea Fumagalli's pieces, is finance's pervasive character in a capitalism that has assumed a radically new character in the last decades to the point where the very distinction between "real economy" and "financial economy" (between "material expansion" and "financial expansion") is today unfounded from an analytic profile in the first place.

It is a problem that regards our historical comprehension of what capitalist production was and is. By now we've learned, based on an ample foundation of historiographic studies, that a capitalism before the industrial revolution existed, a "preindustrial capitalism" with an essentially commercial base. Hence, the possibility that a "postindustrial" capitalism exists is evident and some of the contributions published in this volume provisorily propose to define it as "cognitive capitalism" or "biocapitalism." More important than the pertinence of these terminologies, however, is the problem that they pose, particularly in reference to the role of finance. In an important work published in 1909, Rudolf Hilferding analyzed, based on two key phenomenons of his times (the development of shareholding companies and mixed banks of German-style industrial credit), the transformations that finance was undergoing at the culmination of the process set in motion by the industrial revolution, from the historical caesura with which capitalism made itself industrial.[7] Our conviction is that finance must be investigated today in the same prospective method, which is to say, considering the transformations that have shaped it over the last decades, as symptomatic of an analogous epochal caesura.

3. Let's get things straight, once and for all. When we talk about a radical transformation in the modes of capitalist production, of a capitalism that is no longer "industrial," we are far from negating the importance (that, in a certain sense, is ever growing) that industrial production and labor continue to have on both a global level and in our own territories. Instead, we are insisting on the fact that this production and this labor are progressively "articulated" in

(and commanded by) valorization and accumulation processes of capital that function according to a logic that differs from "industrial" logic.[8] We'd like to call attention to the fact that these processes are increasingly extended over the backdrop of the exploitation and "capturing" of the productivity of abstract and common resources—from knowledge to *bios*, from social cooperation to what Carlo Vercellone defines as "man's production for man." The hybridization between financial capitalism and the sociality of the web 2.0 described by Tiziana Terranova in her piece represents an extraordinarily suggestive exemplification of this new condition. Again, it is on this basis that the thesis of the "becoming rent of profit," presented in this volume by Vercellone and, in the postface by Antonio Negri, must be read.

This thesis results in enormous problems for the definition, on a global level where capital's valorization and accumulation are determined, of what class composition means today. While many contributions take up the category of "multitude" to this proposal, Karl Heinz Roth, in a text originally published in the site of "Wildcat" magazine,[9] suggests reasoning around the formula of a "multiverse, in continual transformation, of the world working class."[10] This seems like a very interesting proposal both from an analytic and a political perspective: here we'd simply like to underline how it also emerges from a productive confrontation with a "global labor history" that has profoundly modified, over the last few years, the historical studies on the proletariat and the working class. It is a long-term prospective, at the same time capable—as Roth writes—of emancipating itself from the narrowness of a "national and eurocentric" point of view, in particular allowing for the redefinition of the debates on labor "precariousness" and "flexibility" and of liberating them from the mirage of a "normal work relation" (a permanent contract tied to a series of "social rights") that in reality is constructed on the characteristics of "Fordism" in the West. However, if it is considered from within the long global history of the mode of capitalist production, it appears much more "exceptional" than "normal."[11] It is worthy of noting, once again, that this is a fundamental question from a political as well as historical and analytic point of view.

On the other hand, there is a question, like many others raised in this volume, that problematically summons a few fundamental concepts forged in the same theoretical laboratory as Italian *operaismo*. We have hinted at it elsewhere in respect to the relation between the "formal subsumption" and "real subsumption" of labor to capital, and the relation between "absolute surplus value" and "relative surplus value"[12] (Antonio Negri addresses the question here, developing it in the realm of revenue analysis). Generally, it is the relation determined between struggle and development as well as between cycle and crisis that doesn't seem to hold up anymore when Carlo Vercellone's discourse on the exhaustion of capital's progressive virtue is taken seriously. In the same method of tendency, the most precious heredity of historic *workerism* must be consequently re-calibrated to the rhythms of a capitalistic development that now appears to register itself in the crisis as its own definitive horizon.

4. Here, too, we should explain further. The idea of re-exhuming a hypothesis of "collapse" is far from our intentions. Capital is crisis, and it can survive in crisis for centuries... Nor can it be taken for granted that after capitalism something better will follow. We are, in any case, inclined to think along with Walter Benjamin, that "capitalism will not die a natural death."[13] What we are reasoning

through is a mutation of the "temporal coordinates" of capitalism (which means, in the first place, of the modes in which capital attempts to organize the time and the lives of the men and women that are subject to its command and that live the reality of exploitation) not any less radical than what has effected its "spatial coordinates" in the current global situation. In particular, we attempt to derive some consequences from the point of view of the political categories with which the crisis must be read. If Andrea Fumagalli underlines the problematic nature of every "reformist" stabilization of contemporary capitalist development, Christian Marazzi and Bernard Paulré, initiating a productive dialogue with the recent literature on the crisis put forth by the French Regulation School, touch on the contortions that the category of governance undergoes in this crisis.

Other considerations could be added from the point of view of the transformation of the concepts and the political problems that emerge from the analysis of the crisis. For example, one could think at length about the vicissitudes of a classic concept of modern politics, that of "public opinion," that—at least since Chapter XII of John Maynard Keynes' *General Theory*[14]—we have learned to investigate in the stock markets. What is the role of public opinion in a situation in which, nearly evoking a "readability" crisis (capital's incapacity to read the composition of labor on whose exploitation it depends), opinion is found to operate within what Tiziana Terranova defines as a "cloud of data"? But again, to briefly and stenographically touch upon a fundamental theme affronted by Stefano Lucarelli and Federico Chicchi in this volume: how can we rigorously define the metamorphoses of power and of the very figure of subjectivity to which the described transformations correspond?

What we would conclusively like to mention is, however, another point: the exact sense that altogether emerges from this book of the risks and opportunities that the crisis presents. The (explicitly racist) attack against migrant conditions that has been underway in Italy in these last few months is a first taste of these risks, and for which precise confirmations could be found in other countries in the world.[15] Then, in the background, there are great geopolitical and monetary tensions described by Christian Marazzi, with the specter of war (those underway and those that are being prepared) always present on the horizon. On the whole, however, the contributions that we present here indicate fundamental areas for social struggles that are opened in the crisis and that actually reveal the possibility of working towards a positive way out. A way out of the crisis, that is, in the direction of constructing a new common terrain where we can reinvent equality and liberty, that constitutes, and will continue to constitute, the guiding thread of UniNomade: the struggles for income and wages and the battles for welfare, in particular, appear completely re-qualified in this crisis. They constitute the privileged area in which to experiment with the synthesis of an unprejudiced use of reformism, aware of its structural limits and reopening a revolutionary prospective that, with different but convergent languages, Karl Heinz Roth's article and Antonio Negri's postface invite us to think about.

Christian Marazzi

The Violence of Financial Capitalism

1. The Becoming of the Crisis

Before interpreting the crisis of financial capitalism, it would be useful to summarize some facts about the macroeconomic and global financial situation that has been emerging for more than a year, as a result of the real estate and banking bubble. Let us say from the outset, citing an article by Martin Wolf, an intelligent supporter of liberal globalization in the *Financial Times*,[1] that, although necessary, the dramatic increase of the American federal deficit and the expansion of credit from Central Banks all over the world will have *temporary* effects, but will not be able to restore normal and lasting rates of development. It is thus possible that over the course of 2009 and beyond we will witness the succession of a false recovery, a hiccuping movement in stock exchange followed by repetitive downfalls and subsequent interventions of governments attempting to contain the crisis. In short, we are confronted by a systemic crisis requiring "radical changes" that, at least for the time being, no one can really prescribe in a convincing manner. The monetary policy, even if it has some efficacy in improving economies during recessions, is entirely ineffective when it enters into a depressive crisis like the one we are going through. The reason is that in a crisis like the present one, which in some sense resembles what Japan experienced in the 1990s, the transmission channels of monetary interventions (reduction of interest rate, insertion of liquidity, interventions in the exchange rate, increase in the banking reserve funds) are beside the point. That is, they cannot transmit the credit impulses to companies and domestic economies necessary to revive the consumption. The difference being that, in the case of Japan, the bubble burst had depressive effects on investments in capital, which up until the 1980s represented 17% of Gross Domestic Product, while the crisis that broke out in the United States had direct effects on 70% of GDP resulting from the consumption in the domestic American economies. Given that "the US consumer is by far the most important consumer in the world, the global implications of America's post-bubble shakeout are likely to be far more severe than those Japan was subjected to."[2]

On the basis of a study by Carmen Reinhart from Maryland University and Kenneth Rogoff from Harvard, we see in what way this crisis is by far the deepest in the last decades.[3] Banking crises like this one, as the authors note in retrospect, last at least for two years with severe drops in GDP. The collapses in the stock markets are profound, with an average fall in real prices of real estate assets equaling 35% over the span of 6 years and a 55% decline in prices of non-real estate assets over 3–4 years. The unemployment rate, always averaged, rose by 7% in 4 years, while the output decreased by 9%. Moreover, the real value of public debt increased, on average, by 86% and this is only in small part due to the cost of bank recapitalization. Instead, it largely depends on the collapse of tax revenues.

An important difference between this crisis and the ones in the recent past is that the present one is a *global* crisis and not regional, like the others. Until, like in the past, the rest of the world is in the position of being able to finance the US, we can anticipate a containment of the crisis on a regional scale, to the extent that the American government can take advantage of a vast program of tax and monetary stimuli financed by the countries in surplus of saving from the purchase of American Treasury bills. But who today can help the US in the long run? The present difficulty consists in the fact that, being global, the crisis broke the very force that allowed the global economy to grow, albeit in an unequal way, over the last decades; i.e., the flux of demand from the countries in the structural deficit of production (like the US) to the countries in structural surplus (like China today and Japan yesterday). But when private spending collapses on a global scale, the efforts to increase the American demand no longer suffice. Actions to revive the demand on a global scale are required, which is to say even in the emerging countries with a surplus of production. At the moment, it does not seem that the emerging countries can compensate for the loss of demand internal to the developed countries (the so-called *decoupling*), since for them the crisis has particularly heavy depressive effects as well. Nonetheless, according to the estimate of the World Bank, it cannot be excluded that, at least in the medium range (2010–2015) and with important differences between China, India, Russia, and South American countries, the growth rates will continue at an average of 4–5%. This possibility depends on the fact that of the total of exports in the emerging countries (which averaged 35% of GDP in the emerging countries over the last 5 years) only 20% are exports to the developed countries, while 15% results from internal exchanges between the block of the emerging countries.[4] In any case, in order to be able to pull the world demand, the emerging countries must—besides raising internal wages—channel their savings no longer towards the Western countries in deficit, but towards the internal demand, which robs the global monetary and financial circuit of the same mechanism that allowed the global economy to function despite, even by virtue of, profound structural imbalances. It is thus possible that, *after the crisis*, the emerging countries will become the hegemonic economic force in which the savings of the developed countries will be invested, thereby inverting flows of capital and somewhat reducing the level of consumption in the developed countries. But no one can foresee the *duration* of this crisis and, therefore, the political, in addition to economic, capacity to manage the cumulative multiplication of social and political contradictions that are already manifesting themselves.

Thus, the least we can do is focus our attention on the trend of demand in the advanced deficit countries, particularly in the US. If we take into account that, in the US, between the third quarter of 2007 and the third quarter of 2008, the fall of demand in private credit equaled 13%, it is certain that the net saving, and not just in the US, is destined to remain positive for several years. In other words, private citizens will do everything to reduce their private debts, which can only annul the monetary actions for the revival of private consumption. Assuming for a moment a financial surplus (that is, lack of consumption) in the private sector of 6% of GDP and a structural deficit in the commercial balance of 4% of GDP, the tax deficit necessary to compensate for the reduction of internal and external demand would have to be, according to Wolf's estimate in the cited article, equal to 10% of GDP—"*indefinitely*"! Reducing public debts of such a scale entails enormous efforts, especially if we take into account that already today the federal American deficit moves around 12% of GDP—at the levels of

WWII. As if this were not enough, we should not forget that the obstacles to debt redemption for companies caused by the effect linked with nominal interest rates tending to zero and the reduction of prices (deflation): in situations of this kind, real interest rates are very high and debt repayment consequently becomes very challenging. It is precisely for this reason that a second wave of banking crises cannot be excluded. As Michael Aglietta writes, "If such is the situation, the banks are risking a second financial shock—return shock, one of the insolvent credits of companies. It is thus that an economic depression can propagate itself by reciprocal reinforcement of debt redemption in finance and economic deflation."[5]

According to Paul Krugman, the $825 billion of the economic stimulus program proposed by Obama is not even remotely sufficient to fill the "productivity gap" between the potential growth and effective growth of GDP at the time of the crisis:

> In the presence of an adequate demand for productive capacity, in the next two years America would be able to produce goods and services worth another $30 trillion. But with the downturn of consumption and investment, an enormous chasm is opening up between that which the American economy can produce and that which it can sell. And Obama's plan is not minimally adequate to fill in this productivity gap.[6]

Now, Krugman wonders, why is Obama not trying to do more? Certainly, there are dangers tied up with the government loan on the vast scale, "but the consequences of inadequate action are not much better than sliding into a prolonged deflationary trap, of the Japanese kind, an inevitable spiral if the actions of intervention are not adequate" (i.e., around $2.1 billion or trillion). Or, Krugman keeps wondering, is it the lack of spending opportunities that limits his plan? "There are only a limited number of shovel-ready projects for public investment, that is, of projects which can be initiated rapidly enough to succeed in the short-term boost of economy. Nonetheless, there are other forms of public spending, especially in the field of health care, which can create assets and at the same time foster the economy at the time of need." Yet again, is there an element of political prudence behind Obama's decision, i.e., the attempt to remain within the limit of a trillion dollars for the economic plan's final cost to ensure the support of the Republicans.[7]

Obama's plan is 60% made up by public spending (health care, investments in infrastructures and education, aids to homeowners risking foreclosure) and 35% by tax reductions. Joseph Stiglitz, in his interview in the *Financial Times*[8] has, however, urged not to squander the stimulus on tax breaks, which, in this crisis, are doomed for a sure failure. For example, only 50% of the tax cut that came into effect in February 2008 increased spending, while the remaining part of the increase in available income was used to reduce private debts. Today a tax break would most likely be used almost completely to reduce the debts, except perhaps in the case of poor families with a high tendency to consumption. It would be much better, if one indeed wants to persist on the path of tax cuts, to limit the breaks of all companies to increases in investments, preferably if they are innovative. "Spending on infrastructure, education and technology create assets; they increase future productivity."

More in general, independently of the fact that the state stimuli result mainly from increases in discretionary expenditures, like in the US, or by the more or less automatic effects of an increase in social spending, like in Europe, the state governance of the crisis depends in the last analysis on the capacity to borrow capital from the bond market. The dimension of the issuance of public bonds scheduled for 2009 is sky-high: it goes from the estimated $2, maybe $2.5 billion in the US, equaling 14% of GDP, to $215 billion of bonds sold in England (10% of GDP), to issuances of significant amounts of bonds in every country of the world, including Germany, which also, at first, tried to resist tax stimuli of the Anglo-Saxon kind (initially accused of "crass Keynesianism" by chancellor Merkel).

The recourse to the bond markets on the part of the US in order to collect capital to cover the growing deficit should not, in principle, be a particular problem, especially in deflationary periods, like the one we are going through, characterized by continuous reductions in interest rates (which for investors in bonds means real fixed and relatively high earnings).

Nonetheless, the expectation of a fall in inflation in the markets and, consequently, a possible increase in state difficulties to honor debt services with growing fiscal entrances (normally induced by inflation), is already provoking an increase in real interest rates on T-bills, and this is also the case in the economically wealthiest countries. (In fact, international investors in public bonds demand substantially higher nominal and real earnings in order to better protect themselves against the risks of state defaults.) According to the analysts, as much as there are signals of economic bubble on the markets that can explain the distortion of prices, "it is nonetheless somewhat unsettling that real interest rates have risen as governments started to borrow."[9] For the countries like Spain, Greece, Ireland, and Italy, whose differential earnings in T-bills had been a little higher than those of Germany until 2007, (the problems with financing public deficits have been increasing) in an obvious way already since December 2008. Despite the ten years of the euro, the markets are working with precise distinctions between the risk countries within this very eurozone—a problem not easily resolvable by the recourse to the creation of a currency by member nations or by releasing union bonds, which would damage the strong countries in the eurozone. This again urgently raises the question of a real unification of state policies, particularly the social ones, within the EU.

In this phase, with few investors disposed to purchase public obligations in the face of an extremely high offer to issue public bonds, the risk of crowding out (of leaving the private bond market) is entirely real. The competition in bond markets between private companies and governments risks further inhibiting the overcoming of the crisis, to the extent that for the companies involved the issuance of bonds can become particularly costly. At this point, the States—as is already happening in the US with the support of the car companies—can be compelled to support private companies directly by purchasing their bonds, which would mean the beginning of a process of quasi-nationalization (without, however, the right to vote from the stockholder State) of non-financial companies, following the one that began in the banking and financial sector with the interventions of Central Banks in the last months. If then, as a hypothesis, the world economy were to start up again, the inverse process of crowding out, i.e., the withdrawal of public bonds towards the private ones, would significantly increase debt service in all the indebted countries.

The scenario in the forefront here is a massive and continuous increase in unemployment on a world scale, of a generalized reduction in incomes and rent, in the face of a vertiginous increase in comprehensive tax deficit. The "socialist turn" of liberal governments to sustain the banking, financial, and insurance system by means of recapitalization and (monetary issuances does not seem to be able to avoid chain bankruptcy of all insolvent decentralized banks as a result of an improbable quantity of toxic assets.) It is entirely likely that in two years the economies of all countries, despite the actions of the economic stimulus, will still be in depression (stag deflation), just as it is possible that each country will try to reintroduce in their native land the quotas of demand by means of devaluations and protectionist actions (deglobalization) in order to try to postpone as much as possible (the rendering of accounts by taxpayers called on to pay public deficits. The margins of economic and monetary policy to effectively manage the crisis are extremely restricted. The classical Keynesian actions lack transmission channels of state stimuli to the real economy, to the demand of goods and services, and investment goods. On the other hand, it makes little sense to speak of a new Bretton Woods without taking into account the profound transformations in the international monetary arrangement, the transformations that reflect the crisis of the national sovereignty resulting from globalization. If one instead wants to speak of a New Deal, i.e., of a process of supporting incomes, employment, and credit system at the "grassroots" level, it will then be necessary to analyze social forces, subjects, and forms of struggle that can substantiate in a politically innovative way the escape from the crisis.

2. Financial Logics

The process of financialization that led to the crisis we are living in now is distinguished from all other phases of financialization historically recorded in the twentieth century. The classical financial crises were situated at a precise moment of the economic cycle, particularly at the end of the cycle, in conjunction with a fall of profit testing as a result of capitalist competition on an international scale, in addition to social forces that undermine geopolitical equilibrium in the international division of labor. The typically twentieth-century financialization thus represented an attempt, in certain ways "parasitic" and "desperate," to recuperate on the financial markets that which capital could no longer capture in the real economy. The accumulation and specific centralization of the "capital bearer of interest," as Marx defined it in Volume III of Capital, also called "fictitious capital," managed primarily by banks with autonomous production of money by means of money, indeed epitomized one of the salient characteristics of the twentieth century financialization processes (and already pointed out by Marx over the course of the second half of the nineteenth century). The financial crises were thus based on a contradictory relationship between real and financial economies, a relationship that today is no longer expressed in the same terms.

Financial economy today is pervasive, that is, it spreads across the entire economic cycle, co-existing with it, so to speak, from start to finish. Today it is in the finances, to speak figuratively, even when one goes shopping at the supermarket, at the moment when one pays with a credit card. The car industry, to give only one example, functions completely in accordance with credit mechanisms (installments, leasing, etc), so that the problems of a General Motors have just as much to do with the production of cars as, if not above all, with the weakness of GMAC, its branch specializing in credit to consumption indispensable for selling their products to consumers. That is, we are in a historical period in which the finances are cosubstantial with the very production of goods and services/ In addition to industrial profits not reinvested in instrumental capitals and in wages, the sources fueling today's financialization have multiplied: there are profits deriving from the repatriation of dividends and royalties followed by direct investments from the outside, flows of interest coming from the Third World's debt, to which are added flows of interest on international bank loans to the emerging countries, surplus-values derived from raw materials, the sums accumulated by individuals and wealthy families and invested in the stock markets, retirement and investment funds. The multiplication and extension of the sources and agents of the "capital bearer of interest" are without a doubt one of the distinctive, unforeseen, and problematic traits of the new financial capitalism, especially if they reflect upon the possibility or impossibility of modifying this system, of "re-financing" it, reestablishing a "more balanced" relation between the real and financial economies.

Like its predecessors, this financialization also begins from a block of accumulation understood as non-reinvestment of profits in directly productive processes (constant capital, i.e., instrumental goods, and variable capital, i.e., wages). In fact, it began with the crisis of growth of Fordist capitalism since the 1960s. In those years, there were all the premises of a repetition of the classical financialization based on the dichotomy between real (industrial) and monetary economies, with the consequent seizing of profit quotas on the financial markets to ensure profitable growth without accumulation. In the beginning of the 1980s, "the primary source of financial bubbles was the trend of growth of non-accumulated profit, the growth caused by a double movement: on the one hand, a generalized decrease in wages and, on the other hand, the stagnation—i.e., decrease—of the rate of accumulation despite the reestablishment of profit rate."[10] For an accumulation rate implies the growth of the amount of net capital, while profit rate implies the relationship between profits and capital: the divergence between the two rates starting from 1980 represents a sure, but not the only, indication of financialization. But, as we said, to the non-reinvested industrial profits are gradually added other sources of "accumulation" of financial capital, a fact to keep in mind in order to understand the transformations of the model of post-Fordist crisis-development.

The transition from the Fordist mode of production to "stock managerial capitalism" which is at the basis of today's financial capitalism is in fact explained by the drop in profits (around 50%) between the 1960s and the 1970s due to the exhaustion of the technological and economic foundations of Fordism, particularly by the saturation of markets by mass consumption goods, the rigidity of productive processes, of constant capital, and of the politically "downwardly rigid" working wage. At the height of its development, in a determinate organic composition of capital (i.e., the relationship between constant and variable capital), Fordist capitalism was no longer able to "suck" surplus-value from living working labor.

> Hence, since the second half of the 1970s, the primary propulsive force of the world economy was the endless attempt of capitalist companies—demanded by their owners and investors—to bring back by different means the profit rate to the highest levels of twenty years ago.[11]

We know how it went: reduction in the cost of labor, attacks on syndicates, automatization and robotization of entire labor processes, delocalization in countries with low wages, precarization of work, and diversification of consumption models. And precisely financialization, i.e., increase in profits not as excess of cost proceeds (that is, not in accordance with manufacturing-Fordist logic) but as excess of value in the Stock Exchange "at the time T2 with respect to T1— where the gap between T1 and T2 can be a few days."

In fact, the recourse to the financial markets on the part of companies in order to reestablish profit testing has really never had anything to do with financing company activities by issuing new bonds—and this is because companies have always had wide margins of auto-financing. American companies, the companies in the largest shareholding country in the world, have used financing by the issuances of assets to supply only 1% of their needs; the German ones 2%. In other words, the financialization of economy has been a process of recuperation of capital's profitability after the period of decrease in profit testing, an apparatus to enhance capital's profitability *outside* immediately productive processes. It is this very apparatus that led companies to internalize in an "irresponsible" way the paradigm of shareholder value, the primacy of shareholder value over that of the multiplicity of "interest bearers"—the latter being called stakeholder value (wage earners, consumers, suppliers, environment, future generations). The (industrial) profit quota of the total income of companies, which in the 1960s and 1970s decreased in the US from 24% to 15–17%, has never since exceeded 14–15% and financialization is structuralized accordingly, becoming to all intents and purposes the modus operandi of contemporary capitalism.

As was shown on the basis of Greta Krippner's complete analysis of available data, the quota of total profits of American societies attributable to the financial, insurance, and real estate ones not only nearly reached in the 1980s, but then exceeded in the 1990s, the quota attributable to those in the manufacturing sector. Even more important is the fact that, in the 1970s and 1980s, the non-financial societies drastically increased their own investments in financial products with respect to industrial plants and machinery and became ever more dependent on the quota of income and profits derived from their own financial investments with respect to the one derived from their productive activity. Krippner's observation is that, within this tendency towards the financialization of the non-financial economy, the manufacturing sector is not only quantitatively predominant, but directly driving the process, is particularly significant.[12]

This is enough to definitively discard the distinction between (industrial) real and financial economies, distinguishing industrial profits from the "fictitious" financial ones. As well as to stop identifying, from either a theoretical or historical point of view, capitalism with industrial capitalism (as Arrighi writes, a typical act of faith of orthodox Marxism that does not deserve a justification). If one really wants to speak of the "irresponsible company" to describe the paradigm of shareholder value—indeed created within companies over the last thirty years—one would do well to speak of the transformation of the production process based on the "becoming-rent of profit," to use Carlo Vercellone's apt expression.[13]

There is no doubt that, in the post-Fordist configuration of financial capitalism where part of the wages are reduced and precarized and investments in capital stagnate, the problem of the *realization* of profits (that is, selling the surplus-value product) remains the role of consumption by means of *non-wage incomes*.

Under this *distributive* profile, the reproduction of capital (characterized by the extremely high polarization of wealth) is carried out partly thanks to the increase in the consumption of *rentiers* and partly thanks to the indebted consumption of wage earners. Financialization has redistributed, although in a strongly unequal and precarious way (if one thinks of retirement incomes derived from supplementary retirement funds in accordance with the primacy of contributions), financial incomes also to wage workers in the double form of non-real-estate and real estate incomes (in the US, 20% and 89% respectively). There is thus a kind of becoming-rent in addition to profit.

The indebtedness of domestic economies, to which corresponds a more or less pronounced reduction of savings according to whether one is in the US or Europe, is what allowed financial capitalism to reproduce itself on an enlarged and global scale. It is possible to affirm that, parallel to the reduction of the redistributive function of the social State, in this period it is assisted by a kind of privatization of deficit spending à la Keynes, i.e., the creation of an additional demand by means of private debt (with a relative displacement of wealth towards the private domestic economies). The explosion of private indebtedness was facilitated, especially after the collapse of Nasdaq in 2000–2002, by a very expansive monetary policy and banking deregulation, a policy that reinforced the securitization of debt-based obligations: Collaterized Debt Obligation and Collaterized Loan Obligations, to which are added Credit Default Swaps, derivative insurance obligations that are swapped (in fact, bartered) between operators in order to protect themselves against the risks of investment. The total of all these credit derivatives amounts to something like $62 trillion, a multiplication of 100 times in ten years.

Securitization allows one to reclaim from the balances of institutions or credit agencies (mortgage, but also credit card) the loans supplied by clients selling them to investment banks. The latter constitute a credit pool with differentiated risks (from good to less good) and on this basis issue assets, which are then ceded to the created ad hoc financial structures (called conduits and special vehicles) that finance the purchase price by short-term debts. Finally, bonds are placed with investors as hedge funds, investment banks, retirement and investment funds. This complex financial engineering, in its good nature, allows for the artificial increase of the total amount of credit (leverage), freeing the balances of the institutions from credit given in this way in order to enable them to create new loans. It is a question of a kind of multiplication of bread because the risk of a split between flows of bonds *qua* right to a part of created profit and flows of purely monetary interests and dividends is inherent in the multiplication of credit by means of securitization.

The American mortgage indebtedness, which reached more than 70% of GDP with a total indebtedness of domestic economies equaling 93% of GDP, has constituted the primary source of increase in consumption since 2000 and, since 2002, the motor of the real estate bubble. The consumption has been fueled by so-called remortgaging, the possibility of renegotiating mortgage loans in order to get new credit thanks to the inflationary increase in house prices. This mechanism, called home equity extraction, has played a fundamental role in economic American growth. The US Bureau of Economic Analysis has estimated that the gains from the GDP growth due to the increase in home equity extraction were, on average, 1.5% between 2002 and 2007. Without the positive impact of mortgage credit and the subsequent increase in consumption, the growth of American GDP would be equal to or outright less than that of the eurozone.[14]

Subprime loans demonstrate that (to grow and make profits finance needs to involve, other than the middle class, the poor too). To work, this capitalism must invest in the raw lives of people that cannot guarantee anything, that offer nothing if not themselves. It is a capitalism that makes raw life a source of profit) Moreover, finance functions on the expectation of growing and "infinite" increase in prices of real estate (wealth effect), an inflationary increase without which it would be impossible to co-opt the potential have-nots—the necessary condition of ensuring the continuity of financial profits. It is a question of a Ponzi scheme or an airplane game in which those who came in last allow those who came in first to be renumbered, as the hoax devised by the ex-president of Nasdaq, Bernard Madoff, teaches us, the hoax that managed to collect something like $50 billion involving an impressive number of respectable financial operators and banks.

The threshold of this inclusive process is given in the contradiction between social ownership of a good (such as a house) and private ownership rights, between the expansion of social needs and the private logic of markets. The social conflict as well as capital's capacity or incapacity to overcome this crisis unfolds on this threshold. It is a question of a *temporal threshold*, if only one thinks of, for example, the architecture of typical mortgage contracts on subprime loans. The formula of 2 + 28—where, in the first two years, mortgage interests are fixed and low, precisely for co-opting ever more "owners," and the other 28 years they are at variable rates, thus subjected to the general trend of conjuncture and of monetary policy—represents an example of the contradiction between social ownership rights and private ownership rights. After two years of relative governance of use-value (the right to the access to housing), we move on to 28 years of governance of exchange-value, with extremely violent effects of expulsion/exclusion. In such a way, the financial logic produces a *commune* (of goods) that then divides and privatizes through expelling "residents of the commune" by means of the artificial creation of *scarcity* of all kinds—scarcity of financial means, liquidity, rights, desire, and power. This is a process that reminds us of the time of the 17th century enclosures where the peasants—living on and off the land as a common good—were expunged by the processes of privatization and division of the common land, the processes that gave rise to the modern proletariat and its bare life.

Speaking of Spinoza and his resistance to the norm and the discipline of sovereignty, Augusto Illuminati highlights the decidedly juridical-normative nature of the processes of enclosures: Spinoza

> does not ignore the land, but his campaign is not circumscribed by the eighteenth century enclosures, fenced in by farming and hunting, where the sheep—to speak with the *Levellers*—devoured men, not by the land where men are reduced to inert sheep learning only to serve, because it is neither peace nor citizenship, but rather *solitude*, desert.[15]

The originary or primitive accumulation, as was shown by Sandro Mezzandra, i.e., the salarization and proletarization of millions of people like expulsion from the land, is thus a process that historically reemerges every time the expansion of capital clashes with the commune produced by social relations and cooperations free from the laws of capitalist exploitation.[16] The commune produced by free social relations thus *precedes* the capitalist appropriation of this very commune.

3. On the Becoming-Rent of Profit

The *non*-parasitic role of finance, (its capacity to produce incomes by ensuring the increase in consumption, the increase in effective demand necessary for GDP growth,) is, however, not explained only from the distributive point of view. It is indeed true that finance nourishes itself on the profit that is not accumulated, not reinvested in capital (constant and variable), and it is exponentially multiplied thanks to financial engineering, just as it is true that the increase in profits allows for the distribution of surplus-value quotas to the holders of patrimonial shares. Under this profile (*distributive*, let us repeat), the analysis of financialization and its intrinsic instability highlights real and indeed perverse processes of autonomization of financial capital from any collective interest (wage and occupational stability, the collapse of retirement rents and of savings invested in stock, the impossibility of accessing consumption in credit, the vaporization of stocks in research), dynamic autoreferentials where the search for ever-higher shareholder earnings generates the increase of fictitious profits by the proliferation of financial instruments—unmanageable because they are outside every rule and control. The crisis-development in this mode of production acquires a discrepancy between social needs and financial logics based on the hyper-profitability criteria: in the developed countries, it is asserted by the anthropogenic model of "production of man by man" where consumption is increasingly oriented towards social, health, educational, and cultural sectors, and clashes with the privatization of many sectors previously managed by public criteria; in the emerging countries, the expansion of valorization spaces provokes processes of hyper-exploitation and the destruction of local economies and environment. The demands of profitability imposed by financial capitalism on the entire society reinforce social regression under high pressure of a growth model that, in order to distribute wealth, voluntarily sacrifices social cohesion and the quality of life itself. Wage deflation, pathologization of labor with increases in health costs generated by work stress (up to 3% of GDP), worsening of social balances, and the irreparable deterioration of the environment are the effects of financial logic and of shareholder delocalizations typical of global financial capitalism.

The *problem* is that, analyzed from a distributive point of view (economistic in the last instance), the crisis-development of financial capitalism leads to a veritable dead-end. As it is thrown out the window, i.e., the common place of a kind that is parasitic on finance, it implicitly reenters through the main door. The *impasse*, more theoretical than practical-political, is before everyone's eyes: the impossibility of elaborating strategies to overcome the crisis, the recourse to actions of economic stimulus that, on the one hand, presuppose the rescue of finance (of which we are really hostages), but, on the other hand, annul the very possibilities of economic revival.

In order to overcome this impasse, it is necessary to analyze critically the crisis of financial capitalism, what it means to begin anew from scratch, i.e., from that increase in profits without accumulation that is at the root of financialization. Which is to say, it is necessary to analyze financialization as the other side of a process of the value *production* affirmed since the crisis of the Fordist model, i.e., since the capitalist incapacity to suck surplus-value from immediate living labor, the wage labor of the factory. *The thesis that is being put forth here is that financialization is not an unproductive/parasitic deviation of growing quotas of surplus-value and collective saving, but rather the form of capital accumulation symmetrical with new processes of value production.*

Today's financial crisis will then be interpreted more as a *block* of capital accumulation than an implosive result of a process of lacking capital accumulation.

Apart from the role of finance in the sphere of consumption, what happened in these last 30 years is a veritable metamorphosis of production processes of this very surplus-value. There has been a transformation of valorization processes that witnesses the extraction of value no longer circumscribed in the places dedicated to the production of goods and services, but, so to speak, extending beyond factory gates, in the sense that it enters directly into the sphere of the *circulation* of capital, that is, in the sphere of exchanges of goods and services. It is a question of extending the processes of extracting value from the sphere of reproduction and distribution—a phenomenon, let it be noted, for a long time well known to women. Ever more explicitly, in the center of both theory and managerial strategies, one speaks of the *externalization* of production processes, even of "crowdsourcing," i.e., putting to use the crowd and its forms of life.[17]

To analyze financial capitalism under this productive profile is to speak of bio-economy or of biocapitalism,

> whose form is characterized by its growing entanglement with the lives of human beings. In its precedence, capitalism resorted primarily to the functions of transformation of raw materials carried out by machines and the bodies of the workers. Instead of this, biocapitalism produces value by extracting it not only from the body functioning as the material instrument of work, but also from the body understood in its globality.[18]

In our analysis of the financial crisis, the reference to the whole of the studies and theories of biocapitalism and cognitive capitalism developed in these years is of a merely methodological kind: here we are more interested in highlighting the link between financialization and the processes of value production that is at the basis of the crisis-development of new capitalism than in an accurate and exhaustive description of its salient characteristics (moreover, already accomplished by a growing number of scholars).[19]

The empirical examples of externalization of value production, of its extension into the sphere of circulation are now abundant.[20] From the first phase of shareholder outsourcing (subcontracts to suppliers and foreign consultants), which, beginning with the 1980s, saw the emergence of atypical labor and of the autonomous labor of second generation, the capitalist colonization of the circulation sphere has been nonstop, to the point of transforming the consumer into a veritable producer of economic value. It may be useful, even at the risk of simplifying the analysis, to discuss the examples that have since become paradigmatic. Thinking of Ikea that, having delegated to the client a whole series of functions (individuation of the code of the desired item, locating the object, removal of shelves, loading it into the car, etc), externalizes the labor of assembling the "Billy" bookshelf, that is, externalizes consistent fixed and variable costs that are now supported by the consumer with a minimal benefit in prices, but with large savings in terms of costs for the company. It is possible to give other examples: the software companies, beginning with Microsoft or Google, usually beta test on the consumers the new versions of their programs, but also the programs belonging to so-called software open source are the result of improvement carried out by a multitude of people, by "productive consumers."

The first important consequence of the new processes of capital valorization is the following: the quantity of surplus-value created by new apparatuses of extraction is *enormous*. It is based on the compression of the direct and indirect wage (retirement, social security cushions, earnings from individual and collective savings), on the reduction of socially necessary labor with flexible network company systems (precarization, intermittent employment), and on the creation of an ever vaster pool of free labor (the "free labor" in the sphere of consumption, circulation, and reproduction, with a more intensified cognitive labor). The quantity of surplus-value, i.e., of unpaid labor, is at the root of the increase in the profits *not* reinvested in the production sphere, profits whose increase does not, as a consequence, generate the growth of stable employment, let alone wage.

Under this profile and with a reference to a Marxist debate about the cause of the crisis ("La Brèche"), it is thus possible to partially agree with Alain Bihr's thesis according to which we have for a while been in the presence of an "excess of surplus-value," but, unlike Bihr and Hudson,[21] this is not the result of a lack of accumulation, of a lack of reinvestment of profits in constant and variable capital. The excess of surplus-value is, *instead*, the result of a *new accumulation process* that took place after the crisis of Fordism *in* the sphere of circulation and reproduction of capital. Francois Chesnais' objections to Alain Bihr's thesis stating that the excess of surplus-value did not just lead to a search for new market outlets, since a significant number of multinational American and European companies have in fact increased their direct investments abroad (in China, Brazil, and, with some difficulties, India), would thus have to be amplified: direct investments, reflective of the typical seat of capital profit, have not been carried out just outside the economically developed countries, *but right inside*, namely, in the sphere of circulation and reproduction. This, for better or for worse, the result of the long march of capital against the Fordist working class; a result that is not necessarily a good one for capital itself.

The studies on *cognitive capitalism*, in addition to highlighting the centrality of cognitive/non-material labor, of cooperation between brains beyond the separation of company and territory, between public and private spheres, between individual and organization in the creation of value added, show the increasing loss of strategic importance of fixed capital (*physical* instrumental goods) and the transfer of a series of productive-instrumental functions to the living body of labor-power.[22]

> The economy of knowledge harbors within itself a curious paradox. The prototype of each new good is costly for the companies because, in order to start producing and commercializing it, huge investments on the level of research are necessary. But the additional units cost little because it is simply a question of replicating the original and it is possible to do this economically thanks to the advantages derived from economies of scale, from available technologies, and digitalization processes. It follows that companies will concentrate their efforts and resources on the production of ideas, having to confront, however, the progressive tendency of the increase in costs.[23]

This characteristic of cognitive capitalism, which refers to the theory of *growing earnings*, is at the origin of both forms of externalization of entire segments of activity in countries with low cost of labor, processes of the creation of *scarcity* (by means of certificates, patents, copyrights) necessary to recoup the initial costs with the prices of monopolistic sales, and, finally, the reduction of direct investment in capital assets. For example, in order to reduce the initial costs, the companies "no longer think of purchasing capital assets, but of borrowing, through various forms of hire contracts, the physical capital they need, deducting both relative costs and exercise costs in the same manner as a cost of activity."[24]

So, it is starting from the salient characteristics of the post-Fordist processes of production that the relationship between accumulation, profit and financialization are to be understood. The increase in profit that fed financialization was possible because the very concept of the accumulation of capital has transformed in biocapitalism. It no longer consists, like during the Fordist era, in investing in constant capital and variable capital (wages), but instead investing in the devices of the production and subsumption of value produced outside directly productive processes. These crowdsourcing technologies represent the new organic composition of capital, i.e. the relation between constant capital diffused in society and variable capital that is delocalized, de-spatialized and dispersed in the sphere of reproduction, consumption, forms of life, and individual and collective imaginaries. The new constant capital, in difference from the system of (physical) machines typical of the Fordist era, is constituted, other than by information and communication technologies, by whole of immaterial organizational systems that suck surplus value by persuing workers in every moment of their lives, with the result being that the work day, the time of living labor, is extended and intensified. The increase in the quantity of living labor not only reflects the transferring of the strategic means of production (knowledge, cooperation) into the living body of the work force, but also allows us to explain the tendential loss of economic value of the classic means of production. Therefore, it is not a mystery why going into the markets over these last years was not aimed at investments for directly generating an increase in the volume employment and wages, but at the pure and simple increase of stock value. If anything, the auto-financing of investments shows that the leverage of accumulation has to do with financialization as a production and subsumption device of value within society.

The increase in profits over the last 30 years is thus due to a production of surplus-value *by* accumulation, although an accumulation entirely unforeseen because it is external to classical productive processes. It is in this sense that the idea of a "rent becoming income" (and in part wage itself) is justified as a result of the capture of a value produced outside directly productive spaces. Today's system of production curiously resembles the eighteenth century economic circuit centered around farming and theorized by the physiocrats. In Quesnay's *Tableaux économiques*, rent represents the quota of the net product, appropriated by the landlord, generated by agricultural labor of wage workers (including the labor of the capitalist tenant where income was considered in the same way as the wage of his workers and not, as it later will be defined by Smith and Ricardo, as profit). In the *Tableaux*, the physical instruments of production are not even taken into consideration. Quesnay defined the producers of instrumental goods (constant capital) as the active part of the *sterile* class, that is, not productive of net product. The exclusion of constant capital, instrumental goods, from the factors of production of net product was certainly a mistake, as was later shown by the fathers of classical political economy on the wave of the first industrial revolution. But it is a question of a mistake that is *productive of knowledge*, if it is true the subsequent discovery of economic value of constant capital and its qualitative difference with respect to variable capital—that is, the discovery of *generic labor*, the labor *abstracted from* specific sectors where it is carried out—was at the basis of the epistemological leap that radically distinguished modernity from capitalism. That is, the qualitative-subjective *separation* between capital and labor, the contradictory *relationship* between the two "factors of production" as the leverage of *crisis-development* of nascent capitalism.

It is possible to say that the forms of life weakening the social body are equivalent to land in Ricardo's theory of rent. Only that, unlike Ricardo's rent (absolute and differential), today's rent is subsumable under the very profit *by virtue* of financialization processes themselves. The financialization, with the logics defining it—particularly the (autonomization of the production of money via money by the directly productive processes)—is the other side of externalization of the value production typical of biocapitalism. This does not just contribute to the (production of the effective demand) necessary for the *realization* of the product of surplus-value, i.e., does not just create the amount of rent and consumption without which the growth of GDP would be low and stagnant. Rather, financialization fundamentally *determines* continuous innovations, continuous leaps that are productive of biocapitalism, thus imposing on all companies, quoted or not, and on the whole society its hyper-productive logics centered around the primacy of shareholder value. The productive leaps determined by financialization are systematically carried out by "creative destructions" of capital, by successive extensions of valorization processes at the very heart of society with ever more sophisticated models of crowdsourcing. By crises ever more frequent and reconciled, crises where access to social wealth, after having been stimulated, is from time to time destroyed.

Starting with the crisis of Fordism in the 1970s, economic bubbles will thus be interpreted as moments of crisis within a long-term process of "capitalist colonization" of the circulation sphere. This process is *global*, that is, explaining globalization as a process of subsuming growing quotas of global and local socio-economic peripheries in accordance with the logic of financial (bio)capitalism. The passage from imperialism to empire, i.e., from a relationship of dependence between development and underdevelopment where the economies of the South functioned as *external* market outlets in addition to being the sources of downmarket raw material, to imperial globalization where the dichotomy between inside and outside breaks down, is also to be included in the capitalist logic of the externalization of the value production processes. *Financialization represents the adequate and perverse modality of accumulation of new capitalism.*

4. A Crisis of Global Governance

Beginning in August 2007 with the explosion of subprime loans, the financial crisis looks ever more like a long-term crisis, a crisis paired with credit crunch, banking bankruptcies, continued interventions of monetary authorities not able to influence the structuring of the crisis, ever more costly actions of economic revival, risks of insolvency of individual countries, deflationary pressures and possible violent returns of inflation, increase in unemployment and income reduction. To all intents and purposes, this crisis is *historical*, in the sense that it contains all the contradictions accumulated over the course of the gradual financialization of economy that began with the crisis of the Fordist way of accumulation.[25]

Nevertheless, the present crisis finds in the Asian crisis of 1997–1999 its moment of determination and acceleration. The Asian crisis marked a change of regime in the international financial order from the moment the Southern and Asian countries decided—in order to overcome the crisis of excessive debt in dollars that caused real estate speculation and industrial over-investment in local currency—to accumulate reserves of international currencies to protect themselves against the risk of subsequent destructive crises implied in the instability of the monetary and world financial system. It is a question of a radical change in the economic model, to the extent that, from a growth pulled by internal demand, Asian countries chose a model of growth based on exports. In this way, the Asian countries went from being dollar debtors to creditors, particularly in the US.[26]

In order to accumulate foreign currencies, Asian countries adopted "predatory" policy in international commerce, resorting to strong devaluations, policy of competitive deflation, and the limitation of internal consumption. If this is what the opening of international commerce in countries like China and India applies itself to, the net result of Asian turn is understood as a deflationary kind: certainly for wages, which suddenly have the effects of redoubling the world amount of active population, but deflationary also for industrial consumer goods produced and exported from China and, to a lesser yet qualitatively important extent, from India. The wage deflation "was, on the other hand, strongly aggravated by the eruption of financial logics in the companies in the real sector of economy, by procedure like reacquisition of companies through debt and leverage effect (the leveraged buy-out or LBO)."[27]

The risk of deflation is revealed as ever more real after the internet bubble crisis. In fact, since 2007, the debt redemption of companies, which have accumulated debts in the expansive period of the internet bubble (1998–2000), compels Alan Greenspan's Federal Reserve to pursue an expansive monetary policy. In order to avoid entering the vicious circle of deflation experienced by Japan in the 1990s, the American monetary authorities decide to keep interest rates low (around 1%) for a particularly long period, also because, with a view to company bankruptcies (Enron, to name just one) called in since 2002, the expansive monetary policy cannot reestablish the confidence of stock markets. In any case, *negative* real interest rates reinforce private indebtedness, but at the same time cause banks to develop the panoply of financial instruments and the famous securitizations under accusation today (the now famous toxic assets) in order to increase the credit amount.

The subprime real estate bubble begins in this context. Companies manage, at least partially, to redeem their debt thanks to real negative rates, while the domestic American economies become exponentially indebted (very often *urged* to go in debt). The increase in consumption by debt aggravates the American commercial deficit and, consequently, reinforces even more the monetary mercantilist policies of the Asian countries (that, as we said, sterilize their realized gains by massively buying dollars to avoid devaluation which would damage their exports to the US and create Sovereign Funds through the budget excesses; the state funds that, for a certain period, seem to be able to resolve the crisis of the Western banks). The deflationary tendency is aggravated also because the commercial excesses of the Asian countries (despite the actions of sterilization) generate investments in these very exporting countries, the investments that, in turn, improve the competitiveness of the emerging countries not only through the low labor cost, but also through the quality of products and the higher added value.

The description, however schematic, of the dynamic that led to the subprime bubble burst shows that the crisis ripened within a precise *world* configuration of the capitalist accumulation process. Within this configuration and this international division of labor, financialization allowed *global* capital to grow thanks to the production of financial rents and consumer debts that endowed international exchanges with *systemic coherence*. The global growth, particularly after the internet bubble crisis and debt redemption on the part of companies following it, witnessed capital restructure itself with subsequent externalization processes so as to reduce the cost of living labor with increases in the quantity of surplus-value, the increases not correlated with increases proportional to investments in constant capital. In fact, particularly from 1998 to 2007, the large companies (S&P500) witnessed a continued and particularly high increase in non-reinvested profits (free cash flow margins), an accumulation of liquidity parallel to the increase, also growing and very high, of consumption, either with reduced family savings or with recourse to indebtedness.

As always, the crises of capital break loose because of the same forces that determined their growth (the typical palindromic movement of the transaction cycle). But *this* crisis illuminates something unforeseen with regard to the preceding crises—which is the loss of capacity on the part of American monetary authorities, even if they manage the international currency par excellence, to manage liquidities arriving at their market as a result of the "mercantilist"-predatory monetary strategy used in the Asian countries since the 97–99 crisis. This specificity (in his day, Alan Greenspan spoke of "conundrum"), already pointed out by Michel Aglietta and Laurent Berrebi,[28] refers to the consequences of a liquidity influx from the emerging countries and from the countries producing and exporting gasoline to the American bond market—particularly Treasury bonds and Fannie Mae and Freddie Mac's obligations. The massive and continued liquidity influx from the emerging countries in fact *reduces* long-term interest rates on bonds, such as T-bills *despite* the Fed's repeated attempts between 2004 and 2007 to restrain the increase in the amount of credits with the increase in direct short-term interest rates (that jump from 1% to 5.25%). "It is this very special situation of inverted curve where long-term interest rates have become less than short-term rates—situation atypical for such a long period—that made it so that the credit cost remained very low for quite some time in the US, despite an ever more restrictive monetary policy."[29] Being able to give out loans to wholesale money markets, the banks thus have the means to give out credits with an ever higher risk to the domestic economies. Consequently, real estate prices in the US were rising until the fall of 2006 and until 2008 in various European countries (in France, rising from 60% to 80%, in England and Spain redoubling over ten years).

The crisis of governance of American monetary authorities is thus explained as the incapacity to manage the effects of liquidity influx from the rest of the world, especially from the emerging countries. In fact, the post-crisis Asian globalization *obscures* inside the developed countries the increase in risk of crisis internal to the transaction cycle because the reduction of premiums on the bonds risks (long-term bonds) reinforce the exposition of the financial sector to the valorization of all patrimonial assets. Once again, in this process, it is the *temporal dimension* that is central in the analysis of the crisis. The signs of a real estate crisis were manifesting themselves already since 2004, so much that the Fed began its race to increase interest rates. But the influx of foreign liquidity annulled the actions of monetary policy so that the bubble was unfolding undeterred until August 2007. And not just that: already in the middle of 2006, real estate prices halted their rise to then drop towards the end of the same year. But the bubble exploded in August 2007 when the rating agencies finally decided to declassify (now toxic) assets issued in credit; thus, a year after the inversion of the transaction cycle.[30]

In other words, the crisis of monetary governance reveals a *gap* between the economic and financial-monetary cycles, in the sense that the former develops in a shorter time than the latter. In the cycle of the real economy, like in all business cycles, the crisis begins at the moment when the inflationary increase in prices (for example in real estate) ends by causing a *falling* increase of demand. (The demand grows, but grows ever more slowly because actualizing the flow of future incomes no longer justifies the "irrational" increase in prices on goods on which the bubble is concentrated) In the "old" economic cycles, this slowdown was usually manifested by the near-full employment. For the banking system, this means a slowdown in the rhythm of repaying the credits lavished in the phase preceding the cycle, the phase during which credit is easy and super-speculation is unleashed on the wave of the increase in profits (the so-called financial overtrading). In approaching the full employment, companies and indebted consumers are, however, showing signs of difficulty repaying their debts because the amount of sales (for the companies struggling with the drop of demand) and available incomes (for the domestic economies confronted by inflation) begins to fall. For the banks, from the secondary to the central ones, this is the moment to increase the interest rates.

The financial globalization, as we saw, *defers* the rendering of accounts, that is, the inversion of the cycle, precisely because the amount of credit to companies and consumers can keep increasing despite the signs of the inversion of the real internal economy cycle (for instance, the prices on real estate beginning to drop). And also despite the trend in the balance of payments that contributes to obscuring the symptoms of the imminent crisis. In fact, until the massive influx of savings from the emerging countries in search of not high, but secure earnings is counterbalanced by the flow of American investments directed abroad (which have earnings greater than the internal ones and which increase the profits of US companies, especially when the dollar is low relative to other currencies), the American monetary authorities can avoid confronting the *all the while evident* problem of the international commercial imbalances.

Moreover, the temporal gap where the crisis of American monetary governance is reversed is at the root of the transformation of regional crises into *immediately* global ones. Certainly, this is due to the dissemination of risks and toxic assets that in this period infects bank portfolios, insurances, hedge and equity funds, retirement funds, and everyone's investments. But, at a closer look, it is a question of a crisis that goes well beyond the world diffusion of toxic assets, as is shown by the total inefficiency of all the actions of intervention undertaken up to now by the governments all over the world in order to recapitalize the banking and insurance system through the huge injections of liquidity. It is thus possible to claim that the crisis of monetary governance explains *only* one part, only the *beginning* of the crisis we are living in. What proves it is that, at the worst moment of the financial crisis—October 2008—contrary to what everyone expected, the dollar was *revalued* against all the other currencies. "The anomaly is that the dollar is reinforced over the course of last weeks against almost all other currencies."[31] But it can happen that, like after the reevaluation of the dollar in August 2007 (in the midst of the subprime crisis!), the dollar starts to devalue again, with inevitable inflationary effects on a world scale (caused, like over the course of 2007–08, by strong increases in the prices on gasoline and food). It is possible that the global imbalances between the structurally deficient countries, such as the US and England, and the countries structurally in surplus, such as the emerging countries, but also Germany and Japan, is destined to still last a long time. A long time, i.e., *beyond* the rescue actions and the redefinition of the banking and financial rules that—from the internet crisis until the subprime bubble burst—allowed the flow of liquidity towards the US to produce the leverage effect of credit that we saw.

It would suffice to pose an only seemingly provocative question: What else could the American monetary authorities and the rest of the world do? Certainly, with hindsight, it is possible to say anything, it is possible, for instance, to invoke (precisely *ex post*) prudential monetary policies, increases in banking reserves, better quality control of issued assets, stricter rules on securitizations based on subprime mortgage loans, and so on. But what could have the American monetary authorities and the Central Banks of the emerging countries done, the former being confronted with the risk of deflation, the latter recovering, shattered, from the 97–99 crisis? The answer is: Nothing other than what has been done. It suffices to say that if the Fed had effected a more restrictive monetary policy in order to restrain or lessen the foreign deficit of the current balance, the result would have been a recession in the US and, consequently, in the emerging countries as well. On top of that, how could the Fed have justified a restrictive monetary policy when the problem was not inflation, but rather deflation?

Let us only recall that a peculiar characteristic of today's financial capitalism and the monetary policy proper to it is the impossibility of managing from outside what occurs inside the economico-financial cycle. The theoretical analyses of André Orléan, Michel Aglietta, Robert Shiller, George Soros, and Frédéric Lordon, to cite the best, show that, in order to interpret the behavior of financial operators on the basis of the value-at-risk models, it is impossible to distinguish between cognitive and manipulative functions, between economic rationality and mimetic behavior of the multiplicity of actors. The neo-classical theory of rational expectations, based on perfect information and the transparency of markets, has for a long time now been beside the point because it removes a central factor of the financial markets, i.e., the intrinsic *uncertainty* characteristic of them, an uncertainty ever more based on the diminishing dichotomy between real and financial economies, between being "inside" and "outside" the global economic system. In fact, there is a particular ontological weakness in the models of probability calculation used to evaluate risks due to the *endogenous* nature of the interactions between the financial operators.[32] It is what explains the "mistakes of evaluation" of risk not so much, or not only, as mistakes attributable to the conflict of interests typical of rating agencies, but as the expression of (ontological) impossibility of making rules or meta-rules in order to be able to discipline the markets in accordance with the so-called rational principles (like the Basel I and Basel II attempts).

It is possible to maintain that the crisis of governance has its origin in a double resistance: on the one hand, the resistance of the emerging countries to every attempt to keep them in the subordinate position with respect to the developed countries, a resistance that led them to modify their growth model after the Asian crisis. The Asian export-oriented model has in fact transformed the amount of savings not reinvested internally into *financial rent*—the rent realized by redirecting liquidity towards the outside; on the other hand, the resistance of the American domestic economies that have played the card of *social rent*, a kind of "in and against" the financialization of economy. For a certain period of time, American families were acting, in however financially unstable form, on the terrain of social property rights, the right to the house and the (indebted) consumption of goods and services. And this was, we would do well to recall, in a period of the state disinvestment in the fundamental sectors such as education and professional training, the disinvestment that caused the impressive increase in the cost of education, forcing the families to go in debt in order to allow their own children to study. The private spending deficit, far from being the reflection of an all-American tendency to live beyond one's own means, is a phenomenon that has its roots in the liberal turn in the beginning of the 1980s and in the crisis of the Welfare State that followed it.

5. Geomonetary Scenarios

The crisis is the capitalist way of transferring to the economic order the social and potentially political dimension, the dimension of the resistances ripened during the phase leading up to the cycle. However, this crisis exploded on the basis of such a tangle of contradictions and rigidity on a global scale that Keynesian actions of intervention on a regional scale are hardly able to undo. It is thus obvious that the overcoming of the crisis is possible only if the actions of economic revival are inscribed in precise geopolitical and geomonetary strategies.

There are, essentially, three medium-term (from 5 to 10 years) scenarios which are extrapolated from the current crisis:

> The first is founded on the US-China coupling (Chimerica), thus on a pact between the dollar and yuan. The second extends the game to Russia and Euro-Western powers, Germany and France come to mind, bound by a special agreement between Euroland and ruble (Eurussia). Thus determining, parallel to the Chino-American axis, the premises of a super Bretton Woods, a full agreement between all the major powers. The third scenario is the exacerbation of imbalances (beginning with the old Europe mayonnaise going bad and ongoing conflicts) to the point of rendering the system completely ungovernable. The catastrophes pile up to then reproduce August 1914, this time on a nuclear and planetary scale.[33]

All these scenarios are based upon the inevitability of the decline of American hegemony, the decline of the *empire without credit*, the formula describing(the paradox of the largest world power that is also the largest global debtor.)On the "self-evident" hypothesis that is to be legitimately doubted if it is true that the crisis strikes the Asian countries in a particularly grave way, from China to Singapore, from Japan to South Korea,[34] while the US continues to be, as paradoxical as it may seem, one of the most secure places to invest one's savings.

Today's crisis ripened within a complex geomonetary order that witnessed the multiplicity of actors bound to one another by autoreferential interests. China can maintain that the Americans would have to save the most, but only as long as the major saving does not affect its exports to the US. And the Americans can ask the Chinese how they managed, repeatedly in the past and, ever more timidly, even now, to reevaluate their currency and to increase the internal consumption, but they are wary of restraining the purchase of T-bills by the Chinese. On the other hand, this crisis is already provoking a strong reduction in the net flow of private capital to the emerging countries (in 2009, it will not exceed $165 billion, at least in the half of $466 billion of 2008 and a fifth of the capital flow of 2007). For their part, the actions of tax stimulus and of rescuing the bankrupt Western banks can only crowd out emerging markets and those of Eastern Europe, increasing, on top of all of that, their public debt service. Which, let it be noted, can cause some Asian countries to try to protect themselves by increasing their currency reserves still more and investing their savings in the debt of the more developed economies, reiterating in such a way the same dynamics that prepared the explosion of the credit in the US.

Thus, it is not the decline of the American empire that compels one to try the way of international cooperation in order to better manage the global imbalances, but rather the fact that this crisis is destined to last a long time without any country being able to assume the role of the leader of the world economy. In other words, the crisis radically undermined the very concept of unilateral and multilateral economico-political hegemony, i.e., that which compels one to explore new forms of multilateral world governance. As David Brooks wrote in an article appearing in the Herald Tribune, what paralyzes capitalism in the current global system is the impossibility of deciding. The dispersion of power "should be a good thing in theory, but mulipolarity means veto power over collective action in practice. Practically, this new pluralistic world has started a global-sclerosis, or the incapacity of resolving one problem after another."[35]

The first step in this direction is to ensure the emerging countries, and not just the Asian ones, that in case of a liquidity crisis they will not be left alone. The offer, in October, on the Fed's part of a line of credit to 4 emerging countries, even though these same countries already had abundant reserves, will be interpreted as an innovation in this direction. The objective is to best coordinate the actions of political economy to reorient the flows of capital so as to stimulate the internal demand in the emerging countries, without, however, jeopardizing the monetary balance between the dollar and other currencies. It is worth noting that this strategy includes the countries in the European zone, since Germany is also structurally in commercial excess and thus has all the interest to pursue policies of a revival of internal demand in order to counteract the drop of the external one.

We should also note that the implementation of this geopolitico-monetary strategy witnesses for the time being the IMF play an entirely marginal role. The amounts in play well exceed the financial availability of the Fund. As a matter of fact, in the medium-long term, such an operative reinvention of the IMF (most importantly, a consistent increase in its liquidity) will reveal itself as necessary for the simple reason that the US cannot guarantee in the medium term to help the emerging countries with "precautionary" lines of credit. The construction of a super Bretton Woods and the IMF as its new armed hand, repeatedly invoked by the French President Sarkosy, must reckon with a characteristic of the Fund that sums up the gist of neoliberal American politics in the last decades. It is a question of writing, highly valued in the US, into the statutes of the Fund, the obligation to the convertibility into a capital account (a convertibility that Keynes, during the preparatory work on the Bretton Woods agreements, resisted with all his force) where before there was only the convertibility into a current account.

> And yet, the difference between the two notions is thus essential. In the second, the accent is on the flows of currencies that cover real transactions, on exchanges of goods and services, on tourist flows or the ones that still correspond to the repatriation of the incomes of the immigrants. In the first notion, all the portfolio operations, all the possible instruments of speculation, are authorized.[36]

The idea of a super Bretton Woods would thus be to remove from the statutes the convertibility into a capital account that since the 1980s represented the precondition of the liberation processes of the international markets and of the accumulation of global imbalances that repeatedly produced the financial crises of the last 30 years. Today the same IMF recognizes that this freedom of movement of capital significantly contributed to the destabilization of the system of commercial exchanges and international financial flows. However, the removal of the convertibility obligation into a capital account from the statutes of a hypothetical new IMF—that has as its fundamental objective the reestablishment of the *economic sovereignty* of nations and the symmetry of exchange relations guaranteed by a supranational monetary system—would have the inevitable consequence of disabling the apparatus that ensured, although with an impressive accumulation of contradictions and financial drifts, the development and affirmation of biocapitalism. To start off, the US would no longer be able to profit from the massive liquidity influx from the emerging countries that, as we saw, allowed American capital to explode consumption through debt of American families. However one values the hypothesis of a new Bretton Woods, it is certain that a reform of it in this sense would have spectacular effects on a model of society that, having dismantled the Welfare State, turned consumption and debt into the motor of its *modus operandi*.

> The breaking point between the partisans of the old disorder and the partisans of a real reconstruction of the financial monetary system will be concentrated on two questions: the control of capital and of the forms of protectionism that allow one to avoid importing the depressive effects of the policies of some countries.[37]

From this perspective, not imminent but real, what is at stake are the possibilities or impossibilities of overcoming the ongoing crisis *politically*, rather than economically. The block of capitalist accumulation on a global scale will be interpreted in the light of these contradictory forces, with, on the one hand, the possibility that this crisis will last a very long time or at least will be systematically followed by similar crises, and, on the other hand, the possibility that, in order to overcome the crisis, the international monetary system will be redefined in the name of national sovereignty and/or regional poles and the symmetry of commercial exchanges.[38]

In the meantime, we would do well to watch how much of the New Deal the Obama administration will be able to realize. Among the different actions of the economic revival plan (*Financial Stability Plan* or FSP), there is one in particular that immediately merits having an eye kept on it. It is a question of the *Homeowner Affordability & Stability Plan*, a law that authorizes bankruptcy judges to change mortgages held by dissolvent home owners.[39] This constitutes a precedent of historical import, since, in the US, the loans for primary residences are currently the only ones that cannot be modified in bankruptcy courts.[40] It also constitutes a totally innovative financial measure in respect to the other interventions to help the banking and insurance system, which have been complete failures up until now. The constitution of mortgage refinance funds for American families is, in fact, the only *technical* action to restore a value, a price, to the derivative assets that are today clogging up the world banking system, an intervention action, above all, without immediate effects on the public deficit, being the financing that is spread over 30 years of loan contracts. In other words, saving families to save the banks. The principle is clear: *begin from the base in order to reform the monetary system.*[41]

As always, *our* New Deal starts from the base, from those resistances that have put financial capitalism in crisis on the level of social rent, simultaneously representing a precondition for overcoming it. The mobilization times around social rent are found in the long-term, through re-conquering a governance able to handle these new contradictions, a governance that institutes the right to the common and the right to live in it.

Andrea Fumagalli

The Global Economic Crisis

and Socioeconomic Governance

Introduction

The financial crisis is already a pale memory. Not because it is over but because it immediately turned into an economic crisis *tout-court*. The current global economic crisis systemically and structurally highlights the inconsistency of the governance mechanism of accumulation and distribution that cognitive capitalism tried to establish up until now. From this point of view, this is not a crisis of saturation but a crisis of growth. It's more a crisis of distribution rather than a crisis of accumulation. Just like in 1929.

As it has already been said, we are facing a systemic crisis. And this systemic crisis doesn't come from the past but rather from the future. In fact, what went into crisis was the attempt of social and distributive regulation that the new paradigm of cognitive capitalism implicitly gave itself. To be more precise, it would be better to talk of "non-regulation" since the dynamic of cognitive capitalism was founded since the early nineties not on discretional and institutional political economic interventions but instead on the market's "all too visible" hand. What we are witnessing is therefore a crisis of governance of the market and its hierarchies.

As already discussed elsewhere,[1] cognitive capitalism is structured as a system of accumulation based on three pillars: 1. The role of the financial markets as motor of accumulation from the financing side of investment and as hinge upon which wealth distribution mechanisms depend (the process of financialization as biopolitical control of life); 2. The generation (learning) and the diffusion (network) of knowledge as the main source of capitalistic valorization on a global scale that redefines the relation between the living and the dead work (the process of cognitive-immaterial accumulation as expropriation of the "common" cooperation, *aka* general intellect).[3] The decomposition of the work force on international scale following the valorization of individual subjective differences in a context of cognitive division of labor (the process of precarization and for controlling cognitive excess).

These three innovations, resulting from the conflictual crisis of the capital-labor relation within the previous industrial-Fordist paradigm, define a new path of accumulation that is aimed at recreating the conditions for monetary valorization from a prevalent short-term point of view with effects of unsustainability in the medium and long-term.

Unlike the preceding Fordist paradigm, here the spatial-temporal coordinates change.

With regard to time, the relation between short—and long-terms is redefined, that is the times of accumulation change: the passage toward forms of immaterial valorization has drastically reduced the time necessary for the process of accumulation to take place and therefore it reduces the possibility of corrective interventions.

As regards space, the processes of globalization and financialization tend to redefine the new international hierarchical structures, in a context where the capacity of autonomous intervention on a national level is highly conditioned by the birth of supranational powers (the crisis of the nation-state).

In the following section, we will further address the limits set by the spatial and temporal dynamic in order to analyze what the institutions delegated to social and economic governance are doing about this and verify not only if regulatory interventions can be envisioned but above all if they are feasible.

1. The Spatial-Temporal Dynamic of the Economic Crisis

a) The Short- and Long-Term Dialectic—One of the factors that best encloses the complexity of the current global economic crisis is the contradiction that arises from the dialectic between short- and long-terms. The dynamic of the financial markets is a short-term dynamic that is becoming increasingly short-term, a necessary condition so that the exchange vortex can never sediment itself into real value while always remaining on the level of symbolic exchange. Such a temporal environment is, however, incompatible with the temporal environment of the subjects that participate in it. The reason is banal: the possibility of obtaining surplus value in the short-term doesn't allow, in fact, to guarantee a protection for the entire lifetime. Whereas in the era of industrial-Fordist capitalism financial investment could be animated by medium- and long-term saving intentions that were consistent with the lifespan and able to guarantee a constant income, in cognitive capitalism the financial markets also represent the place where immediate speculation occurs and only those who possess a large portfolio of stocks can aspire to have positive capital gains; this is the prerogative of few, though.

Such dichotomy between short and long-term refers to a second contradictory element concerning the dismantling of welfare. It is well known that now financial markets play the role of social security (without any guarantee) that was played by the nation state (with a high guarantee) in the Fordist era. A growing part of labor incomes is channeled into the stock market in order to guarantee future and present earnings that are able to face and demand social services which are no longer freely and universally supplied since they increasingly require an individual contribution to the expenses (workfare).

The need to widen the "client pool" in terms of the acquisition of primary goods (such as houses and therefore mortgages) by involving even those social sectors whose income is uncertain and therefore have a higher risk of insolvency seems to confirm this tendency. A mortgage is a long-term investment even though it is "ensured" by short-term derived securities. Here the dichotomy between short- and long-term comes to the fore.

The irresolvable contradiction between short- and long-term heavily and negatively affects also the possibility of performing support and institutional governance interventions.

An average loss of 1% of stock indexes on the main global markets implies the destruction of liquidity equivalent to around $1.45 trillion. Since October 2007, for instance, the Dow Jones index has lost 43% of its value.[2] On average, the Bank for International Settlements (BIS) calculated the destruction of liquidity being around $580 trillion. To put this into context: the entire global real-estate patrimony is valued at $75 trillion; the gross product of the whole planet is not more than $50 trillion. Now, it is true that this is a "nominal" value. But the same BIS (in September 2008) reminded us that it translates into a deduction from the real economy, following the capital loss sustained of nearly $11 trillion, a sum equal to the United States GDP[3] and 20% of the global gross product.[4] Such destruction of currency and real wealth has occurred in the space of 12 months; that is an exceptionally short period for a fall in wealth of such an extent, and whose effects can now be dramatically felt globally. Measures so far undertaken by states and the Central Banks in America and Europe (the areas worst hit by the crash of the stock markets) have led to the injection of around $5 trillion in liquidity.[5] A sum that will start to have effects only in the second quarter of 2009, in a context of possible further losses in stock indexes. It is therefore impossible to intervene at the same time as the financial crisis is biting. The destruction of liquidity travels at a speed that is structurally superior to that necessary for its reconstitution. Also, despite a rapid and immediate introduction of liquidity, it is still not able to face negative expectations and the crisis of trust in the financial markets in the short term. The risk is that in the lapse of time necessary to cure the disease, the patient dies. Thus, the structural problem of "timing" arises.

The second problem of the temporal dialectic concerns the contradiction between the process of accumulation of value determined by the exploitation and expropriation of "general intellect" and its immediate valorization on the financial markets. With the advent of cognitive capitalism, the process of valorization is not immediately computable at the time of production. In the industrial–Fordist paradigm, the material measurement of production was in some way defined by the content of the labor necessary for the production of merchandise, measurable on the basis of the tangibility of production itself and its necessary time. With the arrival of cognitive capitalism, the value of the *immaterial* becomes value of knowledge, affections and relations, of imaginary and the symbolic.[6] The result of these biopolitical transformations is the crisis in traditional measurement of labor-value and, consequently, of the concept of profit as it was characterized in Fordism (as the difference between revenues and costs). As accumulation socializes, the measurement of valorization, embedded in the "communism of capital,"[7] tends to realize itself in the social capital quoted in the stock markets (that is, between the expected future value and the current one): as a result, the exploitation of social cooperation and general intellect partially determines the dynamics of stock values. Profit is thus turned into rent and financial markets become the place where labor-value, which is transformed into *finance-value*, is determined.[8] The current financial crisis, however, highlights how this possible index of measurement is anything but well defined. Its crisis is also the result of the contradiction between short- and long-term: a short-term that would like to immediately realize the future value deriving from the expropriation of general intellect and a long-term that instead defines the time necessary for the production and diffusion of general intellect itself.

The third level of the temporal contradiction of cognitive capitalism regards, instead, labor performance. It has to do with the contradiction between the necessity of the spread of social cooperation and teamwork as a condition to better exploit the dynamic economies of learning and networks (factors of growth of social productivity at the basis of the accumulation process) and the need for an immediate control (in short-term) of labor and knowledge production (such as intellectual property rights). This dialectic pair actuates the production of surplus value, registers cognitive capitalism's process of exploitation and uses new forms of alienation. Here, the new capital–labor relation is defined in its real manifestations. On the one hand, there is the demand for participation, relation and sharing of the productive intentions of business, on the other hand the precariousness of individual relations, anxiety, uncertainty and psychological and existential frustration deriving from it. On the one hand, there is availability for work and medium- and long-term processes of education and learning, on the other hand, individual contractual definition with more or less immediate expiration.

The crisis of short- and long-term dialectics hints at the theme of the impossibility to control and regulate financial markets, that is capitalist accumulation. Contemporaneously, such a contradiction can be used by the multitudes to open new conflict scenarios. We shall discuss these aspects later on. Here, it should be stressed that such a problem was also present during the 1929 crisis. In that case, the state intervened as supra-individual and formally extra-market economic agent able to correct the temporal divergence between the phase of productive accumulation and the phase of realization that was created within that crisis. Keynes' emphasis on the prevalence of short-term in respect to long-term was intended to guarantee the possibility of a *fine-tuned* political economy aimed at "defending the present from the future."[9] If in the crisis of '29 the short-and long-term dichotomy was entirely contained in the productive cycle, precisely between accumulation and realization, today it is entirely contained in the global financial markets.

At that time, the role of the state (together with the emergency of war) was sufficient to recompose the temporal dialectics of the production cycle between debt and valorization, thanks to the role played as guarantor of national economic policy authorities and to the approval of precise rules as regards international payments. The autonomy of the nation-state within the 1944 Bretton Woods Accords (therefore within a precise international hierarchy) allowed for the stability necessary for the Fordist accumulation process insofar as it efficiently neutralized the risk of instability derived from international geopolitical tensions.

Today, we find ourselves in a context in which all of the mechanisms of control and international regulation, yet hierarchical, have structurally come undone to allow the development of a system of cognitive accumulation that founds its growth capacity on global financialization and selective internationalization of production.

b) The International Geo-economic Dialectics—The crisis of the industrial–Fordist paradigm has cracked the international hierarchical structures defined in the aftermath of WWII and sanctioned by Yalta and Bretton Woods. The capitalistic reaction to the crisis of the 1970s, provoked both by social movements in the West and the processes of political and economic liberation of many third-world countries, resulted in structural modifications of the international division of labor. A new division of labor based on different levels of accessibility to the diverse forms of knowledge (i.e. the cognitive division of labor) was added—and in part substituted—to the traditional Smithian division of labor typical of Taylorist production. This happened thanks to the increasingly massive introduction of a new technological paradigm based on information and communication technologies (ICT). In addition to the reduction of transportation costs, there was also the explosion of forms of real and virtual communication that have profoundly influenced the organization of production and labor on a global scale.

In the '80s, when the nation-states were still able to address the economic policy toward the definition of national systems of innovation, we witnessed a technological showdown between

Japan and the US. In the 1990s, after the first Gulf War—which confirmed American military supremacy following the fall of the Berlin Wall and the implosion of the Soviet Bloc—the financialization process gained ground and the outsourcing and delocalization policy reshaped the productive strategies of western multinational corporations. The opening of new labor markets in South-East Asia and Latin America, pushed by the neoliberal policies of the IMF and the World Bank, thanks to Structural Adjustment Plans (the infamous SAP), allowed the massive expansion of the productive base beyond national borders. During the first phase, the one that marked the restoration of American technological leadership in the net-economy, the main international productive companies were firmly under Western control. The process of heavy concentration, both technological and financial, was still under US guidance. During the '90s, the financial crisis of 1997 (caused by the depreciation of the Thai bat)—unlike the crises which occurred after 2000—reinforced the financially hegemonic position of the Anglo-Saxon markets. But it was an ephemeral illusion. The moment in which the paradigm of cognitive capitalism guided by financial markets asserts itself as the tendentially hegemonic paradigm of accumulation and valorization, new contradictions explode within it.

The necessity to extend the markets to the East, the inclusion of China in the WTO, the recent autonomy of Eastern stock markets after the crisis of the internet convention that hit the financial markets in March 2000 brought a new and more marked redefinition of hierarchical productive technological structures. The US began to lose their monopoly over technological control, the Chinese and Indian productive systems, along with the Brazilian one, undermined Western technological leadership in the crucial sector of ICT. With reference to China, the OECD report "*OECD Reviews of Innovation Policy: China. Synthesis Report*" of May 2007 reads:

> In recent years, there has been a spectacular rise in China's high-technology exports. Their share in total exports increased from 5% in the early 1990s to over 30% in 2005. These exports are heavily concentrated in two product categories: Office machinery and TV, radio and communication equipment; high-technology exports such as pharmaceuticals are relatively weak. As of 2004 China is the world's largest exporter of ICT goods (p. 15).

The same dynamics saw both India and Brazil as protagonists, even if in lesser proportions. What follows is that the US is losing the technological hegemony that was at the base of the economic-financial growth of the 1990s.

The shift of the techno-productive axis from the West to the East and South is a factor of economic and political instability of great importance in itself. It is not a process of substitution of technological hegemony from one territory to another, but instead the loss of technological unilateralism. The simultaneous presence of different technological poles must also be analyzed in respect to the other two pillars of international power: the control of financial flows and military power. Until this latest crisis, it was indubitable that financial hegemony was still firmly in the hands of the Anglo-Saxon markets able to condition not only the other main global financial markets, but also the choices of monetary policy of the Federal Reserve, the ECB and the Bank of Japan. Full control of the global economic organisms, from the IMF to the

World Bank, was added to this, while US conditioning power on the WTO had already seen its decline since the failure of the Cancun and Doha meetings.

Nevertheless, after the year 2000, such financial hegemony suffered potential counterattacks due, on the one hand, to the partial loss of control over official international liquidity (not generated by the financial markets but by the official reserves), and on the other hand to the crisis of trust of American goodwill in foreign and military policy, following the *impasse* of the Iraq War.

Regarding the first aspect, it is necessary to underline how a domestic public deficit that rendered the US one of the most indebted countries in the world was added to the structural deficit of the US Trade Balance. First, this pushed towards a depreciation—even if controlled by the FED—of the dollar, favoring a substitution effect between the dollar and valued currencies (above all the Euro) in the composition of the international currency reserves. Secondly, the deficit of US trade balance transformed into surplus in the trade balances of recently industrialized countries which hence become net creditors for the American economy. This created a paradox. The United States held international financial hegemony, but was a net debtor with the rest of the world. In other words, the recently industrialized countries were above all the ones who financed the growth of the American economy, on the one hand by buying public and foreign debt securities issued by the USA, on the other hand by buying securities on the US markets, especially through the constitution of sovereign funds.[10]

Such a financial circuit could not last long. And in fact it didn't. From this point of view, the financial crisis is also the result of the friction created within an empire that is no longer able to define a single and central command. Different geo-economic poles (a center of financial hegemony in the West and a techno-productive shift to the East) can coexist only for a limited period of time and under particular conditions that compensate for its instability.

The monopoly of military force is certainly one of those. But until when does it play a role of effective deterrence and interdictory power? The United States still has such a monopoly, but the crisis that it is going through in the Second Gulf War and in Afghanistan seems to suggest that this monopoly is a blunt weapon, even if it is still formally firm in its hands. After the defeat of the neocon unilateralism of the Bush-Cheney administration and Obama's arrival in the White House, the hatchet seems to be buried again (but certainly not definitively banned). The governance strategy followed by the US—or at least the current attempt—that is compulsorily dictated also by the global economic crisis seems to consider the geoeconomic and geopolitical multilateralism that by now characterizes the global economy. The US seems to recognize Empire. The attempted *coup* has, for the moment, failed.

2. Governance in Action

The institutional strategies put forth so far by the main economic institutions (international organisms, Central Banks and nation-states) seem to proceed along three essential lines:

a) Interventions of business governance aimed at reducing the domino effect of the financial crisis in the real economy. Most of the time, these are interventions to sustain liquidity on the part of the Central Banks and last minute loan interventions aimed at rescuing entities thanks to the intervention of public spending. These are interventions that are not aimed at structurally affecting the forms of valorization or the nature of the crisis. Their main objective is not to resolve the factors of the crisis but instead to give signals that improve the climate of trust. They have no real affect.

b) Interventions of economic governance that begin with the acknowledgement of the failure of the market's capacity to auto-regulate itself. The intention is to create the premises for a process of control over financial markets on an international level through interventions of mixed public-private nature aimed at shaping a new Bretton Woods.

c) Interventions of international political governance aimed at reducing the geoeconomic tensions and at redefining a new international geopolitical structure that in some way takes into account the new international cognitive division of labor. Basically, something like a hypothesis of a new Yalta relative to the international geopolitical structure.

Regarding the first level, there is not much to say. The terms of the current debate essentially concern the following points:[11]

a) The so-called *perimeter of regulation*, that is the deter-mination of the part of the financial and credit system that has a large responsibility for the crisis (the shadow banking sys-tem), constituted by the whole of the financial operators that were not regulated (in the illusion that this could bring about beneficial innovations to the economic system).

b) *The macroprudential dimension*: the analysis of accu-mulated risk, at a systemic level rather than in a single operator case, has proved to be inadequate, and the (few) analyses realized have only resulted in publications and not in political modifications.

c) *The leverage effect*, and the consequent risks that it entails: first of all, the ability to evaluate it and its effects on financial markets should be improved.

d) *Transparency in risk evaluation and in financial tool valorization*: The system of market prices, the evaluations system using internal methods and those done by rating agencies have all proved to be inadequate.

e) *Governance and the incentive system* that has always favored short-term objectives to the detriment of long-term ones.

f) *The cooperation between the regulatory authorities on a European level*, and common tools to face the critical situation. The crisis has highlighted, even in the context of a unified European monetary space, how the anti-crisis interventions have been predominantly made on a national base and without adequate coordination.

Analysts generally agree on the points mentioned. Nevertheless, these points appear completely inadequate to comprehend the real causes of the crisis. With reference to the European situation, official documents only make intervention proposals that start with the necessity of limiting the damages that the "sick" part of the financial markets has caused. Hence, the demands for intervention limit themselves to proposing the following tools:

1. *Transformation of vigilance committees into European agencies*. Yet the risk of their politicization is immediately underlined[12] to the detriment of the principle of total autonomy not only of the CBE but of the rating and control agencies of

the financial markets, too. Thereby, the cause and the effect are confused. It is precisely the total autonomy of the financial markets that, operating in the short-term, collides with the necessity of regulating the same financial markets. Autonomy and regulation are incompatible *de facto*.

2. Creation of roles as *lead supervisor*, with which the responsibility of vigilance is entrusted to the bank's "home country," and yet this clashes with the capacity to intervene in foreign countries and the political will to look after the interests of all the countries involved and not only of the "home" country. The "political" will to maintain autonomous financial markets under national responsibility is therefore not compatible with the necessity of starting a coordination between the European nation-states.

3. *Creation of a European vigilance authority.* Regarding this, it should be noted that such an institution would require the modification of the EU Treaty or at least an unanimous decision by the Council of the European Union. Therefore, this idea is in contradiction with the monetary and neoliberal ideological foundation that serves as a basis for the process of European monetary unification since the Maastricht Treaty.

Beyond superficial declarations, regulatory interventions in the financial markets have no possibility of being effective as long as they move in the direction of Central Banks autonomy in the absence of a higher level of international coordination. It is a type of governance that we could define as "small cabotage," unable to arrive at the heart of the problem. Nor could it do so without tarnishing the foundation on which the new paradigm of cognitive capitalism was grafted. Like never before, the space for "technocratic" reform has been so inexistent.

Interventions of non-regulatory character are certainly more adapted and incisive at least in this phase. They are tied to liquidity injections both through expansive monetary policy (the reduction of interest rates and the creation of fresh currency) and through Keynesian deficit spending policies. It is curious how such a perspective is strongly encouraged by the international monetary institutions (such as the IMF and the World Bank) that until a short time ago advocated the exact opposite economic policy choices aiming at total market deregulation and dismantling the economic role of the state.

Here it is necessary to underline that:

1. Reducing interest rates has less effect in a context of global financialization and under the risk of deflation. The possibility that it stimulates investment clashes against a climate of negative expectations on the demand side. Instead, the possibility that low interest rates can in some way stimulate the demand of securities and recreate higher levels of trust in the financial markets clashes with the scarcity of international liquidity. In fact, self-referential logic of financial markets prevails over the understandings of monetary policy increasingly dominated by the conditions set by financial biopower.

2. Deficit spending policy is not however structurally able to inject enough liquidity into the system.[13] Paul Krugman[14] argues that the nearly $900 million of the American stimulus package plan is not sufficient to fill up the gap between the recessive effect on the GDP and a potential recovery.

3. In a context of cognitive accumulation dragged ahead by the financial markets and which escapes the control of national political economics, resorting to (the rival) Keynesian

policies is no longer enough. A higher goal must be set. That is, an international governance able to propose a supranational, global political economy.

In some recent journalism, often reference is made to this very objective—the creation of a Bretton Woods II. Obviously, Bretton Woods is mentioned because it is believed that there are the conditions to repeat this experience. Let's analyze this aspect closer. The agreement of 1944 was essentially founded on two conditions: the existence of nation-states capable of controlling their own currency by respecting the regime of fixed exchange[15] and the reciprocal relationship between the dollar and gold, that is the last tie that guaranteed a material and quantitative measure of the value of money.[16]

Neither of these conditions are present today. The financialization of the economy has annulled the autonomy of the national political economy, and currency value increasingly depends on the dynamics of hierarchical conventions that from time to time are defined by international relations on an imperial level. Money has finally been completely dematerialized; it has become pure *money-sign*. Its measurement is thus conventional, resulting from the social and international relations, product of the clash between capitalistic rent and the rent of social cooperation, between the production of use-value and the production of exchange value. The inherent variability of the current economic crisis has also had the collateral effect of undermining the conventional structures which are at the basis of some national currencies. Two cases, though different, are emblematic: Iceland and Zimbabwe. In the former (Iceland), the fall of financial indexes and the bankruptcy of various credit institutions particularly active in the securitization processes of derived products brought about a depreciation of the national currency (the

Icelandic Corona) of nearly 30% in 5 months until undermining the level of trust, creating a political crisis which in turn asked for the shift to a Euro based system, thus giving up national sovereignty. In the latter (Zimbabwe), facing an economic and humanitarian crisis as a result of a process of political instability, the national Central Bank gave up the exercising of seigniorage rights (the state monopoly over the emission of currency) by blocking the printing of money. Obviously these were two very different cases, but nevertheless they both involve the loss of monetary sovereignty. History demonstrates that similar situations could come about only as a consequence of the loss of national independence. Today, for the first time in history, monetary sovereignty and territorial sovereignty are no longer two sides of the same coin.

A condition for a new Bretton Woods is the existence of a stable, hierarchical and unilateral structure, that is defined by the acknowledgement of a single convention of accumulation and exploitation, accepted by force or persuasion on a global level. In other words, the question that is posed is whether or not a unilateral governance of the Empire—multipolar and multilateral by definition—is possible. A feasible solution to this paradox is the creation of a new Yalta. The new possible global configuration able to assure the valorization of cognitive capitalism through financial markets therefore passes, above all, through the possibility of controlling and defining the future trajectory of the new cognitive division of labor on an international level, homogeneously and unequivocally.

The Yalta accords of 1945 were the result of a global conflict of great proportions. They marked the pact between the winners of WWII with the objective of delineating the confines of the respective accumulation processes on a national base. Do we have to wait for a new bellicose catastrophe in order to get there?

At the moment, a new bellicose catastrophe is not in sight, also because the foreign policy of the new American administration seems to be more oriented toward developing a process of dialogue. Yet, this shouldn't divert from the fact that in the phase of cognitive capitalism the silence of commercial wars counts more than the rumble of arms. It is, in fact, on this ground that the possibility of defining a new Yalta is measured. Unlike 1945, today international relations are determined more by dynamics of geoeconomic variables rather than by the merely geopolitical variables. Today, Yalta and Bretton Woods cannot prescind from each other: one can't exist without the other, precisely for the lack of economic autonomy on a nation-state level. This is one of the consequences of the coming of the "Empire."

About this, the new American Treasury Secretary, Tim Geithner, asserted in a document presented to Congress for the inauguration of the new government that Chinese currency was "manipulated,"[17] meaning that Chinese monetary authorities artificially kept the Yuan low in order to commercially penetrate the US market. Actually, the Chinese Yuan was revalued by 20% in respect to the dollar after it was separated from it in July 2005. However, such revaluation had but little effect on the deficit of the US trade balance, confirming that the deficit is structurally embedded in the American system of accumulation and it doesn't depend on the simple dynamics of exchange rates. Nevertheless, a few days later, 53 members of Congress signed a letter to ask the Federal government that every public subsidy is to be "conditional on the creation of American jobs in America, not Chinese jobs in China"; at the end of January, the House of Representatives inserted the clause "buy American" in Obama's plan under discussion for the iron, steel and the textile sectors.[18]

Corporative and protectionist tendencies can therefore already be seen, not only as far as the free circulation of merchandise is concerned, but also in reference to the labor market.[19] It is evident that the possibility to imagine a series of multipolar accords relative to the constitution of a new Yalta and a new Bretton Woods lies on the China-US axis.

3. The Latent Conflict Between Economic and Social Governance

We have stated that in cognitive capitalism economic governance is founded on the double role played by the financial markets in funding the expropriation of general intellect and, at the same time, arranging the functions of distribution and social security through surplus value.

Social governance, instead, is ensured on the basis of this double track: blackmail and consensus. Blackmail is founded on rendering life and income precarious as a result of the individualization of labor relations. Consensus, instead, is based on the illusion of "proprietary individualism."

Until 2008, social governance coincided with economic governance. This was the consequence of the mediation induced by concerted union and political action, on the basis of two main conditions. The former, necessarily limited in time, is determined by the redistributive capacity, even if distorted, and the role of economic multiplier played by financial markets. The latter is based on the possibility, already contradictory in itself, of controlling general intellect (through the new proprietary forms of knowledge) and at the same time valorizing it not only as exchange value but also as a moment of the growth of creativity and social cooperation.

Social governance of cognitive capitalism is therefore tied, on the one hand, to the possibility that financial markets expand without limits (therefore growing) up to guaranteeing the illusion of proprietary individualism thanks to a massive diffusion of wealth through debt; on the other hand, it is tied to the existence of a willingness to engage in social cooperation that doesn't ask for anything, or very little in exchange and, above all, that it is characterized by a sort of self-control of the creative excess which is not functional to the mechanisms of capitalist valorization.

So far, such conditions have been imposed with violence,[20] more with blackmail than consensus, with emergency and securitarian policy, the fragmentation of the workforce, with the politics of the control of the symbolic and imaginary, with the fear of permanent war.

But all of this has not been enough, and when, with the financial crisis, the illusion of proprietary individualism dissolved in the tragic reality of debt individualism,[21] even social governance of latent conflicts is put under great pressure.

Elsewhere,[22] it has been discussed whether or not the institution of another New Deal adapted to the valorization processes of cognitive capitalism is feasible as the new face of social governance. The answer is no, not so much on a theoretical level as much as on an immanently political level.

From a theoretical point of view, in fact, the conditions to come out of the current systemic crisis exist. It would consist in operating on the very structure of the valorization mechanisms guided by the financial markets. In particular, on the level of accumulation, it is necessary to recognize that in cognitive capitalism the source of (surplus) value is derived from the exploitation of learning and network economies. Cognitive-relational labor, or *biolabor* (life put to work, outside of times officially certified by private law), represents the node around which both accumulation and distribution hinge. Financial market dynamics represents this bioeconomic valorization *in fieri*.

In the last analysis, not recognizing the value of biolabor is the central factor of the governance crisis in cognitive capitalism. To prevent this, it would be enough to operate on three levels:

a) Regarding accumulation, to define the productive social cooperation inherent to learning and relations as institutions of the Common, basing it on the formation of a "Law of the Commons" that limits the processes of private expropriation of knowledge;

b) As regards distribution, the institution of a basic income as remuneration (and not assistance) for socially diffused general intellect;

c) Concerning welfare policy, the definition of a Common welfare that supports the distribution of basic income and guarantees the institutions of the common during general intellect's development cycles. In fact, a new type of social conflict able to define the foundations of welfare of the common (commonfare[23]) can be opened through the reformulation of a welfare adapted to the new modalities of accumulation.

The dialectic between the capitalistic attempt to recover the wealth that originates in social cooperation and the re-appropriation of Common value by the multitudes is what is at stake here. And it seems there are non-negotiable points at the political level. Economic governance is theoretically possible only through giving up social governance.

The introduction of basic income as direct payment of general intellect's productivity weighs on the possibility of capitalistic economic command of actuating forms of control over the labor process. By guaranteeing an unconditional income as payment for the social cooperation that exceeds the current certified forms of traditional labor performance to all citizens, the blackmail of labor deriving from the necessity of income in order to survive vanishes. As Marx already found,[24] such blackmail is one of the tools of domination of one class over another. It is therefore not possible to maintain such social governance over labor that today is made possible by precarious conditions and the working proletarianization within what we have defined as the double track of blackmail and consensus.

Likewise, as concerns accumulation, the necessity of a working capacity founded on the free and productive circulation of knowledge as a condition to restore an accumulation mechanism violates one of the foundations of the capitalistic system, that is the principle of private property of the means of production (yesterday the machine, today knowledge *too*).

Economic governance thus leads to the possible overcoming of the capitalistic structure of accumulation. It means that it opens the road to the development of postcapitalistic forms of social production. In other words, the reform of the process of accumulation, made necessary by the reasons that are at the basis of the current crisis, implies renouncing social governance practices. There is no longer any space for reformist politics.

The wedge of the social mobilization of the multitudes can and must insert itself into this irremediable contradiction.

This is the true meaning of the slogan: "We will not pay for your crisis!"

Carlo Vercellone

The Crisis of the Law of Value and the

Becoming-Rent of Profit

Notes on the systemic crisis of cognitive capitalism

Introduction

This article aims to provide a few elements of theoretical reading of
the current crisis, taking the thesis of the "becoming-rent of profit
and the crisis of the law of value" as a starting point. Following the
crisis in the Fordist model, the current transformation of capitalism
is characterised by a full-fledged comeback and proliferation of
forms of rent parallel to a complete change in the relationship
between wages, rent and profit. Theoretically and politically, this
evolution has been interpreted in different ways.

In particular, according to a widespread opinion in the Marxian
theory deriving from Ricardo's political economy, rent is a pre-
capitalist legacy and an obstacle to the progressive movement of
capital's accumulation. On this premise real, pure and efficient
capitalism is capitalism without rent.

A similar view wholly substitutes the key role of ground rent
with that of financial rent, is being proposed nowadays to interpret
the systemic crisis that hit capitalism following the popping of the

speculative bubble created by subprime loans, but more generally founded on the securitization of credit under the form of *fictitious capital*. According to this analysis, the meaning of the current crisis lies in a conflict between, on the one side, a tendency of financial capitalism towards rent, and on the other, the 'good' productive capitalist defense of an accumulation logic that favors the growth of production and employment.

As the analyses of several economists of the Labor Left in France and Italy suggest, this interpretation leads to the proposal of a sort of neo-Ricardian compromise between wage labor and productive capital against the power of finance. Such a compromise would allegedly bring stability back into the hegemony of the managerial capitalism of Fordism, alongside the necessary conditions for a growth that approaches full employment; all of this in a context of significant continuity with Fordist modes of labor organization and regulation of the wage relation. At the same time, it would restore the good functioning to the *law of labor time value* as the norm for the distribution and measurement of value, against the distortions that finance has inflicted on them by making the prices of immaterial and material assets (e.g. houses) rise in a speculative way and appropriating a disproportionate quota of the profit created in the real economy for itself.

In our opinion, this reading is mistaken on four accounts:

a) It is mistaken on the role of rent in capitalism because it regards it as a category that is external to the movement of capital and opposed to the category of profit;

b) Its denunciation of the return and perverse effects of rent is disconnected from any analysis of the underlying transformations that, following the crisis of Fordism, intervened to shape the forms of division of labor and the capital-labor relation. Transformations that, as we will see, are for the most part tied to the growth in potency of the cognitive and immaterial dimension of labor. However, the development of financial services represents only one of the aspects of these dimensions, even if it is the most unclear among them;

c) Omitting the importance of the evolutions that ended the hegemonic role of capital accumulation's industrial logic and that have lead to an increasingly pronounced tendency towards rent and speculation of productive capitalism itself;

d) It does not really perceive, whereas Marazzi strongly underlines it in his fundamental contribution to this volume, finance's *pervasive nature*, the way in which it "is spread over the entire economic cycle" of the production-distribution-realization of value. Thus it involves a multitude of social subjects and economic agents and making it increasingly difficult to clearly distinguish the financial economy from the real economy.

Certainly, it is not about denying the relative autonomy that finance enjoys and the systemic power that it possesses. A power that is manifested both during the growth phase, when finance appropriates an exuberant part of the profits,[1] and during the phase that it goes through after the burst of a speculative bubble. In this frame, the threat of transforming a local crisis into a global crisis allows finance to *take hostage* numerous institutions, obtaining formidable and unconditional concessions from Central Banks and from governments.

However, underlying finance as if it was a quasi-absolute autonomous power that could engulf the so-called real economy too often leads to the omission of the permeation between financial and productive capital just as the other socioeconomic causes at the origin of the contradictions of the crisis in capital valorization.

Such a view omits, for example, the way in which the passage from the crisis of internet market conventions to the crisis of the real-estate market conventions lies not only in the cyclic repetition of the logic of finance, but marks a fundamental turning point in the dynamic of cognitive capitalism. In fact, the crisis of March 2000, tied to the fall of NASDAQ, sanctioned the end of the myths of the New Economy. In so doing, it reveals the structural limits that capital meets in the attempt to subjugate the immaterial economy and the internet to the logic of commercialization, where the principle of gratuitousness continues to predominate despite the attempts to establish economic barriers to the access and the reinforcement of intellectual property rights.[2] When the old sectors driving Fordist growth entered into decline and clashed with market saturation and the competition of developing countries, a formidable accentuation of the subjective and structural contradictions of cognitive capitalism is seen. These contradictions are in fact related to the impossibility of the part of capital to integrate the immaterial and knowledge economy into a progressive growth dynamic as a basis for the new expansion of outlets and its own legitimacy in social and productive organization. Proof is the globally disastrous balance of the macroeconomic Bush age legacy. After the NASDAQ crisis, the rare years of economic dynamism (2004–2007) were almost exclusively due to a speculative bubble, in which the development of real-estate and financial sectors fed one another, assuring a 40% growth in the American private sector. At the same time, wages compression and the explosion of distributive inadequacies in income that pushed the abnormal development of consumer credit cannot be thought of as simply resulting from financial avidity. Their structural reasons are also and especially found in the strategies of putting labor in precarious conditions by capital in order to guarantee the control of an increasingly autonomous labor-force at the level of productive organization.

All in all, financialization and more generally the growth of the role of rent are for a large part the consequence and not only the cause of these global conditions within cognitive capitalism. The same consideration is valid for understanding the nature and the cause of the opening of the current crisis that would be erroneous to consider—as most economists do—essentially as a crisis of financial origin that, for its systemic consequences, ends up involving the real economy in a second moment. Looking closely, this framework could be overturned. Numerous economic, social and ecological indicators of a global crisis were quite visible before the financial crisis exploded. It is enough to think about the inherent difficulties of the commercial development in the New Economy sectors, the latent crisis of the automobile industry, the unsustainable family debt as well as the international economic and financial imbalances and the spectacular rise in the prices of primary and alimentary goods.

To use the categories of the French Regulation School, the current crisis of cognitive capitalism is not merely, as in 1929, a "great crisis" of the regulation mode, in relation with the foundations of an accumulation regime that could be substantially viable. Therefore the meaning and the possibility of coming out of the crisis cannot be reduced to the research of a new capital-labor compromise able to limit the power of finance and reestablish the Fordist connection between wages and productivity assuring, in this way, a harmonious development of its own productive and consumption norms founded on knowledge and the immaterial.

Instead, the thesis explored in this article is that the depth of the current crisis expresses more the irreconcilable character of cognitive capitalism with the social conditions at the root of the development of an economy founded on knowledge and necessary for the preservation of the planet's ecologic equilibrium.

We are talking about a structural crisis that most fundamentally hits the contradiction between the development of productive forces and the social relations of production. To use André Gorz's wonderful formulation, it indicates the way in which "capitalism has reached a frontier in the development of productive forces beyond which it cannot reproduce [...] without superseding itself into another economy."[3]

This contradiction is closely tied to the crisis of the law of value and the tendency that we have defined through the thesis of the becoming-rent of profit.

What should be understood by crisis of the law of value?

Overall, such crisis is presented as a crisis of measurement that destabilizes the very sense of the fundamental categories of the political economy; labor, capital and obviously, value. But even more fundamentally, the crisis of the *law of labor time-value* is not limited to a measurement crisis, but corresponds to two elements that particularly show, in the advanced capitalist countries, the exhaustion of the progressive force of capital and its increasingly parasitical character.[4]

The first element corresponds to the exhaustion of the law of value as the criterion of capitalistic rationalization of production capable, as in industrial capitalism, of making the abstract labor, measured in a unit of time of simple, non-qualified labor, the tool allowing for the control over the labor and simultaneously favoring the growth of social productivity. This crisis is associated with the return and the growth of the power of labor's cognitive dimension. It corresponds to the assertion of a new hegemony of knowledge incorporated in labor with respect to the knowledge embodied in fixed capital and the managerial business organization. In this framework, profit, like rent, increasingly depends on mechanisms of value expropriation that proceed from a position of exteriority in respect of the organization of production.

The second element consists in the exhaustion of the law of value understood as the social relation that makes commodification logic the key and progressive criteria for the development of the production of use values and the satisfaction of needs. In order to better understand this assertion, it needs to be remembered how for Marx, or even Ricardo, *value* (of merchandise) depended on the difficulty of production and therefore on labor time. Thus value concept is radically different from the concept of wealth that instead depends on abundance and use value. The capitalistic logic of production had found, in industrial capitalism, a sort of historical legitimacy in the capacity to favor the development of *wealth* through the production of a growing quantity of merchandises with a unitary value and thus relatively lowering prices, satisfying a growing quantity of true or superfluous needs. In this sense, the capitalistic development of productive forces and the profit could present themselves as an instrument of struggle against scarcity. In cognitive capitalism, this "positive" relation between *value* and *wealth* is broken and it evolves toward a veritable disassociation. The survival of the dominance of the logic of exchange-value, like that of capitalistic property, in fact is increasingly based on the destruction of non-renewable scarce resources and/or on the creation of an artificial scarcity of resources. This process operates through mechanisms where profit is confused with rent.

It should be pointed out right away, without ambiguity, that it does not mean that labor is no longer the substance and the source of the creation of value and surplus value. It simply means that the law of value-surplus value and the exploitation survives as an emptied shell in respect of what Marx, wrongly or rightly considered as the progressive functions of capital, i.e. its active, demiurgic role in the organization of labor and in the development of productive forces as means of struggle against scarcity and of the passage from the *rein of necessity to that of liberty*.

It also means that capital-labor antagonism increasingly takes the form of antagonism between the institutions of the common as the foundations of knowledge-based economy and the logic of expropriation of cognitive capitalism that develops itself under the form of rent—a rent whereof finance is only one of the expressions even if it often synthesizes all of them through the transformation of fictitious commodities[5] into fictitious capital.

To demonstrate our thesis, the following of this article is divided into two parts.

In the first part we will come back to the definition of the categories of wages, rent and profit. We will insist upon the flexible and mobile borders that separate the category of rent from profit. To do so, we will base the argument on some points that Marx develops in the third book of *Capital*, when he sketches a theory of the becoming-rent of capital, a theory that can be put into relation with the hypotheses of *general intellect*.

In the second part, we propose a reading of the historical transformations of the capital-labor relation which have simultaneously lead to a growth in the power of rent and to a crumbling of the distinction between rent and profit.

I. Wages, Rent and Profit: Some Definitions

According to Marx, wage, rent and profit are the three major categories of income distribution emerging with capitalist relations and, in the same way as the latter, are historical. In this perspective, we will here try to produce a few conceptual tools to understand wage, profit and rent transformations within contemporary capitalism, focusing on this last category in some depth.

From a logical point of view let us start with wages. Why? For the simple reason that wage in capitalism designates remuneration of productive labor, i.e. the labor that produces the surplus-value that is at the origin of both profit and rent production.

As Marx has already pointed out about the factory, this surplus-value is not intended as a simple sum of the individual surplus-labor of each wage-worker. On the contrary, it is conceived of as the gratuitous appropriation of the surplus generated by the social cooperation of labor. This is a crucial aspect of the following analysis. In this context, the concepts of wage, productive labor and exploitation are necessarily to be thought inside a framework where this cooperation is no longer confined within the factory but extended to the whole of society. On the other hand, it organizes itself more and more autonomously from capital.

After wages, we are going to examine rent and profit as forms of revenue which permit the surplus-labor's product appropriation. Theoretically, the notion of rent is very complex.

We would like to suggest a definition that starts from three closely related aspects. They will enable us to describe rent's role in the reproduction of productive relations as well as in the relations of distribution which constitute the other side of rent's concept.

From the standpoint of production relations, the first aspect is used to chart the genesis and essence of capitalist rent as the result of a process of expropriation of the social conditions of production and reproduction. The formation of modern ground rent coincides with the process of enclosures, the first expropriation of the common that was the 'preliminary and *sine qua non* condition' for land transformation and labor power into fictitious commodities. We can already draw a theoretical lesson on this premise. The varying significance of rent's role in the history of capitalism is closely linked to what, following K. Polanyi, can be defined as the historical alternation, inside economy, of stages of de-socialization, re-socialization and then new de-socializations.

Therefore, rent can be grounded in the epoch of primitive accumulation. The different forms it assumes throughout the history of capitalism tend always to lead to privatization of the social conditions of production and to the transformation of the common into fictitious commodities.

Here we identify a common trait that subsumes under a single logic both the first land enclosures and the new enclosures based on knowledge and life. This analogy can be applied to the role of public debt during the first stage of primitive capitalist accumulation at the time of mercantilism. Similarly, it can be used to describe the important role privatization of currency and public debt has played in the development of financial rent and in the destabilization of welfare state institutions in the current historical conjuncture.

Despite these elements of continuity, it is nevertheless important to emphasize a decisive historical particularity in the current process of neoliberal de-socialization of the economy. Nowadays, the expropriation of the common does not only rest on pre-capitalistic conditions such as land, which, in Rosa Luxemburg's sense, belong to the external sphere of capitalism. The contemporary process of de-socialization of the economy mostly depends on the expropriation of elements of the common. Those elements have been constructed by social struggles there where the development of productive forces is most advanced, and where some institutional and structural bases of a knowledge based economy are oriented beyond the logic of the capital. These are what we could define, at least potentially, as elements of a post-capitalist *exterior*. Its worth referring, for example, to the guarantees and to the *collective productions of man for man*, historically insured by the welfare state's institutions, such as the healthcare, education and research systems. We will later come back to this point that plays, in our opinion, a central role in rent's recovery and in the characterization of what is at stake in the current crisis.

The second aspect of rent is that resources on which *rentier* appropriation is based do not generally tend to increase with rent; indeed they do exactly the opposite. In other words, quoting Napoleoni's definition, rent is "the revenue that the owner of certain goods receives as a consequence of the fact that these goods are, or become, available in scarce quantities [...]"[6] Rent is thus linked to the natural or, more frequently, to the artificial scarcity of a resource, i.e. to a logic of rarefaction of such resource, as in the case of monopolies. Therefore the existence of rent is based upon monopolistic forms of property and positions of power that permit the creation of scarcity and the imposition of higher prices, justified by the cost of production. Scarcity is induced in most cases by institutional artefacts, as shown today by the policies of reinforcement of Intellectual Property Rights.

Finally, in its third aspect, unlike feudal rent, capitalist rent can be seen as a pure relation of distribution because it no longer has any "function, or at least any normal function in the process of production."[7] Therefore, rent presents itself as a credit title or a right to the ownership of some material and immaterial resource that grants a right to drawing value from a position of exteriority in respect to production.

On this basis, we can now turn to profit and to the criteria that distinguish it from rent, which are much less evident than what is normally thought. In order to do this, it is useful to return to the example of ground rent, which consists in the remuneration of the land owner by means of the use of the land he owns. In this sense, according to an idea inherited from the classics, rent can be conceived of as what is left once everyone who contributes to production has been remunerated. Noticeably, in this conception, everything depends on one's understanding of 'contribution to production' and of 'who contributes to production.' Thus, if we accept the classical and still valid definition of profit, profit is the remuneration of capital and it requires the obtainment of a revenue proportional to the mass of capitals invested in production.

As Smith has already pointed out, profit as such has nothing to do with the retribution of coordination and surveillance functions of production, carried out by the entrepreneur or company executive. This given, one could also consider capital remuneration as rent, the same way as land remuneration. In fact, owner's capital can easily limit himself to providing the means of production without putting them to work in person.[8]

In effect, Keynes himself, in his *observations on the nature of capital* in the *General Theory* proposes a strong and original answer to this question: he considers that the return on capital as such depends on scarcity: we are thus dealing with an instance of rent and Keynes will connect this affirmation to the support for the theory of labor-value in the classics of political economy.

Faced with this unresolved aporia of classical political economy, the two most serious arguments developed in economic theory to effect a rigorous distinction between rent and profit derive from Marx, and they are the following:

i) The first argument claims that, unlike rent, profit is essentially conserved within business in order to be reinvested in production. In this way, profit would play a positive role in the development of productive forces and in the struggle against scarcity;

ii) The second argument concerns the internal character of capital as related to the process of production (still unlike rent). It is here considered as the necessary condition for the management and organization of labor. This interiority rests on the correspondence between the figure of the capitalist and that of the entrepreneur. It also informs the managerial logic embodied in productive capital and plays a key role in the management of production, innovation and the expansion of productive capacity. In both cases, the interiority of capital presupposes a distinct opposition between conceptual labor (an attribute of capital and its functionaries) and the labor of banal execution (an attribute of labor);

To better understand this second argument it is necessary to remember how, according to Marx, the capitalistic process of production is the contradictory unity of two dimensions.[9] The first dimension is the *labor process* aiming at the production of use-value: from this point of view the potentially directional function of capital is an objective function of the organization of production. The second dimension is the *valorization process* aiming at the production of commodities through the exploitation of wage-labor. From this point of view, capital's form of direction is despotic and marked by an antagonism that leads capital to restructure the *labor process* according to the *valorization process*. In Marx's opinion, in the age of industrial capitalism and *real subsumption*, it is the capacity to simultaneously assure these two functions that make of the capitalist an *agent of production*. Thus, this capacity gives the appearance of an objective and necessary condition to the management of the labor process to capital's power over labor. For this reason, profit appeared as a category of distribution internal to the productive process, unlike rent which is considered as *a pure relation of distribution*.

However, as we will see, the realization of these two conditions which are necessary to the distinction—or better—to the opposition of rent-profit, is not but the transitory product of an epoch of capitalism, of industrial capitalism. More precisely, these two conditions are fully realized in the golden age of Fordist growth, during which both the logic of real subsumption of labor to capital and mass production found their expression. These borders are instead increasingly blurred in cognitive capitalism. But before developing this first element of our analysis, it is useful to make another brief theoretical digression through Marx, when in the third Book of *Capital* he delineates the hypothesis of capital rent.

Excursus—From Book III of Capital to General Intellect: The Hypothesis of Capital-Rent in Marx

In several of his writings, Marx seems to distinguish between rent and profit according to the following two criteria:

Like classical economists, in the analysis of capital in general (volume I and II), Marx seems to assume that the industrial capitalist owns his own capital and manages his enterprise, which in fact was often the case at the time of the writing of *Capital*. The industrial capitalist thus seems to be opposed to the figure of the *rentier* as far as the former is directly involved in production relations and makes investments towards the development of the productive forces (and the reduction of scarcity of capital).

Marx's thought identifies the second and more important criterion within the framework of a tendency towards real subsumption. It is here that, as Marx puts it, the purely despotic functions of production and the objective functions of the capitalist organization of production seem to merge. This convergence depends on how far the embodiment of science in fixed capital and in the separation of conceptual from executive labor provides the management of capital with an objective foundation inscribed in the very materiality of the productive forces. For this reason Marx claims that "the capitalist and the wage laborer are the only two agents of production [...] whilst the land owner, an essential agent of production in the ancient and medieval world, is a useless excrescence in the world of industry."[10]

However, in volume III of *Capital*, whilst developing his analysis of capital as the bearer of *interest* and *profit of the enterprise* [Unternehmergewinn], Marx questions the terms of the opposition between profit and rent as well as the limits of a definition of rent reduced to ground rent only. He takes this reasoning further and eventually comes to consider the becoming rent of profit and capital ownership. In order to do so, he introduces a conceptual distinction between two determinations of capital, namely ownership and function [performing capital], and links this distinction back to that between interest as revenue from capital ownership and the active profit of the entrepreneur who manages production. On this premise he goes on to develop two complementary theses.

The first concerns the manner in which the tendency of the development of credit and stockholdings companies was leading to a deep separation of capital ownership from its management. According to Marx, capital ownership was following a similar path to that of ground rent in the shift from feudalism to capitalism: it is to say that it was becoming external in relation to the sphere of production and, like land ownership, capital ownership was extracting surplus value whilst no longer exercising any function in the organization of labor.

Thus, it "remains only the functionary and the capitalist, as superfluous, disappears from the production process."[11] Marx distinguishes between the passivity of the ownership of capital and the active character of the performing capital. Resulting from the separation of property from management, this last becomes increasingly embodied in the figure of the manager, where functions of leadership and exploitation of labor take on the false appearance of a wage laborer practicing conceptual and organizational tasks in production.

In many ways, here, Marx anticipated Keynes's analysis of the *General Theory* where the figure of the entrepreneur is opposed to that of the speculator and that explicitly extends the concept of rent to the ownership of capital. On this basis, Keynes forecasted "the euthanasia of the *rentier*, and, consequently, the euthanasia of the cumulative oppressive power of the capitalist to exploit the scarcity-value of capital."[12] In fact, Keynes argued that "interest today rewards no genuine sacrifice, any more than does the rent of land."[13]

However, in volume III of *Capital* Marx went further than Keynes and profiled a situation where the *rentier* and parasitical character of capital becomes associated with productive capital itself. In fact, the second hypothesis concerns an evolution of the capital/labor relation where the position of exteriority of the ownership of capital from production goes hand in hand with a crisis of real subsumption linked to the workers' process of re-appropriation of knowledge.

In this framework, Marx tells us that the coordinating functions of the manager's production, of the functionary of capital, becomes superfluous too and thus appears to be purely despotic when confronted with a productive cooperation that is capable of organizing itself autonomously from capital. On this issue, Marx quotes a passage from Hodgskin—who would be largely influential in the development of his theory of the general intellect—where he claims that "[t]he wide spread of education among the journeymen mechanics of this country diminishes daily the value of the labor and skill of almost all masters and employers by increasing the number of persons who possess their peculiar knowledge,"[14] thus making the managerial and intellectual functions exercised by capital increasingly redundant.

To conclude our digression, we would claim that this theory of capital-rent, merely drafted in volume III, acquires strength and theoretical and historical relevance in the context of a thesis on the general intellect for two main reasons.

Confronted with the emergence of a diffuse intellectuality, the Hodgskianian thesis on the unproductivity of capital becomes an attribute of all the functions of capital (ownership and management). In this framework, Marx claims that "even the last pretext for the confusion of profit of enterprise and wages of management was removed, and profit appeared also in practice as it undeniably appeared in theory, as mere surplus-value, a value for which no equivalent was paid, as realized unpaid labor."[15] Hence, profit derives from a simple appropriation of free labor operated, just like for rent, without having any real function in the process of production.

In an economy based on the driving role of knowledge the law of value founded on labor time is in crisis. One of the implications of this crisis is that, since the directly necessary labor time for production is weak, there is a risk of a drastic reduction of the monetary value of production and its related profits. As a result, in an attempt to forcedly keep the prominence of exchange value in place and guarantee profits, capital is led to develop *rentier*-logic based on the rarefaction of supply.

To sum up, with an extraordinary power of foresight, the development of the analysis of volume III of *Capital*, together with the *Grundrisse*, helps us see how from the standpoint of the objective as well as the subjective conditions of production, the becoming rent of capital was inevitable. Yet Marx does not make this association because his hypothesis was only a potential becoming and a tendency situated in the long run at the time, and quite rightly so. After his death and despite the turbulence and expansion of financial rent that characterized the historical period between the great depression of the end of the 19th century and the crisis of the 1930s, the framework for the development of industrial capitalism was still largely characterized by a deepening of real subsumption.

II. From Industrial Capitalism to Cognitive Capitalism

Let us now turn to the analysis of changes in the relationship between wages, rent and profit in the historical shift from industrial to cognitive capitalism.

a) The Marginalization of Rent in Fordism—After the crisis of 1929 and during the postwar period, rent was progressively marginalized as industrial capitalism—directly involved in the creation of surplus-value—became hegemonic. Four main factors explain this marginalization in the golden age of Fordist growth:

— A set of institutional tools relative to financial market regulation, progressive taxes on income and Keynesian regulation of currency availability contributes to limit the power of patrimonial property, favoring at the same time an inflationist process associated with very low, sometimes negative, real interest rates;
— The development of welfare institutions allows the socialization of the conditions of labor-force reproduction and excludes a growing amount of incomes from capital's logic of valorization and of financial power;
— In the leading firms involved in mass production, the development of Taylorist and Fordist principles of labor organization facilitated the accomplishment of a trend to separate conceptual from executive labor. Consequently, the hegemony of managerial capitalism in Galbraith's sense could be established. Here we underline the power of a technical structure that grounded its legitimacy on its role in the planning and development of innovation within the organization of production (around the white collar offices and laboratories of research and development). This resulted in a managerial logic that relegated the interests of the share holders and other 'unproductive' modes of capitalist valorization to a secondary role. Besides, the managerial organization of big business seems to prioritize productive investment and therefore the development of production as a struggle against scarcity.

— Lastly, consistent with this logic of accumulation centered on fixed capital, the role of intellectual property rights was very limited.

In this framework, the distribution of income is thus concentrated around the conflict between wages and profit, and more precisely between company profit and a wage dynamic that found its main drive in the large Fordist enterprises. Moreover, this allows wages to grow closely to productivity.

Rent featured in a secondary role, especially in relation to the increase of ground rent taxation that was connected to urbanization following a logic that almost defied that of profit. As evidence of this we recall Agnelli's proposal at the beginning of the 1970s to form a neo-Ricardian alliance between patronage and trade unions against the urban rent which he believed to be responsible for the inflation of wage rise demands in the Hot Autumn.[16]

b) The Return of Rent in Cognitive Capitalism—This arrangement was threatened with the social crisis of Fordism and the development of cognitive capitalism. Our times are characterized by a proliferation of forms of rent and, in the meantime, by a blurring of the distinction between rent and profit. In new capitalism, profit rests increasingly on two mechanisms, related to what, following J.M.Chevalier (1977), may be defined as the "improductive valorization of capital."[17]

— The first mechanism concerns the key role of different forms of property (from shareholders' ownership to patents) *as well as* credits titles, which corresponds to a formal right to collect part of the generated value from a position that is external to production.

— The second mechanism consists in the progressive substitution of direct command over the production process with marketplace command, and this through the construction of a monopoly position that, through capital's ability to found the appropriation of value created on the outside of the business context, imposes itself as an intermediary between labor and market, according to a logic that recalls the putting-out system.[18]

More importantly, this exteriorization of capital with respect to production concerns both the organization of labor within companies and their relationship with the outside.

Two trends follow the tendency outlined in our thesis.

On one hand, with the shift towards a cognitive division of labor, business competitiveness increasingly depends on external circumstances and on their ability to seize the rent linked to a differential productivity that arises from a location in terms of its knowledge resources and the quality of its education system and public research. In other words, contrary to the Smithian model of industry based on the central role of the technical division of labor in the factory, the source of the 'wealth of nations' rests on a productive cooperation that is external to the company grounds.

On the other hand, the main source of value now resides in creativity and knowledge that are mobilized by living labor rather than fixed capital and the routine labor of execution. In so far as the organization of labor becomes increasingly autonomous, Taylorist engineers either disappear or become the avatar of times past. In this framework, control over labor no longer takes on the Taylorist role of direct allocation of tasks; it is mostly replaced by indirect mechanisms based on the imperative to deliver, the prescription of subjectivity and a pure and simple coercion linked to the precarization of the wage relation.

Thus, capital has to recognize that work has a growing autonomy in the organization of production, even if this autonomy is limited to the choice of the means with which to attain heterodetermined objectives.

In this context, the old dilemma about the control of labor reappears in a new form. Capital has not only become dependent on the knowledge of laborers again, but it must also obtain a mobilization and an active implication of the entire knowledge and social times of wage workers. The *prescription of the subjectivity* to obtain the interiorization of the company's goals, the client pressure but also and above all, the pure and simple coercion associated with precarious labor, are the main ways in which capital tries to answer this new form of dilemma.

Therefore, precariousness of labor-power is presented as a factor, largely structural, of the neoliberal regulation of cognitive labor, despite its counterproductive effects regarding an effective management of the knowledge economy. This fact greatly helps to explain wage stagnation and frozen buying power of the so-called middle classes.[19]

In this logic, we find the explanation for the monetary and incomes policies that, disregarding the hypothesis of a reform of the distribution and redistribution mechanisms have deliberately favored in the United States the explosion of consumer credit and family debt. This choice, in particular since 2002, should have played a triple function: i) compensating with credit the risk of consumption stagnation which in the United States, as in France, reached 70% of the GDP; ii) assuring to capital, through the accumulation of interests charged on families, a new indirect source of surplus value extraction; iii) creating through the generalization of debt, a dependent subjectivity, a subjectivity conforming to capital, and in which the rationality of *homo oeconomicus*, of *human capital*, replaces the idea of social rights and common goods.

Two conclusions can be drawn from this analysis.

Firstly, the very concept of productive labor (of surplus value) and therefore wages as well as the content of collective negotiation should be rethought integrating a whole of temporalities and activities that exceed official work hours done inside the company.

Secondly, as Paulré underlines, large companies are today essentially concerned with their financial architecture and ultimately seem to occupy themselves with everything but the direct organisation of production. To paraphrase Veblen's prophetic expression, "large companies have become a place of business rather than of the creation of industry,"[20] and in this respect company profits could increasingly become assimilated to rents.

It should be noted that even from this point of view, financialization is not simply the product of a change in the power struggle between management and stockholders. Above all it also results from an endogenous change in the logic of valorization of large industrial groups. All this occurs as if the movement of autonomization of labor cooperation corresponded to a parallel movement of autonomization of capital in the abstract and eminently flexible and mobile form of money-capital.

In addition, this tendency goes hand in hand with a distortion of the traditional functions attributed by *economic science* to financial markets. According to mainstream economics, financial markets are assumed to be able to assure the best risk management (!) and an optimal allocation of capital. Moreover, contrary to the theory according to which stock markets finance firms, what we have observed all over these years of the development of a speculative bubble is that firms have fueled with liquidity (dividends, interests, etc.) and stock-market surplus-values their stockholders, often with negative returns.[21]

Moreover, such dynamic is associated with a stagnation of productive investment in Europe and, in particular, in France. We are dealing with the reason why some economists have spoken of *a model of profit without capital accumulation.*[22]

In short, the driving role of profit in the development of the productive forces and thus in the struggle against scarcity also appears heavily compromised. This evolution participates in the more general tendency of capital to transform profit into a *rentier* mechanism of drawing surplus-value from a position of exteriority in respect to production and/or founded on the creation of an artificial resource rarefaction.

However, at this stage of our reflection and before embarking on a more detailed analysis of different forms of rent, the following question arises: what is the new role of rent, not only at the level of the sphere of distribution, but also in the expropriation of the common and the regulation of the capital-labor relation in cognitive capitalism? To answer this question, a crucial political and theoretical point needs to be made. That is, there is a contradiction, if not actual antagonism, between the logic of cognitive capitalism, on one hand and the dynamics of collective creation and emancipation that lie at the origin of the development of an economy founded on the crucial role and spread of knowledge, on the other.

In fact, in our opinion, the point of departure and main feature of the current transformation of capitalism are neither financialization nor the Information and Communication Technologies (ICT) revolution; but two other phenomenons at the core of the crisis of the Fordist wage relation:

a) First and foremost, the constitution of a diffuse intellectuality generated by the development of mass education and the rising of the average levels of training. This new intellectual quality of labor power brought about the affirmation of a new prevailing quality of living knowledge, which labor incorporates and sets into motion in relation to the knowledge embodied in fixed capital and the managerial organization of companies.

b) Secondly, conflicts that led to the spread of social income and welfare services incompatible with the Fordist regulation mode. This dynamic has often been interpreted as a simple factor in the crisis of Fordism, given the increase of the cost of reproduction of labor-power. In reality, *a posteriori*, we can see that in fact it provided two crucial conditions for the development of a knowledge based economy.

In order to understand the importance of this dynamic we should insist on the "stylized fact" often evoked by economic theory to characterize the genesis of a knowledge based economy.

This stylized fact refers back to the historical dynamic through which part of so-called immaterial capital (R&D, software, but especially education, training and health) which is essentially embodied in men, has surpassed the part of material capital in the real stock of capital and has become the principal factor of growth.

The interpretation of this stylized fact has three other major meanings, which are systematically occluded by mainstream economists but, in our opinion, essential for understanding the origin and the stakes of the current crisis.

The first is that the tendency to increase in immaterial capital is therefore strictly linked to factors that are at the basis of the formation of a diffuse intellectuality and the new hegemony of cognitive labor: it is the latter that explains the increasingly significant part played by growth of that which is mistakenly called intangible capital.

The second meaning is that so-called immaterial capital really corresponds, for the most part, to the intellectual and creative capacities which are embodied in and mobilized by labor-power. It thus corresponds to the way in which, to quote Tronti 'labor-power as non-capital' now exercises a hegemonic role with regard to science and the knowledge incorporated into fixed capital.

In this sense, the notion of immaterial capital is a symptom of the crisis of the very category of constant capital that affirmed itself with industrial capital, where C (constant capital) was presented as dead labor, crystallized in the machines that imposed its dominion on living labor. Despite the torsion introduced by terms like "intellectual capital," "intangible capital" or "human capital," such capital is nothing other than collective intelligence. It consequently escapes any objective measurement. Its value can't be anything but the subjective expression of the expectation for future profits effectuated by financial markets who procure themselves rent in this way. This helps to explain why the "market" value of this capital is essentially *fictitious*. It is based on a financially self-referential logic destined, sooner or later, to fall apart, threatening the global credit system and the whole economy by provoking a systemic crisis. In brief, as emphasized by André Gorz, the dynamic of new capitalism, characterized by the succession of progressively serious crises, is not simply produced by "bad" finance regulation, but expresses "the intrinsic difficulty to make immaterial capital function like capital and cognitive capitalism to function like capitalism."[23]

But that's not all. Not only capital, but the very product of labor is increasingly immaterial and is incorporated in innovation, knowledge and digital services that constitute fictitious commodities.

Why fictitious commodities? They are fictitious commodities because they are outside of the criteria that define traditional goods because they are non-rival, cumulative and difficultly *excludable*.

Thus an eminently contradictory situation that, as we have already explained, was at the origin of the crisis of the New Economy, is created and continues to get worse. On one hand, from the point of view of demand, despite the reinforcing of intellectual property rights, immaterial production doesn't reach enough commercial outlets to be able to truly replace the traditional sectors of the economy where demand is close to saturation and increasingly subject to international competition based on its costs. On the other hand, the way in which capital's attempt to transform knowledge into a capital and a fictive commodity generates a paradoxical situation, a situation in which the more the exchange-value of knowledge artificially increases, the more its social use-value diminishes by virtue of its privatization and rarefaction. In other words, cognitive capitalism cannot perpetuate itself except by blocking the development of the productive forces and the creativity of the agents on the basis of a knowledge-based economy.[24]

The third meaning is that the truly driving sectors of an economy founded on knowledge are not found in the private R&D laboratories. Such a driving role is instead played by the collective *man for man productions*, traditionally assured by the common institutions of the welfare state according to a non commercial logic. This element explains the extraordinary pressure exercised by capital to privatize collective welfare services, and this is both for its strategic role in the growth of the social demand and in biopolitical and bioeconomic control of the population.[25]

Even in this case, just as in knowledge-based goods, the subordination of this sector to commercial logic and profit cannot but lead to an artificial resource rarefaction in subjection to the solvent demand and a destructuring of the creative forces at the base of the development of an economy founded on the driving role of knowledge and its diffusion.

In fact, three factors, on a social and economic level, make the extension of the capitalist rationality of the law of value to *man to man production* entirely counterproductive, depriving it of that progressive force that, for certain aspects, had pushed industrial capitalism in the production of standardized material goods. The first factor is tied to the intrinsically cognitive and affective character of these activities in which labor did not consist in acting upon inanimate material but on man himself in a relation of coproduction of services. The second one depends on the impossibility of raising measured productivity according to quantitative criteria if not to the detriment of the quality that qualifies the effectiveness of a service relation, like, for example in the health sector and/or in transmission of knowledge. The third factor is tied to the profound distortions that the application of the principle of solvent demand would introduce in the allocation of resources and in the right to access to these common goods. By definition, common productions are founded on gratuity and free access. Their financing therefore can only be assured through the collective and political price represented by taxation, social contributions or other forms of resource collectivization.

Hence the crucial stake that, as social conflicts have shown in the last few months in Italy, France, and Greece, is represented by the clash between the neoliberal strategy of *rentier* expropriation of the common and a project of economic re-socialization founded on the democratic re-appropriation of welfare institutions and *an alternative development model based on the centrality of man for man productions*.

It should be stressed how, in the near future, this battlefield will be aggravated by social costs tied to public interventions put into work to save the banking system and to finance the stimulus plans to rekindle the economy. *De facto*, one of the principle consequences of such intervention measures has been the following: the development of private debt as support for consumption has been substituted by the exponential growth of public debt as a mechanism for the socialization of loss. Now, if the titles of public debt can still be collocated on the markets without great difficulty to the extent that they appear as a pure and simple guarantee of liquidity, almost certainly the competition between states will rapidly lead to an increase in interest rates and debt service.[26] The necessity of strongly increasing fiscal pressure will result from this and will serve as a pretext to resort to more cuts in public spending and a new privatization of public services leading to a further deepening of the process of the expropriation of the common.

Conclusions

In cognitive capitalism, financialization and more generally the development of rent constitute structural dimensions of the logic of valorization of capital and the objective and subjective contradictions that it generates. The explosion of the crisis was the condensation point of the whole of these contradictions as much on the level of the capital-labor relation as on the antagonism, more and more intense, between the social character of production and the private character of appropriation.

In this sense, to cite a Gramscian formulation, the current crisis is a "great crisis," a tragic moment that "consists precisely in the fact that the old dies and the new [still] cannot be born; in this interregnum, morbid phenomenon of the most varied kind come to pass."[27]

But if nothing will ever be the same, it is dutiful to admit the difficulty of precisely defining the possible escape routes from the crisis.

In any case, in our opinion, it is extremely difficult to share the hypothesis, sill maintained by other scholars, that the current crisis can lead capital to realize the necessity of a contemporary New Deal able to reconcile *cognitive capitalism* and *knowledge economy*, resolving the imbalances inherent to the inequalities of income distribution, demand insufficiency and financial instability.

More precisely, the possibility of a contemporary New Deal, a new capital-labor compromise, clashes against, other than the wall of financial power, two major obstacles, hurdles that are translated in, as we have seen, the exhaustion of the progressive force of capital and the crisis of the law of value. The former is tied to the way in which a possible reinforcement of welfare assurances and new distribution mechanisms of income that substantially reduce the monetary limit of wage relations could result in a major risk for capital: that of profoundly destabilizing the mechanisms of control of cognitive labor founded on precarious labor. The development of increasingly acute conflicts that would interest not only the level of income distribution but the very question of the definition of the organization and the social scope of production could also result from such a risk. The latter depends on the way that, at least in the advanced capitalist countries, the major part of the needs that the development of production is susceptible to satisfy are situated outside of the sphere of activity in which the economic rationality of capital has been able to play a progressive role in industrial capitalism. Deindustrialization and market saturation of mass-produced goods of the old Fordist economy in fact goes hand in hand with the structural difficulty of subjecting those informational goods and services to the logic of capital which had fed the speculative

Nasdaq bubble and the myths of the New Economy for a short time. In an even more fundamental way, the driving sectors of an economy founded on knowledge, as we have seen, corresponds to activities, like *man for man productions*, to which the logic of commercialization and profitability cannot be applied if not at the cost of unsustainable inequalities and a drastic diminution of the social production of these goods and of their external effects on the effective development of a knowledge based economy.

For these reasons, the return of the intervention of the state as macroeconomic regulator and last minute savior of the imbalances in capital doesn't seem to be the prelude of a contemporary New Deal. This evolution instead seems to design the contours of a "social totalitarianism of capital" at the service of the continuity of the neoliberal politics of expropriation of the common as a tool to expand the parasitic nature of the commercial sphere and the precarious character of the labor-force.

Proof is the orientation of the management politics for the crisis and the economic stimulus packages put into act within the EU and the United States. Independent of their size (insufficient in any case), they have as a common denominator a social policy that aims at maintaining unaltered the pillars of neoliberal market regulation of labor and welfare. Even Obama's plan, much more ambitious in the level of financial resources substantiated, left the Senate amputated of a large part of the initially planned measures in favor of income support for the unemployed, education, the extension of health care, and all this despite the notorious delay of the American welfare system in comparison to Continental European and Nordic models.

The reformist capacity of capital thus seems carved by the same limits that have impeded cognitive capitalism from re-establishing the struggle-development dialectic that had characterized industrial capitalism, particularly in the Fordist era. The result of all this is a situation of structural uncertainty that helps to explain the inefficiency of the economic stimulus packages to effect market expectations and the structural causes of the crisis.

Despite its devastating dynamic and the risks of implosion that it brings, the historical crossroads created by this crisis thus presents itself as a complex, open and profoundly conflictual process that can give way to oppositely oriented evolutions. Particularly, it allows us to foresee an alternative scenario that social struggles, through a long positional war, could, by defining the contours, open a model of society and alternative development founded on two principle axes.

The first axes refers to the democratic re-seizing of welfare institutions, based on the associative and self-organized dynamic of labor throughout society. It defines, as much from the point of view of the norms of production as from the norms of consumption, the bases of the construction of an alternative social model founded on supremacy of the non-commodity logic and the *man for man productions*. In this framework, the collective services of welfare must not be seen strictly as social costs to be financed by taxation, e.g. through value appropriated on the merchant sector. They must be recognized as key driving sectors in a mode of development founded on intensive knowledge production.[28]

It is in fact these sectors that depend on the rhythm and the quality of a developmental logic whose measurement becomes the satisfaction of essential needs that, in an advanced and aging (for its demographic evolution) society, assure the simultaneous reproduction of a diffuse intellectuality and, to use Christian Marazzi and Robert Boyer's expression, the *anthropo-genetic* reproduction of society from one generation to the next.

Anyway, health, education, research, and culture orient not only consumption norms and the lifestyles of the population; they also constitute a source of highly skilled works in activities whose cognitive and relational dimension of labor is preponderant and where fresh forms of self-direct production, founded on a coproduction of services that closely involve users, can develop.

The second axis indicates the struggle to overthrow the power of rent and transform the "socialism of capital" into a process of resocialization of money that puts the former at the service of the expansion of the common and the multiplication of the forms of access to income (from students to temporary workers), freed from unconditional wage labor. The horizon and the common thread of this constituent dynamic is, in a mid/long-term period, the creation of a universal Guaranteed Basic Income independently on employment and conceived as a remuneration for the totality of social times that contribute to the creation of wealth and value is meaningful.

From the perspective of a knowledge based economy, the guaranteed basic income or wage should be understood both as a collective investment of society in knowledge and as a primary income for individuals. That is, as a social salary directly stemming from a productive contribution and not as mere social security deriving from a redistribution of income (like, for example the *RMI*[29]).

It should be remembered in this regard that the proposal of a Guaranteed Basic Income, as primary income, rests on a re-examination and an extension of the notion of productive labor, conducted from a double point of view: the first refers to the concept of productive labor, conceived according to the dominant tradition of political economy, as labor that generates profit and/or participates in the creation of value. Here it is the contestation according to which today a significant extension of unpaid labor time is being witnessed that, beyond the official work day, directly or indirectly participates in the formation of value captured by business. Guaranteed Basic Income, being a social wage, would correspond, from this point of view, to the remuneration of this increasingly collective dimension of an activity that creates value and that is extended over the whole of social times, giving way to an enormous mass of unacknowledged and unpaid labor. The second point of view suggests a concept of productive labor thought of as labor that produces use value, a source of wealth that escapes both commercial logic and subordinated wage labor. In short, it sustains that labor can be unproductive of capital even while being productive of wealth and thus generating an income. It should be worth noting how the ambivalent relation, both antagonistic and complimentary, of these two contradictory forms of productive labor are contained within cognitive capitalism. The expansion of free labor in fact goes hand in hand with its subordination to social labor that produces surplus value for the very tendencies that lead to a crumbling of the traditional confines between labor and non-labor, the sphere of production and the sphere of free time. The question posed by a General Basic Income is then not only of an acknowledgement of this second dimension of productive labor, but also and above all, of its emancipation from the sphere of the production of value and surplus value. It would permit the re-composition and reinforcing of contractual power of the whole labor-force, by reclaiming a part of the value captured by capital through rent. At the same time, the weakening of the monetary construction to wage relations would favor the development of forms of labor that escape the commercial logic of subordinated labor as well as the transition toward a non-productive model, based on the pre-eminence of non-commercial forms of cooperation that are able to free the general intellect society from the parasitic logic of cognitive capitalism and finance.

Stefano Lucarelli

Financialization as Biopower

Introduction

Speculation is a reoccurring risk in free market economic systems.
Even so, if we look at the current crisis while keeping the new character of capitalism in mind, speculation needs to be analyzed in a
new light: this crisis is not simply the fruit of financial insanity,[1] but
instead should be understood starting from the specificity of the
existing accumulation regime. An accumulation regime delineates a
long-term growth model. This term, introduced by the scholars
who identify themselves with the research program of the so-called
French Regulation School, refers to the set of regularities that assure
a general and relatively coherent progression in the accumulation of
capital; thus allowing for the re-absorption of imbalances that arise
from the duration of the process of accumulation.[2]

My thesis is that contemporary capitalism is characterized by
an accumulation regime that tends to lead every specific moment
of individual existence back into the process of valorization. The
means through which this happens do not only include economic
politics of neoliberal inspiration, but also include the command
devices that are only understandable if they are put in the hybrid
zone where the political economy meets social psychology (I'm

referring to the *wealth-effect*). I will therefore try to analyze financialization as a practice of social control. In fact, it seems to me that to understand an accumulation regime unable to construct long-lasting modes of regulation, there is only one alternative: assume a new point of view that immediately focuses on the problems of command and power. This new capitalism needs a social control compatible with democratic societies where order is based on the formalized participation of great masses.[3] One of the new characteristics of the financialization process that involves us is its mass participation, its formal democracy.

In order to articulate this line of reasoning, I will borrow a few categories from Michel Foucault, in particular *biopower* and *governmentality* (§2);[4] I will then adapt them to my object of analysis, concentrating on the role that the wealth-effect assumes in the financialization process (§3). I will then illustrate the role assumed by monetary policy in the described accumulation regime (§4). Lastly, I will refer to the American economic model—intended as *ideal-type*—and I will propose a personal reading of the financial crisis (§5): the roots of the crisis are to be sought in the instabilities in the new accumulation regime that is characterized by a dominant technological paradigm. The new technological paradigm started with the crisis of Fordism and the so-called Smithian division of labor. In the new division of labor, along the whole productive assembly line, knowledge plays a key role in the redefinition of the capital-labor relation.[5] The so-called subprime crisis then will be explained as a phenomenon endogenously produced by the dynamics of the new accumulation regime that has affirmed itself ever since the crisis of Fordism; an accumulation regime—it is important to stress—compatible only with non-authentic modes of regulation, or ones that don't assume the exercise of conflict as a necessary premise for a social pact. Social control (biopower) thus emerges in a new form, more difficult to perceive and contrast.[6] Here, I'd like to limit myself to simply indicating another moment for the necessary consideration on the political-economic proposals in response to the crisis.[7]

1. Foucaultian Categories

The term *biopower*—coined by Foucault in the area of a vaster reasoning on the rationality of western politics—refers to the great structures and functions of power; in his own words, it is a great two-sided technology, anatomic and biologic, that acts on the individual and the species: the comprehension of power cannot stop at the specific social places in which discipline is exercised, but also presupposes the analysis of the regulation of populations in their daily lives (the anatomic and biological aspects therefore participate in a political dimension). This all began to be discovered in the 18th century, when it was realized that the relation of power to the subject or, more precisely, to the individual, cannot be based merely on subjection—that permits power to take goods, riches and, possibly, even the body and blood from subjects—but that power must be exercised over individuals in as much as they constitute a kind of biological entity which must be taken into consideration if the population is to be used as a machine to produce wealth, goods or other individuals.[8] The logic of biopower is the production of wealth through the daily use of the population, in opposition to anatomo-politics, which is to say the whole of mechanism and procedures limited to disciplining subjects. The new mechanisms presuppose that the population is not simply perceived as a sum of the individuals that inhabit a territory.

As Adelino Zanini has rightly pointed out, what must interest the scholar is the passage from the art of government to political science, from a system dominated by *structures de souveraineté* to one characterized by *techniques du gouvernement*. A passage made possible by imposing a new paradigm of the political economy.[9] Political economy—according to Foucault—is the science which is able to identify the law necessary for the scope of governing according to the modern logic of the *gouvernment de la population*: "The new governmentality, that in the 17th century had thought itself capable of entirely investing itself in a complete and unitary policing project, now finds itself in the situation of having to refer to a neutral area, which is the economy."[10] The logic of biopower therefore takes us to the exact modalities of control that Foucault called *governmentality*:

> With the word "governmentality" I mean three things. [First,] the whole of institutions, procedures, analyses and reflections, calculations and tactics that permit the exercising of this specific and quite complex form of power, that has the population as its main target, in the political economy the privileged form of knowledge and in the security devices the principle technical tool. Second, for "governmentality" I mean the tendency, the driving force that, in the whole West and for a long time, continues to assert the preeminence of this type of power that we call "government" over all of the others—sovereignty, discipline—with the consequent development, on one hand, of a series of specific government apparatuses and, [on the other hand,] a series of knowledges. Lastly, for "governementality" we should mean the process, rather than the result, of the process through which the state of Medieval justice, having become the administrative state in

the course of the 15th and 16th centuries, gradually found itself "governmentalized."[11]

Foucault didn't elaborate his research in the direction of financial and monetary history. Yet, a history of governmentality—as I see it—cannot leave out the financial and monetary apparatuses that came into existence in the 18th century. As many important studies conducted on the history of money have shown, this century represents an incredibly significant moment for the history of money in Europe: it is the moment in which European money frees itself from the traditional configuration, that of guaranteeing account correctness and payment stability in the whole Empire. Before then, in fact, it was

> the duty of the Prince of conserving a treasure from which it is possible to draw upon if needed, which is to say if the community's need imposes it, and its regulatory function is limited to this. [...] The "nature" of money is exhausted in its distributive capacity and is naturally delimited by the measure in which the goods are present. In respect to such measure, money is constantly able to take account of the presence of things, but can never solicit that they come into presence: it is both measure of abundance and scarcity starting from their natural alternation in time.[12]

In modernity—in the course of the 18th century—the need to strengthen the territorial states shattered the imperial political-administrative equilibrium just described. The dominant need became that which money can change value in relation to the changing needs that are manifested in nation-states, which is the valorization of money. Money's "nature" is no longer delimited by the measure in which goods are present, but consists in the urge to get rich. Grasping the trait that joints both this function of money and the regulation of populations for the production of wealth, clarifies the concrete meaning of biopower.

In order to transform the Foucaultian concept of biopower in a political category useful for the analysis of the current process of financialization, it must be understood simultaneously in the two dimensions proposed above. If the quickest way to produce abstract wealth, i.e. money, is trying to realize it minimizing the risks that are run and the conflicts that come up when raw goods production is organized, it is only rational to minimize the costs of production, including state and bank control over economic activities, thus maximizing the possibility of money's autonomously deciding what it has at its disposition. In such a way, a new power of control over the population is exerted. The risk distribution inherent to the production of money through money becomes the strategy to employ.

The power that is exercised within an accumulation system dominated by finance is something different from the power exercised by a sovereign state over its citizens. The search for *governmental freedom* that markets claim goes right along with the management of the populations which nation-states take responsibility for. So that the population produces wealth within money's valorization cycle, a form of social control that substantiates the different relations both between master and slave and between state and citizen. My thesis is that financialization represents the very form of social control necessary for such scope. It is in fact a form of socialization (of risk but also of the prospectives of enrichment that are complementary to it) that leads to a revolution in the concept of sovereignty. What financialization puts at stake is no longer the immediate application of sovereign power but the directing of the whole of the human behaviors necessary so that sovereignty is coherent with the financialization process.

2. Financialization and the Wealth-Effect

First of all, financialization can be defined as the diversion of domestic economy savings to stock market shares.[13] Ever since the 1980s, the American economy has been characterized by the process of financial market liberalization and the consequent explosion of new financial tools: thus the passage from a Keynesianism built on a pact between producers in an environment of a monetary system that binds currency and financial maneuvers—already weakened by president Nixon's declaration of the inconvertibility of the dollar to gold in 1971—to a financial Keynesianism based on private deficit spending, in which the largest financial market deregulations are accompanied by the diminution of social incomes distributed by the welfare state. We are facing an evolution in liberal governmentality. In other words, financial Keynesianism is a modality of liberal governmentality. Shareholder value[14] becomes the principle macro-economic indicator, the scepter and the pastoral that govern both investment and consumption through the wealth-effect.[15]

For a psychological dynamic that would be worthy of further study but that represents a necessary condition of stability of the *American economic model* (here intended as *ideal-type*), the wealth-effect induced by an increase of value in the markets affects consumption behaviors more than the expected wealth due to an increase in wages.[16] The model has a high risk of instability; the fact that financial crises have followed one after another so quickly over the last few years is proof of this. The exercising of liberal governmentality means that this form of specific command over individual behavior is reintroduced each time: the rule that has been consolidated consists in passing from one bubble to the next,[17] forcing individuals to believe that their wealth depends more on financial markets than demands for wages or other forms of possible claims. Following this approach, the wealth-effect represents the form of command typical of financial Keynesianism, here understood as liberal governmentality. The dynamic that goes from profit to financial market and vice-versa substitutes the principle political decisions in the Fordist-Keynesian paradigm: the productivity-wage connection and the production-mass consumption connection.

The impact of financial returns on patrimonial decisions becomes the key factor in investment decisions; these must keep count of the financial returns, and not only on the variations in demand. Consumption continues to depend on the accumulation of traditional income from labor (i.e. wages) but a variable that measures the value of the financial tools that families own intervenes too. If financialization is highly developed—which occurs when family wealth depends more on the quote of income coming from financial markets than wages—wage moderation, favoring companies' profitability, increases financial returns; thus a dynamic founded on the wealth-effect aimed at favoring private consumption while even facing falling real wages can be triggered. The level of production becomes a consequence of financial value. This inverts the relations between the real sphere and the financial sphere that prevailed under Fordism: the market dynamic replaces wages as source of cumulative growth. This inversion also revolutionizes social control mechanisms that concern the individuals in the modern world.

In other words, the wealth-effect that supports the financial world's thought process depends on the degree of subsumption not only of labor, but of life itself and finance (this is where biopower's feature lies).

In macroeconomic terms, this dependent relation is translated in the growing liquidity that financial markets attract starting with private savings that were previously invested in State bonds. Even so, this growing liquidity is not enough by itself. There is a second explanatory variable necessary so that the wealth-effect continues: it is the common sense that forms between individuals about the reasons that should explain the production of money by means of money, and about the hierarchy of needs to satisfy in order to maintain an acceptable social status. The logic of valorization leads to the transformation of social relations. More precisely, this means that financialization is a form of socialization that makes liberal governmentality evolve.

So, it is comprehensible as to why the analysis of financialization cannot be limited to the study of the conditions of the macroeconomic sustainability of the system; it also requires paying particular attention to the social codes through which human relations are reciprocally limited. We must thus understand these *conventions* that settle in the population, starting from the business world. A convention furnishes a valuation system *a priori*, pointing out the whole of the social rules able to make the different behavior of single individuals homogeneous. Therefore, it presupposes a theory of imitation. This is the observational point that Keynes uses to explain the generation of long-term expectations:

> There is, however, not much to be said about the state of confidence *a priori*. Our conclusions must mainly depend upon

the actual observation of markets and business psychology. [...] Thus certain classes of investment are governed by the average expectation of those who deal on the Stock Exchange as revealed in the price of shares, rather than by the genuine expectations of the professional entrepreneur. How then are these highly significant daily, even hourly, revaluations of existing investments carried out in practice? In practice we have tacitly agreed, as a rule, to fall back on what is, in truth, a *convention*. The essence of this convention—though it does not, of course, work out quite so simply—lies in assuming that the existing state of affairs will continue indefinitely, except in so far as we have specific reasons to expect a change [...] Nevertheless the above conventional method of calculation will be compatible with a considerable measure of continuity and stability in our affairs, *so long as we can rely on the maintenance of the convention.*[18]

However, the analysis of conventions cannot be limited to the business world. The state of trust defined by conventional valuation is in fact legitimated by public opinion.[19] It spills into the business world, involves the populations and becomes political object. Hence it helps in focusing the (Foucaultian) problem of the *governmentality* of civil society.

3. Boom, Boom. Boom, Boom.

The dominant accumulation system in contemporary capitalism supposes more than one change in the political sphere: first of all, growth conditions depend on the acceptance of a new productive model in which labor assumes a different role. It is not only a deconstruction of the Fordist union; nor is it merely the reduced importance of wages in as much as a fundamental macroeconomic variable for accumulation and therefore the annihilation of the inherent conflict in wage claims. Instead, it is the construction of a valorization process in which the acknowledged objective reasons that are at the base of the production of wealth change; valorization becomes dependent on the conventions that are asserted in the financial community.

Macroeconomic stability depends largely on the interventions of the Central Banks that, facing a scarcity of liquidity in the financial markets, must be quick enough to prevent a financial crisis. The Central Banks react facing the need for liquidity, aware that they are sustaining the wealth-effect on which it plays—in Foucaultian terms—the security of the territory's population delimited by the financial markets.

The levers of power are no longer in the distribution of banking credit, nor in deficit spending. The independent variable is neither wages, nor profit, but is the accumulation rate from financial appreciation. The offer of currency is freed by the *quantum* of currency held by the Central Bank and is tied to the reorganization of the division of labor and the redefinition of social relations in the circulation-reproduction sphere. In other words, money supply is tied to the dynamic of capital-(living) labor: as the contributions by "Primo Maggio" workgroup on money show, monetary policy represents a modality of capitalist command.[20] Today this task is no longer accomplished through the control of the quantity of currency in circulation nor merely in the name of inflationist thrusts. In the Central Bank and academic worlds, throughout the 1990s a principle was established according to which the credibility of monetary policy must realize itself either through pegging the exchange rate or through delegating monetary politics to a foreign Central Bank with elevated inflation aversion. First, this *New Consensus* negates Friedman's monetary policy: the main instruments for monetary policy control are interest rates, no longer money supply. In theory, the role of the Central Bank consists in assuring the equality between the monetary interest rate and the real interest rate that regulates the balance between loanable and investment funds. When market rates (in real terms) are fixed under the natural rate, inflation is created. A restrictive monetary policy would have no negative effects and would help to control inflation. In reality, to support the rate of accumulation from financial surplus value, the highest monetary policy institutions didn't hesitate in behaving differently:

> At the head of the Federal Reserve there are still people with good sense that have sacrificed, as in Greenspan's case, their philosophic maximalism in the name of the preservation of the system even with tools completely contrary to that maximalism. But even in Europe, the maximalism of the very ECB statute was substituted by the good sense of those that manage our highest monetary organism. Greenspan didn't hesitate to cut the Federal Fund rates 11 times in one year, bringing it to the lowest nominal level of the last 40 years. And the ECB willingly followed his example![21]

Monetary policy in a finance-led growth regime *must* follow the needs of valorization, supporting the conventions. The monetary creation influenced by financialization is substantialized in a recovery process of capital's profitability that involves people's lives in financial risk. Financialization determines the times of capitalistic reorganization, facilitating the subsumption of *circulation* within the entire process of valorization.[22] This last element is the one that connects the three phases of the financialization process ever since 1993: the boom of the New Economy (1993–2000), the reaction to its crisis (2000–2003), and lastly the real-estate bubble (2003–2007). All three phases occur in the same technological paradigm. For this reason, the *conventions* that regulate financial valuation are not subjected to radical changes. The valuation logics in the financial community are, for the most part, the same.

4. The Dynamic of Financial Governmentality

In the 1990s, financialization, as investment of the collective savings in the stock market, generated additional incomes. The incomes were created in the markets through business debt to the banking system.[23] In the period between 1993 and 2000, the New York Stock Exchange upwardly exploded (the Dow Jones from 4000 to 11700, Standard & Poor's from 450 to 1530): the appreciation obtained in the market favored real growth thanks to the exploitation of the knowledge and productivity of labor involved in the high-tech sector above all. The valuation of financial markets began to depend on the organizational change geared toward favoring innovative cooperative forms between relatively autonomous workers. The dynamism of the organizational change became— thanks to the attention that the financial markets gave it—a new modality of valorization of productive capital.

Thus a system of finance-led growth regime[24] asserted itself where governmentality rested on the promise of a new world, or what Christian Marazzi has called the "internet convention" and which was passed off as the New Economy in the press. "In the second half of the 1990s, the idea of a digitalized society, with liberating effects on the world of work and life, became a convention. Whether true or false, there is no doubt that this convention pulled the *real* transformation processes of the world ahead."[25] Joseph Stiglitz's lucid critique of the roaring '90s confirms this:

> Modern American-style capitalism was pivoted around what would later be called the New Economy, symbolized by the so-called dot-coms that were revolutionizing the way that America—and the rest of the world—did business, modifying the rhythms of the very technological shifts and increasing the growth rate of productivity to extraordinary levels, that had not been seen for over 25 years. [...] Halfway though the '90s, the manufacturing sector had slipped to a scarce 14% of total production, with a percent of employees even lower in respect to the active population.[26]

As a matter of fact, the lever of innovation passed from research & development laboratories to the work force's living bodies while capital from the rest of the world flowed into the stocks and business bonds quoted on the US markets. In this accumulation system, various forms of remuneration tied to the whole of business yield developed: not only stock options for managers, but also the very retirement or investment funds that mostly involve wage laborers. These forms of remuneration made financial market liquidity grow but, in the absence of an adequate redistribution rule, inside a capitalism in which the rule is to command living labor in any case, this also compressed wages, leading to systemic instability. This is what happened in the March 2000 crisis. Beyond having distributed new stock incomes unequally, the command bridge of the New Economy made them by destroying wages and employment stability, in line with a new common sense: the conditions over financial markets to create stock value encourage extreme organizational innovation, promoting the processes of downsizing, reengineering, outsourcing and Mergers & Acquisitions. Hence, finance translates and betrays the real innovative processes in act by devaluating living labor. To attract investors to the stock markets, companies offered increasingly higher yields precisely through merger and acquisition operations of other companies, acquiring their own shares, and even rigging their accounts. The necessary capital for this restructuring aimed at controlling the technological trajectory was done by taking remuneration from the labor-power.

The March 2000 crisis marked the passage toward another diffusion and generalization of financialization: a new phase characterized by a marked decline, with losses of 40% in the Dow Jones, 50% in Standard & Poor's and 80% in the NASDAQ. In the meantime, wage deflation advanced, under the effects of the Asian (Indian and Chinese) industrial reserve army but also put into action by outsourcing. The market recovery came in 2003. Christian Marazzi has talked about this as the "China convention";[27] a convention—which, in our opinion, should be understood as a change on the margins of the internet convention—that rests on the idea that valorization depends on the outsourcing towards developing countries with a high exploitation of labor and the environment, but still within the same technological paradigm. This triggered a mechanism that could be defined as an industrial reserve army of financial origin.

The fact that the New Economy did not precipitate into a depression equivalent to the 1930 depression depends, on one hand, on the monetary policy of the FED, and, on the other, on precise financial innovations. In the two-year period following the March 2000 crisis (2001–2002), the FED drastically lowered the interest rate from 6% to 1%. That pushed the economic agents to go into unreasonable debt to benefit from the discrepancy between their own capital yield and the interest rate. This incentive to accumulate debt means that the wealth-effect was articulated in different ways in respect to the roaring years of the New Economy: the prices on real-estate markets rose and the FED's monetary policy supported the buying power of American consumers. American families could thus obtain practically unlimited credit from the banking system, putting up a real-estate patrimony with increasing value as a guarantee. The expected earnings came back high, sustained by a negative real interest rate. Stock prices came back up in March 2003 (at the eve of the American intervention in Iraq). It is possible to find a precise description of financialization as practice of social control in the words of Stiglitz:

> The story goes back to the recession of 2001. With the support of Federal Reserve Chairman Alan Greenspan, President George W. Bush pushed through a tax cut designed to benefit the richest Americans but not to lift the economy out of the recession that followed the collapse of the Internet bubble. Given that mistake, the Fed had little choice if it was to fulfill its mandate to maintain growth and employment: it had to lower interest rates, which it did in an unprecedented way— all the way down to 1%.
>
> It worked, but in a way fundamentally different from how monetary policy normally works. Usually, low interest rates lead firms to borrow more to invest more, and greater indebtedness is matched by more productive assets.

But, given that overinvestment in the 1990s was part of the problem underpinning the recession, lower interest rates did not stimulate much investment. The economy grew, but mainly because *American families were persuaded to take on more debt, refinancing their mortgages and spending some of the proceeds.* And, as long as housing prices rose as a result of lower interest rates, Americans could ignore their growing indebtedness.[28]

In other words, the population was involved in the production of (financial) wealth, first through the construction of the New Economy, then—after the diffusion of a new swarm of innovations and innovative instincts that fed financial euphoria, but over time transformed into positional rents for only the most aggressive businesses—repositioning the financial level to the real-estate sector after having disciplined a euphoric society through outsourcing toward developing countries that highly exploit labor and the environment. Monetary policy facilitates this process without governing it: from Spring 2003 to January 2007 the FED extraordinarily increased the liquidity available to the markets. 97% of the American population hit by wage deflation—through which the devaluation of living labor is understood—continued to preserve its quality of life through rising real-estate prices, the generosity with which the American credit markets operated and the low price of imported goods. Nevertheless, this financial lever sustained financial earnings without any relation with the capacity to generate profits in the "real" economy: insolvency risk was high. Credits of the same nature were grouped and converted into bonds and derivatives that were put into financial markets. Thus risk was transfered to the operators of these financial activities, which increased bank solidity, but was susceptible to leading to a bigger crisis. As Boyer, Dehove and Plihon warn in a 2004 study, the fact that a reduced number of actors (insurance companies, non-financial corporations, etc.) can assume a large part of the risk can put the financial system in danger if an ugly turn in the market dries up liquidity is seen:

> The severity and thus the outcome of the crises depend on the degree of concentration/dispersion of risks and the banking system's degree of resiliency. Indeed, we find that financial crises are all the more serious because the risks tend to be concentrated on the banks, which are essential to the continuity of the payments and credit-relations system.[29]

The real-estate market boom moves parallel to wage deflation: after having exhausted wage prospects and aspirations by selling market dreams, the selling of another dream begins: a house that can be payed for with credit, an infinite credit and a high insolvency risk (this is where subprime loans come in, high risk mortgages for buying a house conceded to families with few income guarantees). The goal once again was to bolster the wealth-effect by compressing real wages. Those responsible, beginning with the chief economists of the financial institutions involved, cannot but recognize that the American crisis is so bad because it started from a real-estate bubble that touched the most crucial part of the US economy, housing property. The Fannie Mae and Freddie Mac affairs represent a parabola of the American dream: a house at any cost. The two institutions with a $83.2 million capital sustained— thanks to federal help—$5.2 billion, half of all the existent mortgages in all, an unsustainable relation of 1 to 65.[30]

In the meantime, finance's subsumption of life sharpened, the transformation of social relations favored the concentration of financial risk in the weakest sectors of the population. The August 2007 crisis came after many years of strong expansion of real-estate credit that followed the internet bubble. The financialization of the economy in order to function requires the inclusion of a growing number of domestic economies in value creation. On the one hand, the securitization of subprimes represents a formidable lever for the creation of credit. On the other, the distribution of risk to the wallets of an elevated number of investors on a global scale, through credit bond markets, make the relations between monetary institutions more fragile.

Conclusions

This contribution is intended to be a mere premise to reach a more complete theoretical framework. The problem has to be posed again since, at the moment, a few fundamental questions still have to be answered: where does the value that is fixed in financial markets come from? What connection is there between living labor and the growing liquidity captured by stock markets? What is the political dimension of finance in this phase of capitalism? These questions inevitably lead to pondering the forms of resistance facing financialization processes. From the analysis developed so far, a limit to financial market power emerges, which, if not respected, introduces a series of macroeconomic pathologies. This limit lies not simply in the effective fall in demand, nor in the low levels of real wages, but more precisely in the devalorization that living work is subjected to.[31] Foucaultian categories can constitute an important tool for analysis. In using them, the process of financialization is revealed as a practice of social control, that subsumes life into the process of valorization, spreading an ideology of the wealth-effect to annihilate the exercisable conflict not only over wages, but also over the contents and the modalities of production and reproduction.[32] Following Foucault, we reach the problem of the relation between biopower and biopolitics. It seems to me that Judith Revel's reading of biopolitics points to a useful direction to continue a discourse like the one we've developed up until now.

> While "biopower" remains the term with which a new investment of life is designated (again: not only biological but social, affective, linguistic, etc., too) on the part of power relations, in Foucault, "biopolitics" seems more tied to a prospective of resistance, of "subjectification," or at the same time subtraction from power and reinvention—elsewhere—of that which exists (better yet: new relations with the Other, new organizational figures, new ways of life, new institutions…). Far from being equivalent, the two terms actually each describe a specific side of the same investigation: a new analysis of power on one hand, and a new analysis of resistant subjectivities on the other.[33]

What determines the very functioning of financialization as a form of biopower is the constitution of biopolitics. The possibility to re-appropriate what finance controls depends on this constitutive process which implies new institutions and new conflictual democratic practices. What is at stake is not only the *a priori* system of valuation on which financial valuation of the real is based (conventions), but even the "whole of the social rules able to make different behaviors of single individuals homogeneous."

Federico Chicchi

On the Threshold of Capital,

At the Thresholds of the Common

Sidenotes on the ambivalences of biopolitical capitalism

1. Reflections and Proposals on the Recent Financial Market Crisis

It is appropriate to note that the following arguments are only a partial—anything but definitive—attempt to circumscribe a few relevant questions concerning the *knowledge-power* connection in contemporary capitalism. More specifically we are interested in focusing our attention on the ambivalences that the recent crisis of global financial capitalism highlights in the very body of post-Fordist capitalism.

In the first place and for these reasons, therefore, we believe it is useful to underline how, in the last decades, the increasingly pressing rhythm of economic crises on one hand and the complexity of the plot through which they are articulated and strike social bodies on the other, once again show capital's ability to produce, within an edulcorate but at the same time poisonous and violent mix of power, a strategic management of its intrinsic internal ambiguities. Capitalism's structure is necessarily dynamic; the unveiling—the first intuition being certainly Marxian—of this paradox allows us to reveal and therefore understand how the *crisis* is the driving force of its accumulation process. In other words, as the most shrewd *workerism* has already made clear elsewhere, it is *resistance* (class struggle) that is produced at a grassroots level against coaptation devices of valorization forces,[1] the social opposition to their *translation* into portions and forms that are measurable in the anthropologic background of proprietary individualism, that triggers a process of progressive refinement, deviation, deepening and widening of its horizons of growth. The fact that the necessary process of accumulation is not smooth and clear but, to the contrary, dense, jagged and to a certain point even dangerous for its hegemony; it hasn't cracked, up to now, much of the structural capacity of capital. Better yet: in a certain sense, the bigger the ambivalences internal to its composing principles are, the bigger they appeared to be spaces of valorization that are produced to its advantage. Capital actually is a social structure and as such functions because it is *problematic.*

Here it might be useful to pick up, structurally and only within a fleeting parenthesis in our argumentation, the Deleuzian lesson on the intrinsic structural paradoxes in one of his best works: *The Logic of Sense*. There is always an *excess* to play on, a rift, an empty box between the signifying series and the series of signifieds that is a part of and makes a structure work (that is, in this sense, always definable as an open relation between two series). A structure that is a *totality* outside of a never definitively closed relationship topologically or temporally, a form that historically wields, once and for all, the values of a finite series, in an ordered and quantitative *measure of being* doesn't exist, nor can it exist. Ontology is and can only be intemperance, disparity, movement. *The living exists according to becoming*, to put it in a Simondonian way. Therefore, in this sense, identity and measurement are its perversion, or more precisely, its pathological paranoia, its symptom. Exploitation (of *value-power*), its social declination, is the symptom of capital: simultaneously the fusion point of its (accumulative) functioning and the point where mobilizing political energies to provoke its functional collapse is possible.

However, the current crisis that is manifested, above all but not exclusively, in the crisis of international financial institutions is a crisis that presents new radical characteristics. It seems to undermine the very layer on which capitalistic social and economic structure has always sunk and still sinks the roots of its ordinary functioning practices. It actually confuses, destabilizes and delegitimizes the fulcrum on which it realizes the form of commercial exchange, the very form of the social tie to modernity: money as *counting unit* of the social relations of debt and credit.[2] The lesson that was first Keynesian, and then Regulationist, teaches us, in fact, how money is considered as the fundamental institution of the modern economic system. "Money, as value operator, is the normative institution *par excellence* because payment is prescriptive."[3] Money, in order to be able to maintain its hegemonic function of generalized *measure* of social relations and its role of general equivalent operationalized through currency, must actually rest on an extra-economic trust structure that preexists it and through which institutions regulate and/or govern social relations. "It logically comes before commercial relations because it is the condition of possibility and the base of evaluation. *It comes from sovereignty.* It is the center of a common belief of individuals in commercial relations, because money is what confers them their belonging in economic terms."[4] The deep crisis of the institutional structure of finance in contemporary capitalism could then trigger a *money* crisis (of its value form based on countable measurement), and therefore, a crisis of the social and economic forms within which the relation of monetary power is managed today. The crisis of the "monetary institutions" is, in fact, generalized and transversal, it concerns almost all the most relevant organizations/institutions that preside over the management of economic relations.

This, it seems, is a now visible and manifest aspect of the crisis (and the hardest effects of the economic crisis, such as increasing unemployment, poverty and an increasingly unfair distribution of wealth, etc., are dramatically being added to this). The loss of trust in neoliberal capitalist institutions therefore seems inevitable and if, on one hand, it vividly and urgently reveals the political opportunity to imagine a radically new institutional architecture to organize the production of social wealth, on the other hand it also poses the problem of risking a *great new transformation* (in the Polanyian sense), characterized by an authoritarian and violent drift in power, still today, despite everything, hegemonic and called upon by the state to try and restore trust in money/measurement.

All of this constitutes, therefore, a new and extraordinary *density of contradictions* within the capitalist structure. Capital's knowledge-power connections, that are today organized to capture the valorizing powers of general intellect (surely cognitive, but also mass affectivities) by short-circuiting them into the *prisons* of the owner and in the inducted buying motive, are severely put to the test today. The *gaps* that can be highlighted within the vicious cycle of *fetishistic* production of life into merchandise/measurement is now shown, in this sense, as a new political opportunity (with everything still to be constructed) to escape its command. The short-circuit between subjectification and subjugation seems to finally show its violence, previously phenomenologically opaque to most, which is characteristically appropriative/dispositive.

In this perspective, the financial crisis and the widespread perception of its social gravity are not anything other than an ulterior revelation of the previous crisis, now definitive, of the Fordist com-promise between capital and labor[5] as the key *regulator* of value production; compromise that had, up until the end of the last cen-tury, instituted the theme of progress as symbolic sum of social legitimation of economic growth at any cost.[6] From this point of view, the processes of precarious labor and the fragmentation of the modern institution of labor that have characterized global economies for the last few decades are nothing other than the first layer of a systemic cri-sis that capital has tried to manage in its favor, first dumping the costs of the crisis of fordist accumulation on labor (the socialization of business risks), and then reorganizing itself in a new model of power and expansion of exploitation that identifies, as the components of valorization, no longer *labor-time*, but directly the *specific* qualities (material and above all immaterial) of *bios* and social territories (bioeconomy). The (illusory) financial production of wealth (the *wealth-effect*) has been in this sense the referent of one of the most effi-cient operational devices of post-fordist regulation and stimulation.

To orient analysis and antagonism in contemporary capitalism, in the light of the economic crisis in act, it is therefore useful to consider and subsequently attempt to develop three main interpre-tative paths: the first, in epistemological and methodological order, concerns the need to abandon a paradigm centered around the ana-lytical categories of the Modern Era. These categories, organized around an "oppressive" and "discrete" form, now reveal all of their heuristic and interpretive insufficiency. Labor/consumption, pro-ductive labor/unproductive labor, rent/profit, wages/income, subjectification/subjugation, etc., are all conceptual forms today crossed by new complexities and their empiric emergency is undoubtedly characterized by their progressive coalescence and internal short-circuiting. In synthesis, an effective analysis of contemporary capitalism should probably be collocated beyond (even if not completely outside of) the paradigm of political economy. As Claudio Napoleoni understood at the end of the 1960s, the analysis of value (absolute value) can no longer be included in the paradigm of the political economy, be it classic or neoclassic. Particularly, the aporias of value theories, the Ricardian and Marxian matrix, had, despite Sraffa's attempts, already become manifest and insurmountable if seen in an investigative scheme completely contained in economic grammar.

What the author seems to have demonstrated in his praiseworthy, even if in a certain sense shaky, attempt to save Marxism within the themes of alienation (of the subject-object turnover) and of exploitation, classically based on the production/appropriation of a surplus, it is the very need to read and deconstruct the economic problem through a more elastic and less linear device such as philosophy. "That is: if it is still true that the bourgeois society is characterized by the reduction of every reality to the economic, of quality to quantity, it isn't true on the other hand that the modalities of this reduction can be argued by economic science; the latter remains defined (and delimited) as a reified analysis, while the process of reification must necessarily escape analysis."[7]

The second question, closely related to the first, is more substantial, and concerns the necessity to think of the crisis of financial capitalism inside a phase of general crisis in the mode of capitalist production. In this sense, we believe it necessary to realize that the modalities of value production (and with this the subjectivities of value) have deeply changed (from the factory to the *social* factory) and that along with these changes the strategic devices of exploitation that make the process of accumulation possible and sustainable have changed too. We are therefore firmly convinced that in order to interpret the current phase it is necessary to refer to the analyses that describe the emergence of *cognitive capitalism*[8] (based on an economy of knowledge, communication, and social cooperation) and above all the appearance of an architecture of accumulation of capital, definable as *bioeconomic*. The third and last point concerns the urgency and the opportunity to organize a new practice of antagonistic social movement that sets its primary mission in the production of a new political lexicon (but we could also say "anthropologic"), which is able to build a common *telos* in the background of production to orient the *power* of its general becoming. In this sense, the central political question results as being the *putting to form* of "modes of life" capable of expressing such necessity, that is first of all, in our opinion, the production of a new *ethic*, that is and must be sociality, of the common.[9]

We have talked at length about this premise, purposefully forgetting the specific theme that we have been called to discuss only because we believe that it is extremely important to stress that in order to understand and act politically within the current crisis of capitalism, it needs to be absolutely clear that it should be done, epistemologically and methodologically, outside from the interpretive (and binary) forms of the Modern Era: those are too limited to a linear logic that doesn't comprehend the weight of contemporary paradoxes.

It is even more important to stress that if every structure has a blind spot that makes social relations possible, a point that is never assimilable without inevitable and progressive self-destruction, every crisis in a structure that expects to function also presents itself as a *radicalization* of its internal and unresolved ambivalences. The crisis as a densification of ambivalences becomes, or can banally become, indeed, a political opportunity that insists and must insist on the new visibility of a *novum* that suddenly shows itself under a new light of possibility and practicability. When the impossibilities of the *structure in dominance* (in an Althusserian sense) become phenomenologically more visible and if they gain experience, they conversely increase the possibility of acting as a new (counter-)power (a new knowledge) inside capital's strained hegemonic plan. There actually is in play, inside the spaces opened by the recent, and already defined by most as epochal, financial crisis, as we see it, the very survival of the post-Fordist accumulation system.

2. The Bioeconomic Texture of Contemporary Capitalism

It is appropriate to underline how financial markets aren't merely interpretable as one of the regulatory mechanisms of the new productive system of proprietary wealth, but Foucaultianly must also be considered, above all, as a *knowledge-power* device that exercises a pervasive action of capture of conduct, emotions, orientations—in a word—of the *lives* of *social individuals*, immersed, frequently in spite of themselves, in the growing and radical instability of the post-Fordist economic environment. In other words, "with financialization we enter directly into the field of *bios*. What is at risk with stock market investments? Our future lives are, our future income, our retirement, our possibility to live with dignity once we've left the labor market to retire, and not only: at risk, for the first time in a peremptory, explicit way, is *bios*, through the financialization of the economy and, thus, society."[10] The post-Fordist financial economy exercises, in this sense, a *biopower* over human behavior, it tries to create and possess within its functioning field, free but docile subjects, "obedient, subjugated to certain habits [and] rules"[11] so that they actively accept being subjectified as *value-power*, being transformed and refined, in order to maximize and better exploit their valorizing resources, forces and energies.

The *wealth-effect* that stock and financial markets produce (with a dangerous, *ad libitum* dilatation of the debtor-creditor relation) as a sort of illusory social insurance for the crumbling of Fordist social security, generates a new impulse to accumulation processes of capital in its whirling and immediate appetite (this is what Christian Marazzi has defined as the *privatization of Keynesian deficit spending*). Such a device creates new wealth (above all for those who control these knowledges), new illusions (for people who let themselves be subjectified in these devices) and new poverty/expropriations (suffered by those who are excluded from these knowledges) but above all confuses and redirects the interests of the wage workforce inside the very body of capital, politically fragmenting it and weakening it. "The transposition of constant capital into the workforce, which we previously referred to, in reality means that the previous contradiction between capital and labor is now directly preset in our bodies; it is difficult, in this sense, to find an outside in this space of financialization."[12] It is here, in this perspective, that global financial markets can be described as the key element in a capitalism that becomes *bioeconomic*.[13] What is meant, in a first approximation, the structuring of an economy that is sustained through direct and pervasive biopolitical exploitation and valorizing *qualities* of the human race, generally speaking. In our opinion, to fully analyze this fundamental aspect it is necessary to articulate the theme of a *bioeconomic paradigm* in two questions that are co-substantial to it and that the unfolding of the financialization process of the economy makes particularly evident. First: the production of a *schizophrenic* social tie, within which the individual-social relation appears imbalanced in a pathological way on the individual side of the constitutive social relation,[14] making it politically more difficult to promote non-local and collective antagonistic actions on a general level. Second: the overcoming of the Marxian *sphere of productivity* as the exclusive space of production of value (that is accompanied with, in economic analysis, the progressive impossibility of distinguishing between rent and profit).

The first question therefore concerns the social theme of the *financialization* of contemporary capitalism in the sense that it "acts as an aggregation device for individuation processes, a sort of 'communism of capital,' an extension of the 'property of the means of production' in the diffused workforce. It is financial capital, in as much as social capital quoted in the market, that is presented as the 'collective representative' of the multitude of subjects that populate civil society."[15] In this way, the rarefied public environment of postindustrial civil society is directly reconstructed in the heart of the sum of particular-singular (financial) interests, a space that is therefore completely contained in capital's proprietary logic of privatization. However, this aspect also assumes a relevance that we could label as "anthropological" because it acts, altering it, on the "quality" of the social connection. Post-Fordist capitalism would actually induce the subject to represent himself, illusorily, as enough for himself, a complete and self-sufficient monad, a single operator of his personal destiny, without acknowledging the necessary and unavoidable connection of the *I* with the *preindividual* (and the *transindividual*) field for the production of his own autonomy, showing in such a way the typical traits of a *schizophrenic* clinical inclination. The progressive disconnection of the subject from his socio-historical dimension, his reduction to his own punctual individuality, would provoke, in other words, the risk of a narcissistic separation (*Spaltung*) of *living labor* from the public sphere (in this perspective the labor becomes *individual business* and/or *human capital*), excluding the fold of *subjectivity* from a participated and constitutive construction of a *sense* of the inhabited world. Here then the paradox of the subject becomes clearer, just as post-Fordist capitalism tries to define it within its most recent power devices: representing and recognizing legitimacy in the individual as disconnected from its social existence (deprived of the *praxis* and crushed in his illusory egocentric freedom) in order to re-comprehend and assume the social capacity to valorize, although negated and ideologically obscured in its structural code of production.[16] The *subejctivity*, disoriented and mutilated on his social and political side, disconnected from the "property" of his intrinsic *social being* and cooperative nature, and therefore subjugated to systemic imperatives, begins to turn on himself in the deadly vortex of trivial consumption and his illusory acquired freedom. Certainly this scenario, that of a subjectivity rendered schizophrenic by the constitution of bioeconomic and cognitive capitalism, doesn't tell the whole "truth," it only deepens a perspective of the question of power that focuses on the *impression* of the subject within the imposition of value measurement, and not on the question of subjectivity as a prospect of resistance and insurgent excess. "However," to quote Antonio Negri, "the capitalist illusion is strong, and effectiveness of its command is even stronger."[17] We have to keep this in mind.

The second element to reflect upon with regard to the bioeconomic nature of contemporary capitalism concerns the progressive overcoming of the sphere of production as the exclusive space and *theater* of capitalistic *valorization*. In this sense, but from a different perspective, we could say that *financialization reveals the becoming-rent of profit*.[18] The theme is complex and controversial but of crucial importance. In fact, only by clarifying the new processes of value production is it possible to fully understand the contemporary transformations in capitalism and the dynamics of power over life that are co-substantialized in them. However, not being able to fully unravel the question here, given the limited space of this work, we will limit ourselves in showing how the dualisms of production/circulation and productive/reproductive in the definition and therefore production of value have today, in the spreading of cognitive capitalism, structurally exceeded. To say it with the very effective words of Antonio Negri, we can note "that the rate of surplus value, on the level of real subsumption of society/labor in capital, is the exact expression of the degree of exploitation not only of the workforce (of the laborer) by capital (by the capitalist) but also of the totality of the common powers of social production that are included in the social workforce."[19]

The political perspective of the multitude, the construction of new social forms of organization as *subjective power* and expression as a new scenario in the becoming common of life, cannot in fact be separated from the specification of the central role of the *social and metropolitan laborer* in the new mechanisms of value production. With one warning though: "when we say production, we are not only saying an economic reality but we are speaking about, above all, a biopolitical reality. The social operator therefore acts inside biopolitical production."[20] The breaking point, the space between subjectification and subjugation, the *exodus* movement that is continuously re-actualized is, as we see it, tied by a double bind to the overthrowing of the negative and parasitic sign of rent towards an immediate institution of a "positive" availability of the common wealth. Hence, *changing the sign* of rent. This is the political challenge that awaits us.

3. Conclusions: An Ontology of the Common as Necessary Background for Insurgent Antagonism

However, it would be an error to read contemporary capitalism only as the capitalism of financial markets. It is much more. Financialization is an internal and coherent device of its movement, an institution of regulation of its broader post-Fordist structural organization. Contemporary capitalism is an economy that tries to institute itself without any mediation (be it legal or political), as a *univocal texture* of sense that puts subjects and their cooperative and biopolitical behaviors directly at the center of its imperative of accumulation. Contemporary capitalism organizes the excesses of value and the power of social cooperation (of the productive common) not by governing them but, rather, by inserting them into a variegated and complex *control* device that produces and *imprints* life in monetary measurement. Such "mechanisms" of pervasive subsumption of *social being* to capital no longer needs to be instituted in the theme of labor, it functions immediately inside and outside of it, in consumption, care, relations, languages, affects, and we might say with a rhetorical provocation, in human activity *sans phrase*.

In conclusion and in the light of what we have asserted up to now, there are two political questions that await an urgent articulation. It exists a reality of emerging social wealth that is continually produced with extraordinary valorizing power. It is the fruit of a social and multitudinary knowledge that finds its infrastructure in communication technologies (the *network*) and mobility (the medium of the potentially unlimited and reflexive propagation of knowledge and living labor). These spaces are, to put it briefly, the spaces of *making* in social networks and *metropolitan* creativity. Rent is the economic tool that capital uses today to obscure the *specificities* and therefore to put them to value inside the quantifiable measurement of accumulation.

Changing the sign of rent means creating a movement of appropriation and multitudinary distribution of this wealth, showing the "ethical" insufficiency of the proprietary device in order to understand it and develop it, throwing down the yoke to which common making is subjected through forms of capitalist power.

In order to do that, it is necessary to operate a political investment that goes in the direction of imagining and constructing new *forms* of democracy that institute and render practicable a new social and anthropological (metastable) space in which *social individuals* can meet, share and allocate social time to develop their multiple singularities. The struggles that have been fought in these last few years and that, in proximity to the cooperative subjectivity and its "infrastructure," mostly through the defense of their particular aspects and/or territorial instances, produce *gaps*, partial and local collapses in capital's capturing devices (that, as we have seen, function through a short-circuit in the valorizing *novum*). The political problem (and the tactics that are derived from it) is therefore the production of resonance among these insurgencies of biopolitical subtraction, allowing in this way the multiplication and therefore the generalization, on a higher and composite ethical scale, of an *affirmative biopolitics* and, subsequently, of the "common conditions" that are produced there.[21] Consequently, we have to immediately pose the problem of how to build the conditions to "make possible the slow invention of the common as a space that is always re-elaborated by subjectivations and ways of life."[22] In fact, only through the progressive and contingent construction of a social architecture of the common that is phenomenologically *real* is it possible to imagine a subjectivity that has the ethical and political force to subtract itself simultaneously from both the sounding and deadly *jouissance* and the violent and repressive *command* that contemporary capitalism continues to play and exercise on our bodies and our lives.

Tiziana Terranova

New Economy, Financialization and

Social Production in the Web 2.0

Initially, in the 1990s, beginning with the decision to suspend the ban on the commercial use of the internet and with the introduction of the Web protocol, the meeting between the New Economy which the famous "dot.com"s were an expression of and financial capital was a happy pair. It was an economy of abundant capital and new labor cultures that developed in these short years from the mid-nineties to the May 2001 crash and saw a generation of 20 to 30 year olds, mostly North Americans and Northern Europeans, who founded a whole series of micro-businesses in the empty frontier space opened by internet commercialization. In this gold-rush atmosphere, these new North American and Northern European generations were literally invested by enormous flows of capital in a kind of generalized gamble that led the mass of investors to heavily finance a multitude of micro-businesses based above all on the selling of products and services online.[1]

The capital that invested in this young workforce was used to finance labor cultures that were very different from the previous ones. In fact, during this period, pushed by countercultural movements tied to the invention of the personal computer, there was an open polemic with the model of corporate computer labor *à la* IBM (suit and tie, the corporation hymn sung in the morning all together, the company as family).[2] The young entrepreneurs and dot.com workers used this capital to finance ludic cultures, where the classic divisions in the type of labor (with men responsible for the most part for programming and women responsible for design and social relations) still persisted, but in an informal atmosphere that prolonged the soft heterosexuality of university life (think Douglas Coupland novels, particularly *JPod*).[3] While the workplace atmosphere became ludic and more informal, wages as fixed income were integrated into a participation of variable income constituted by rent earned through stock actions. Sprinkled by a potent flow of financial capital—also in mutation—hardly anyone seemed to care that the rhythm of digital labor made agreements and compromises like those of videogames (see for example the traumatic and theatric un/masking of the true "boss" in Lars Von Trier's 2006 film *Direktøren for det hele* [*The Boss of it All*]) and that the wages of the most part of new media employees were much lower than those of traditional media workers.[4] Under this financializational push, schizophrenically, a new labor culture emerged that, as noted by Andrew Ross, absorbed the refusal to work and transformed it into a new modality of labor that partially accounted for the needs for liberty and informality that had come from the precedent cycle of social struggles, imported the partial dissolution of the borders between life-time and work-time from academic and university labor and, in many cases, an entrepreneurship that combined self-education and self-exploitation.[5]

In the May 2001 crash, the so-called "dot.com" bubble clamorously popped, and for a moment it seemed that the New Economy—that dream of diffused financial liquidity able to sustain a new way to work and produce—had vanished. Was this the scrapping of general intellect, as Franco Berardi sustained at the time, in favor of returning to a war economy, with its new police and security inflection, catalyzed by September 11th?[6]

Yet, the 2001 crash didn't so much mark the end of the New Economy, but rather its re-calibration. The process of financialization re-invested in the internet, but on new bases. It was, using the discourse of the New Economy guru Tim O'Reilly, a remodeling of investments towards a selection and an individualization of the new cultural and technological tendencies, and of the new economic models capable of building a "new New Economy" out of the net.[7] Enough with the simple re-mediation of economic models imported from the Old World, it was a matter of reflecting on what were the innovative economic models in the web. The key words in the post-crash New Economy were "social web" or "web 2.0." Web 2.0 businesses, O'Reilly says, all have something in common. Their success is based on their ability to attract masses of users who create a world of social relations on the basis of the platforms/environments made available by sites like Friendster, Facebook, Flickr, Myspace, SecondLife and Blogger. Nonetheless, O'Reilly underscores, the web 2.0 is not limited to these new platforms, but also involves applications like Google, in the extent to which they manage to harness and valorize user browsing; or other applications that again allow the extraction of surplus value from common actions like linking a site, flagging a blog post, modifying software, and so forth. Even Amazon, which first seemed like a simple bookstore re-mediation, survived the dot.com crash because, according to O'Reilly, it adopted a web 2.0 model. Amazon.com doesn't only sell books, but organizes the publication of reviews written by users about the books for sale and uses algorithms that, starting from the selection and acquisitions of the users, are able to regroup and connect similar publications to then propose "suggestions" to site visitors.

The web 2.0 is a winning model for investors since it harnesses, incorporates and valorizes users' social and technological labor. The frontier of innovation of the capitalist valorization process in the New Economy is the "marginalization of waged labor and the valorization of free [user] labor," which is to say an unpaid and undirected labor, but which is nonetheless controlled.[8] It's about attracting and individuating not only this "free labor" but also, in some way, variate possible forms of surplus value able to capitalize on diffused desires of sociality, expression and relation.[9] In this model, the production of profit for a business through the individuation and capture of "lateral" surplus value (selling advertising, the property and sale of data produced by user activity, the capacity to attract financial investments on the base of the visibility and the prestige of new global brands like Google and Facebook). In numerous cases, the surplus value lies in the savings of the cost of labor in that it is "externalized" to the users (like the externalization of videogame evaluation and beta-testing or user technical assistance).[10] For example, in Italy the mobile telephone company "3" has in all effects externalized technical assistance to a community of experts that answer user questions.[11] In exchange for their participation, the user-collaborators receive some type of more or less immaterial return (being a part of a community or social network; or, much more materially, having access to credit and various free products).[12]

The web 2.0, therefore, in its business version, seems to move on a terrain that is common to another movement in computer networks, the movement of social production or "peer to peer" (p2p). The p2p movement explores the possibility of creating an economy based on the mechanisms of social production in the net that is autonomous from the mechanisms of the valorization of capital, but not necessarily antagonistic to social production valorized by the capitalist organization of the web 2.0. The p2p movement maintains that it is possible to put into act forms of voluntary cooperation organized in the net able to give life to a new participative economy outside of the juridic system of individual property.

The idea of evolution is central in some forms of discussion and exposition of the p2p principles, and it is often posed explicitly against an antagonistic interpretation of social production from the Marxist tradition.[13] The evolutionist motif is preferred to antagonism and is used to sustain the possibility of thinking of the economy as an ecological system, that would allow for, at least at first, the coexistence of different forms of productive organization and social cooperation valorization that can coexist side by side, at least until the day when the success of p2p will render other forms of economic organization obsolete.[14] The p2p movement aims at developing autonomous financial tools (like a network of donators for example) or the production of new types of money able to make up the income of those that participate in it.

Thus, the strategy would seem like a partial "escape" from the capitalist economy that however doesn't exclude cohabitation and parasitism, able to, for example, take advantage of moments of "crisis" like the present one to impose the effectiveness of its models. A criticism that can be made against the p2p movement, in some way tied to the refusal of conflict as a determining element of the relation between p2p and the capitalist economy, is that it tends to produce a model of social cooperation mechanisms that is paradoxically poor from the point of view of the integration between the subjectivities that participate in it.

Sometimes this is translated, like in the exemplary case of an often cited and appreciated text on p2p, *The Wealth of Networks: How Social Production Transforms Markets and Freedom* by the jurist Yochai Benkler, in readapting the idea of the classic economy's invisible market hand, that this time becomes the invisible hand of social cooperation miraculously able to assure the harmonic production of common wealth starting from the interplay of individual interests.[15]

1. The Internet's Guilt and Model Financing

The fundamental problem (and the fundamental resource) of the New Economy is therefore social cooperation, but a cooperation that crosses numerous degrees of sociality and activity, starting with the "lowest" level constituted by the simple cumulative action of clicking a site or searching for multimedia materials up to a "higher" level like open source software production.[16] In this sense, it is possible to individuate an abstract line that crosses the "new New Economy" of the web 2.0 and the mass financialization of the 1990s through to the new millennium. What seems to be fundamental in theorizing and reflecting upon the new network economy and the standard financing of micro-operators is the problem of the multiplication of interactions and individual choices able to produce surplus value. Such interactions are dispersed outside of capital's commanding capacities but nonetheless inside a more or less experimental logic of control.

It is significative that in the hottest days of the financial crisis that hit the global markets in October 2008, *Newsweek*, in an editorial entitled "The First Disaster of the Internet Age," turned the reflectors on computer networks in general, accusing them of being among those responsible for the catastrophe.[17]

Here, it is worthwhile to go over what the argumentation is according to which the *Newsweek* editorial attributed the responsibility for the financial crisis to the internet. The editorial makes an explicit attack against the president of the US Federal Reserve, Alan Greenspan, who, before the dot.com financial crisis of 2001, had maintained that the internet would have transformed finance, making a "re-allocation of risk" possible through the "creation, valuation and exchange of complex financial products on a global base."[18] *Newsweek* reproached Greenspan for not having foreseen how breaking up financial products (like the famous subprimes) would have created problems for the valuation of titles, triggering a search for cash that went beyond any rational valuation of titles and thus igniting the fuse of the future credit crisis.

For *Newsweek*, while it is true that the internet lowered transaction costs, it also "contaminated" financial capital insofar as it promiscuously grafted it into a new type of sociality, that of the web 2.0. The web 2.0 isn't explicitly cited by the article, but it is significant how the criticism brought forth by *Newsweek* against internet financing repeats what has become a commonplace criticism of the web 2.0, which is the fact that it often leads to the production of closed worlds, or the so-called "echo chambers," spaces, that is, where it is possible to confront oneself with similar people, closing oneself off in group narcissism from relations with different viewpoints.[19] It is within these echo chambers that the *Newsweek* editorial identifies spaces of aggregation of "builders of exotic new products for the now $668 trillion [...] derivatives market."[20]

Likewise, instead of rendering markets more democratic and transparent, the internet would have also created a "fog of data" that would have helped some wiseguys on Wall Street to derail the global economy as easily as playing a videogame. If the dot.com financial crisis had been, all in all, an adolescent internet crisis, now it is the "first financial crisis of the mature internet age—a crisis caused in large part by the tightly coupled technologies that now undergird the financial system and our society as a whole."[21]

The internet would have therefore brought on an intolerable multiplication of the number of economic operators whose joint behavior lacks that intrinsic rationality that permits the market to correctly assess commercial value. On the other hand, the ease with which it became possible to buy and sell shares exponentially multiplied the number of transactions that became practically untraceable and consequently increased market volatility. This interaction with the screen was also identified by an important scholar of financial markets, Karin Knorr Cetina, as a fundamental component of financial markets that fundamentally distinguish it from other market models like anthropologic ones based on gifts and those based on the production of consumer markets.[22] Financial markets would then be based on a particular visual or scopic system, where the market becomes "fully visible on the screen—as a whole of pieces subjected to rapid, interchangeable, altogether contextualized changes on which to act through a whole series of financial tools." As a result, financial markets produce, for Knorr Cetina, a "global inter-subjectivity that comes from the characteristics of these markets as reflexively observed by the participants on their computer screens in an immediacy, synchronicity and temporal continuity."[23]

According to *Newsweek*'s editorial, this global inter-subjectivity driven by computer screens gave life to a "shadow-banking system" that, in 2007, was as big as the traditional one. What happened in the financial markets after the year 2000 was an inter-subjectivity not merely global, but also porous in respect to web 2.0 cultures, inserted in Facebook's social networks, influenced by the most famous bloggers' evaluations, that communicated through instant messaging tools like MSN used to conclude financial transactions. For *Newsweek*, the internet allowed for the proliferation of the "invention" of new financial tools in the same way in which it had facilitated technological innovation and at the same time made the financing of derivatives a kind of cross between

> gossip and videogames. [...] Trivial conversations over instant messaging can mutate into trades. Everything gets flattened, with chatter about the weather right alongside setting up a $100 million default swap. What matters when everything looks the same and is bookended with a happy face?[24]

Newsweek concludes sustaining the necessity of another level of technological innovation, wishing for the creation of a new interface for financial operators on the web, a kind of electronic dashboard with quadrants able to indicate, through a color-coded system (curiously similar to the alert system created by the Bush administration to warn the population about the risks of terrorist attacks) that can facilitate the evaluation of financial markets.[25] In short, a new web protocol for finance capable of rendering communication transparent and in some way disciplining, through a correct evaluation, the irrational euphoria of financial operators.

The proposal to create a "financial dashboard" for the web would therefore discipline mass financial transactions, making them transparent through a new technological mediation and defusing the dangerous convergence between the social web of bloggers, Facebook, MSN and Myspace with finance. So, the "dashboard" would add to another fundamental way in which computers become a part of the financial market assemblage, tied to the necessity of building a market "meaning" that can somehow make the chaotic dynamics of multiple interactions globally comprehensible and significant, as it would function in the realtime of distributed electronic communication. Actually, the "sense" of the market is increasingly constructed on the level of the formation of public opinion, like the aggregated meaning, nevertheless intelligible, of an ideal entity able to emit definite signals on what its perceptions, sensations and affects are. The post-crisis financial market is a market that, in newspapers and television reports, is capable of emotions like fear, anxiety, and panic, that trusts or doesn't trust, and that, put synthetically, reacts like a single body to the signals that come from economic indexes, political statements and consumer behaviors.

For some financial operators, this global sense that the "financial dashboard" on one hand and the public opinion machine on the other attempt to take from the market comes from the use of econometric models and simulations. For example, "risk managers," a specialized group of financial operators with technical skills and higher pay than simple operators, widely use statistical models and stochastic simulations taken from mathematicians and physicists from the ex-Soviet Bloc and India and now converted for use in the economy.[26] For example, the Black-Scholes model represents financial products over time, or the famous Monte Carlo, which Nassim Nicholas Taleb, a Lebanese professor of the "science of uncertainty" at the University of Massachusetts (Amherst) and discretely successful "risk manager" on Wall Street, speaks about in his editorial success *Fooled by Randomness: The*

Hidden Role of Chance in Life and in the Markets.[27] In fact, the Monte Carlo simulator, originally developed by physicists at Los Alamos to study the chain reactions of the atom, can simulate a whole series of scenarios over time, determining a series of "evolutive paths" within a "phase-space" that can determine the possible variations of highly volatile market prices.[28]

Inspired by the work of the economist Robert Schiller, author of *Irrational Exuberance*, and famous for having doubted, already in the early '80s, the "efficient market" model,[29] Taleb relates price trends, which is to say the way in which the various scenarios dealing with price trends can vary according to the Monte Carlo simulation, not only to statistical and physical factors, but also behaviors, conducts and even physiological reactions of stock market operators. For example, Taleb stresses the importance of emotional kicks, the emotional sea-saw and the consequent shifts in the chemical state of the operators' body as a result of their continual exposure to market highs and lows.

What these models aim to simulate, maybe in vain, is therefore the behavior of an assemblage, that of the financial markets, that encompasses a multitude of variables and cultures like the social web and MSN instantaneous messaging cultures, mathematical and physical cultures dedicated to financial advising, and even the culture of financial operators in global cities like London, New York and Tokyo. Let's take, for example, the culture of the financial operators in the City of London, close to fundamental places of the English New Economy of Hoxton and Shoreditch.

Every weekday, a mass of deathly pale men in suits and ties pour from buses, trains and subways into the zone around the Liverpool Street station, only to reemerge eight or nine hours later in the bars and pubs of Old Street, Brick Lane, London Bridge,

Clerkenwell Road and Hoxton Square in the search for extreme highs and mercenary erotic experiences. For those who live in the areas neighboring the City (populations of artists, New Economy workers and African and Middle-Eastern ethnic minorities), the City operators are a particularly noisy and visible presence in the evenings and weekends, when they can be seen going in and out of night clubs to meet up in smoked-glass limousines (inside which the consummation of sex sprinkled with champagne and cocaine are easily intuited) around Hackney Road's strip clubs.[30] Adding another variable to the physiology of the financial markets, the surplus testosterone produced by these nocturnal activities actually makes the financial operator, according to a study by the Department of Physiology Development in Neuroscience of University of Cambridge, more efficient.[31] Here we might ask ourselves what uses these high levels of testosterone will be put to in the new working sector for financial operators that have lost their jobs following the crisis, which is mainly in university teaching education.[32]

2. Networks vs. Network and Ethic-Artistic Experimentation

From the point of view of new technologies, therefore, financial capital works like an assemblage of assemblages in which technical, cultural, social and physiological components intervene.

What Sandro Mezzadra has defined as being the process of capitalistic capture and valorization of the common concretely unfolds along a long chain where there is an attempt to construct the impossible measurement of the forms of biopolitical life that Toni Negri speaks about. It is difficult to understand what effects the new regulation efforts announced by many as an antidote for the financial crisis will have. However, it is along this chain that any effort aimed at disrupting the dynamics of rent accumulation and exploitation of the common must act.

The question of how to struggle from assemblage against assemblage, which is the question of "net wars," has been the object of numerous studies over the past few years, both by groups close to the American military establishment and from the point of view of the elaboration of new political practices calibrated for the net society.[33] In a recent publication, Eugene Thacker and Alexander R. Galloway propose a new political tactic for the age of assemblage (net) wars—the "exploit."[34] Defining the struggles tied to the deployment of protocol net-vs.-net conflicts (from protocols that organize and control computer networks among others), Thacker and Galloway maintain that political resistance in the net (technological and biological, vital) implies the discovery of weaknesses or holes in existent technologies as its fundamental modality. The political practices connected with net vs. net struggles, assemblage vs. assemblage, characterized by a lack of distinction between organic and inorganic, technological and biological, imply the identification of leaks or holes in the very composition of networks and their immanent modalities of control. "The scope of political resistance in vital networks, then, should be the discovery of these exploits—or better yet: look for traces of exploits and you will find political practices."[35] Such political practices, however, are not simply acts of resistance, but also involve the projection of potential shifts through the opening glimpsed and utilized by the exploit.[36] Obviously, this idea isn't declaring traditional forms of political struggle obsolete, but rather asserts the necessity of working on another level, one constituted by the specific forms of control (and inevitable weaknesses) of the great technological and biological assemblages that are organized in networks.

In reference to the notion of exploits, here I'd like to propose two ethic-artistic experiments that use a strategy parasitical to the economic-financial concatenations at the scope of inserting themselves in systemic holes to provoke catastrophes: the activity of a group of activists known as The Yes Men (a collective name associated with the Americans Andy Bichlbaum and Mike Bonanno and their admirers/imitators) and the GWEI project (Google Will Eat Itself, by Ubermorgen.com, Ludovico and Cirio).

The Yes Men, a noted group of cultural activists, act on the particular assemblage constituted by the network of corporate and government public relations that, in the Edward Bernays' public relations tradition, manipulate public opinion in order to produce consensus and benevolence levels for the corporative politics that they represent. Taking advantage of the systemic chaos induced by the multiplicity of communicative sources active in the net, and starting with the assumption that the practice of public relations consists in masking the brutally cynical ideological assumptions of corporations and governmental organizations, the Yes Men create, for example, websites that perfectly imitate the ones of the targeted organization, and accept invitations sent to the site to participate at events, conferences and interviews in the name of the imitated organizations.[37]

Assuming the authoritative aura of official spokespeople (for example they have pretended to be the spokespeople from the World Trade Organization, McDonald's, Halliburton, Exxon, Dow Chemical and even the Department of Housing and Urban Development of the US government), they've made proposals that, if shocking for many, they believe correspond to the base ethos of these organizations. For example, they have proposed to audiences of investors and lobbyists to make vote selling legal and even making the poor eat recycled human excrement. It seems that the majority of these proposals were received in a relatively favorable way, or at least without indignation or shock, by their listeners. The Yes Men see to the publication and diffusion of both their proposals and the reactions of the investors and lobbyists in the general public.

Another strategy used by the Yes Men is again pretending to be spokespeople from large corporations and governmental organizations and publicly announcing events like the closure of the WTO or the admission of guilt, and consequently the responsibility for compensation, of the damages made to the civil population by their toxins. In 2004, for example, one of the Yes Men was able to get himself invited by the BBC and publicly announced that Dow Chemical would compensate the victims of Bhopal, paying $12 billion to the survivors. This false announcement, even if unmasked in a timely fashion by Dow Chemical, caused a 3.4% fall in the Dow stocks on the Frankfurt market and fifty cents on the New York market.[38] The Yes Men therefore identify, in the "information fog" mentioned by *Newsweek*, and in the proliferation of communication sources, a weak point in the assemblage of public relations that plays an important part in establishing, for example, stock prices on the financial markets. It seems that with carefully planned actions, they intend not only to cause micro-shocks that in the end are easily handled by the corporations under attack, but also to show the vulnerability of the assemblages dedicated to forming public opinion to these types of actions and to construct the market sense as it is expressed in the value of financial titles.

Another example of experimentation with protocol struggle

practices, in an ethic-artistic version, is seen in the Google Will Eat Itself project (GWEI), an Italo-Austrian collaboration between Ubermorgen.com, Alessandro Ludovico and Paolo Cirio. GWEI works in a very simple way. The fundamental source of income for the search engine Google is its "Adsense" program that connects hundreds of thousands of little advertisements to web sites in the whole world. The authors of GWEI have opened a large number of Adsense accounts and put them in a series of hidden websites. Every time someone visits one of these sites, a mechanism is activated that pays the site network a micropayment from Google. Google pays monthly for these visits: once the necessary level has been reached, the amassed funds are used by the project authors to buy Google shares (therefore using Google to buy Google).

The provocation launched by this act of computer cannibalism is explicitly contextualized by a criticism of Google's economic model and what the authors consider a fake benevolence. In "Hack the Google self.referentialism" (the theoretic text that explains the project's assumptions),[39] the authors accuse Google of being a dictator who confines its subjects, not like an authoritarian or monopolistic government such as Microsoft, but a new type of monopoly in a certain number of strategic sectors in the net economy. Particularly, Google's database seems like a veritable priceless patrimony of value that is in every effect privatized. Google's database is immense and includes a series of preferences relative to news, images, prices, and email that can "be localized and statistically analyzed by cross checking locative, general and product searches."[40] The recording of all this data, of user requests, is therefore "simply ignored by the users, which are hypnotized by an almost perfect virtual machine."[41] The web 2.0 has also allowed

Google to get into the network of bloggers that, through a program like Adsense, feel they can participate in the profit generated by Google.

> They accept to display this tiny text advertisment [sic] in exchange of a small amount of money for every click on them. This process is protected and monitored for preventing abuse. The final (actual) scenario is Google as the giant middleman. It sucks money from the advertisers offering a targeted portion of the global webspace. And it gives spare changes to the publishers for their collaboration. It sucks infos from the websites (and news, images, prices) and it releases it to the user's queries. Being in the middle it is more and more the unavoidable balancing center of the system. But we're not talking about a natural system. We're talking about business and predominance.[42]

The GWEI authors conclude highlighting this loophole, the leak or exploit, as Thacker and Galloway would call it, through which it seems possible to pick at the benevolent dictatorship of Google and others. "The greatest enemy of such a giant is not another giant: it's the parasite. If enough parasitites [sic] suck small amounts of money [...], they will empty this artificial mountain of data and its inner risk of digital totalitarianism."[43]

Can these micro-leaks, individuated and exploited by the Yes Men and the authors of the GWEI project really sink the boat of financial capital and its perverse mechanisms? This isn't the level on which these ethic-artistic experiments should be judged. It seems to me that they have an essentially heuristic value, in the sense indicated by Galloway and Thacker.[44] Individuating exploits implies the necessity of opening an experimentation that touched the most ample series of concatenations possible, able to cross through all sectors of neoliberal society hit by the effects of an economic governmentality that intensifies exploitation levels, mortifies life, barbarizes social relations and impoverishes subjectivities. On the other side of the black holes, maybe there isn't the horizon of a financial market reform or revolution, but a surmounting of financial capital and its dominion over society.

Bernard Paulré

Cognitive Capitalism and the Financialization

of Economic Systems

Introduction

In order to correctly address the problem of the very nature of contemporary capitalism, we believe that the only pertinent criteria is
the question of accumulation—with the understanding that what
is at stake is its very nature rather than its relevance. The kind (or
the system) of accumulation characterizes the ways in which a society intervenes upon the conditions of its production; it specifies the
nature and the importance of the curve along which the conditions
of the productive activity can be changed; it establishes the degree
and the level in which a society defines its very possible existence,
characterizing its potential to intervene and organize historically
determined changes. Through the forms that it assumes, the accumulative system also implies a dominant conception concerning
both the modes in which a society projects itself in the future and
the way in which it conceives the notion of progress.

In our opinion, the essential feature characterizing the accumulation system of contemporary capitalism is cognitive accumulation,
broadly assumed as including knowledge, information, communication, creativity: in a nutshell, everything that constitutes
intellectual activity.[1] It is the central role of this kind of accumulation

that distinguishes cognitive capitalism from the historical period that we have just abandoned, i.e. industrial capitalism. In the previous context, accumulation was principally geared around physical capital and the organization of labor. Although still present, in the post-industrial (or cognitive) context physical investment and the organization of labor ceases to be central, no longer constituting the only essential basis of accumulation and progress.[2]

Keeping in mind the different positions held by scholars in dealing with the problem of the nature of capitalism, we shall address the question whether it is possible to consider financial, rather than cognitive, accumulation as the essential form of accumulation. Are these two kinds of accumulation juxtaposed or complementary? This contribution is dedicated to clarify such an issue.

We shall look at some finance activities that will be dealt with according to a long-term statistical approach and discuss the relevant features necessary to identify seminal changes that could justify the thesis of the advent of financial capitalism. Within an economy in which essential accumulation increasingly rests upon immaterial rather than commercial factors, to address the issue of the specific role of finance generates new and original problems that will be dealt with in the last section.

Essentially, our conclusion is that finance must not be understood as a sphere where accumulation occurs against real investment. The contemporary development of finance can be explained on the basis of the emergence of a new stage of capitalism, characterized by new forms of "real" accumulation. In this framework, it is the weight assumed by uncertainty, along with the difficulties and the instability associated with knowledge that determines the importance of finance through its desire of keeping liquid titles, realizing rapid transferals and to be able to limit risk. Obviously, this is not the only reason that explains the current development in the sphere of finance; this is because the creation of financial activities necessary for sustaining growth constitutes, as always, its principle function. However, this is the reason that allows us to understand the co-evolution of cognitive capitalism and financialization.

Thus, finance plays a pivotal role in amplifying and strongly structuring the curve through which the conditions of productive activity can be changed. And, in a subsequent stage, it allows the transformation of the very nature of accumulation; namely, it contributes to the transformations that allow the emergence of cognitive capitalism.

1. Financialization and the Possible Justifications of a Financial Capitalism

We shall evaluate some of the main arguments aimed at sustaining the thesis of the emergence of financial capitalism, or, even better, that justify the existence of the new phenomenon of financialization. According to some scholars, the present financialization of the economy is an original and sufficiently localized phenomenon, able to justify the idea of a new era of capitalism. Our objective is to discuss the relevance of this argument.

Generally speaking, it is possible to identify some of the conditions that underpin the hypothesis of a new era of capitalism. Certainly, one of them is that the proposed configuration presents a certain structural stability *per se*. In other words, the institutional conditions and the behaviors of both public and private agents guarantee that the fluctuations and evolutions come about without destabilizing the system or provoking a worse crisis. In this way, the functioning of the system itself is never put under discussion.

Another condition is that the new period is substantially distinguished from the previous ones and that, without imposing the existence of decisive ruptures, through observation, it becomes possible to indentify thresholds or significant stages. It is not far from the truth that qualitative changes are the result of progressive changes. Dynamic models sometimes show "inflection points"[5] of maximum and recursive paths that reveal how continuity allows the emergence of something new. However, in order to define and justify the modifications of the representation (or the interpretation) of the system studied changes must become sufficiently perceptible.[6]

We shall examine different aspects of the economic system upon which scholars of financialization have focused their attention: (i) first and foremost the question of governance; (ii) the role assumed by the buying and selling of financial activities and debt; (iii) the relative importance of financial accumulation in relation to real accumulation (investments).

In doing so, we shall not offer a complete analysis. We shall limit it by discussing and illustrating a few aspects concerning of the financialization process in developed economies. Our main objective is to introduce a hypothesis rather than immediately producing a complete defense of this thesis.

2. Is Governance the Manifestation and Principle Stake of Financialization?

Among all of financial phenomenon that can legitimize the idea of a rupture, it is worth analyzing the practices considered directly accountable for some of the biggest changes in the industrial world, namely, contemporary governance and its presumed consequences on the increase in retirement funds. In these regards, the literature often refers to the financialization of companies and/or of their strategies. In this vein, we shall review the evolution of the norms established by the management and the main strategies that result from the pressure exercised by shareholders—sometimes represented by institutions and professional managers, sometimes by themselves— in order to obtain the highest value. Therefore, the reflection on governance and its derivatives is not only useful but also necessary. We shall limit our thoughts to a few notes.

To begin with, we have noted how the transformation of the norms of evaluation, modes of management, and strategic business logic is undeniable. Here we shall not give a detailed review. Nonetheless, it seems clear that these evolutions move towards what is called the financialization of business strategy that allows a deep internal penetration of an essentially financial logic concerning functioning and investment.[7] However, a financialization of wage relations can also be seen in parallel.

However, the issue regarding the channels of diffusion and the motives that govern the evolution of management strategies and practices still awaits an answer. Many analysts point out the direct effect of institutional shareholder interference (retirement funds, etc.) and their consequent "activism." At any rate, such an approach seems to be unconvincing as a substantial number of studies, in particular those conducted on the US case and aimed at verifying this point, have not been able to offer sufficiently clear conclusions. Obviously, shareholder activism does exist and many examples can be pointed out. But what about both its extent and relevance? It is difficult to say. However, if this activism were to be realized and recognized as a property of the present form of capitalism, it would be difficult to forecast what kind of conclusion could be reached. In fact, like some Marxist authors have pointed out, in a capitalist system shareholder domination is a new phenomenon or even a disorder? Certainly, we can always argue that the bases on which the Fordist period rested were quite different and that, to use M. Aglietta's expression, *carnivorous* capitalists were rather rare.[8] At any rate, this situation should not be generalized for two specific reasons: the maintenance of a dynamic and robust domestic capitalism and the considerable development of the *non-quoted*, i.e. private equity, in favor of the development of *risk-capital*.[9]

In such an evolution towards the financialization of firms, there could indeed be seen a new conformism and the manifestation of the diffusion of new norms interiorized by directors, without it being necessary to explain it using a form of direct power on the part of shareholders and the modes of business control. It should also be considered that, in the context of excessive liberalization, the expansion of the financial market created the conditions for the emergence of new behaviors, especially those of market shareholders.

The imperfect character of capital markets and their relative inefficiency facilitate the influence of the financial world over economic activity (and not only in the industrial sphere). This is translated in the diffusion of practices and norms considered normal in a contemporary context, above all when they are able to help, or even to reinforce, these firms. Financial derivatives of any sort are the manifestation of market imperfection, insufficient control, absent counterbalances, and the capacity of initiative, all aspects that are beneficial to the financial élite.[10] Certainly, governance is a point upon which it is worth focusing our attention as it lies at the very heart of capitalism: it poses questions concerning power, distribution of profit, and business management (with the well-known consequences on employment, profitability, innovation, activity portfolios, etc.). This institutional perspective can lead to important reform proposals. However, it could be asked if an institutional reform of the way in which administration boards and general member assemblies work could be sufficient to undermine the influence of finance over contemporary societies.

Another reason that calls for a prudent use of the arguments attached to corporate governance is that it is often considered as *the* characteristic phenomenon of financial capitalism, and that the whole question of financialization seems to have been reduced to that of the nature of governance. Now, the financial system is nothing else but share markets, and is not geared around governance.

The fact of privileging the issue of governance has a certain advantage: it allows the virtual construction of a connection between the articulation of finance and the question of the management of capitalism and the issues of wage relations, business organization, and the control of the productive system. Nonetheless, in doing so, it is possible to grasp that there is a way of embracing a vision centered on the productive system and that of treating post-Fordism in terms that, in the end, are not too far from the traditional representations of Fordism.

In brief, a consideration of governance is pertinent, but not exhaustive. Thus, the liberalization of finance is an essential process even if its beginning is not recent.

3. Some Quantitative Manifestations of Financialization

There is no general agreement on the meaning of financialization. Especially if it is addressed from an empirical point of view: the quantitative manifestations are sufficiently diverse to justify different viewpoints. This is due to the fact that some authors propose a definition that we believe to be too broad. A clear case in point is the one proposed by Gerald Epstein who defines financialization as "the growing role of financial motives, financial markets, actors and financial institutions in the functioning of national and international economies."[11]

In order to attract the attention to the incredible extent of financial operations, other scholars have lingered over the evaluation of a certain number of market maneuvers,[12] like currency operations. We prefer an approach that, in order to justify the legitimate preoccupations, focuses upon the speed of financial exchange in particular sectors. It seems reasonable to refer to the size of stocks and annual operational flows that are not subject to many and to speculative maneuvers, even if in many areas market maneuvers and the speed with which they happen—as shown for example, by the (downward) evolution of medium duration of share holding—are growing.

a) *The Evolution of Long-term Debt in the United States*—The simplest way to evaluate the weight and the importance assumed by finance consists in studying the way in which the evolution of the relationship between financial activity and GNP evolved. If we take the United States as the benchmark (cf. Chart 1), with reference to the period between 1956 to 2006, we shall see a significant increase of the debt GNP relationship, with a regular increase between 1973 and 2000 that, at the end of the century, began to accelerate slowly. Between 1959 and 1968, the ratio has always been close to 1.5. From then onward, except for few and very rare falls it constantly increased. There is no authentic historical rupture in this series. Does the most recent period indicate an accelerated growth in the ratio? The highest growth rates are situated in the 1982–1987 period (values between 3.1% in 1983 and 8.2% in 1985). Various analogies could be found in 1998 (+4.4%) and in the period between 2001 and 2003, but the three highest values of the entire period between 1960 and 2006 occurred during the 1980s.

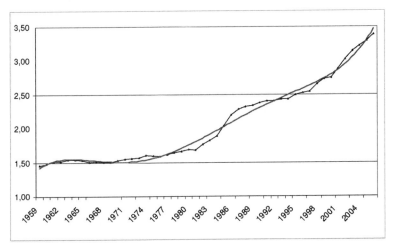

Chart 1. Accumulated debt report from all agents (stock)/GNP United States, 1959–2007. Source: Flow of funds of the United States, 6 December 2007. Table L.4 Credit Market Debt, All Sectors. Annual sums, 4th trimester values. 5th degree polynomial tendency curve.

Likewise, considerable evolutions could be observed in the relative size of debt carried by different agents in the non-financial sectors (cf. Chart 2). A first evolution is produced between the beginning of the series (1952) and a plateau that covers the period from 1973 to 1980. Whilst the debts carried by families concerned amount to 33% of the total debt of non-financial agents those carried by businesses account for 39%. At the end of the 1980s the percentages began to rise considerably. The percentage

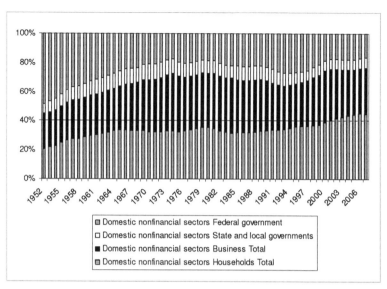

Chart 2. Decomposition of debt (stock) in US non-financial sectors, 1952–2007.
Source: Flow of funds of the United States, 6 December 2007. Table D3 Debt
Outstanding by Sectors, Annual sums, 4th trimester values.

referring to families is currently 44% and the one referring to
businesses is 32%. This part has more than doubled; as this trend
took over 50 years to reach its apex, we could not speak of a
strong and/or sudden rupture. On the contrary, the part that has
considerably decreased is the amount of internal debt of the federal
government. It went from more than 40% in 1952 to less than
20% in 2007.

Also the debt of non-financial agents *vis-a-vis* the total debt
is decreasing (cf. Chart 3). It went from 94.6% to 63.9% at the
end of the period, favoring the financial sectors that went from
2.3% in 1952 to 32.2% in 2006. This trend assumed a relatively
stable feature after 1952. It began to slow down only after the
year 2000.

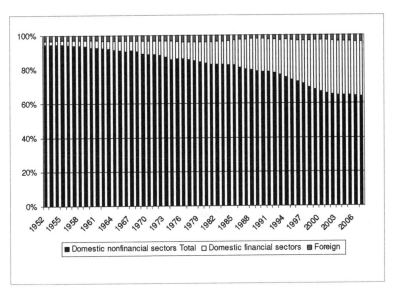

Chart 3. Decomposition of debt (stock) in the United States 1952–2007, according to three main sectors: domestic nonfinancial sectors, domestic financial agents, foreign. Source: Flow of funds of the United States, 6 December 2007. Table D.3 Debt Outstanding by Sectors, Annual sums, 4th trimester values.

b) The Evolution of Net Business Financial Investment—One of the variables which it is necessary to take into consideration in order to study these trends is the net business financial investment: namely, the acquisition of net financial activities minus the net passivity increase. We have calculated, for Nonfarm and Nonfinancial Corporate Businesses, the given ratio between the net financial investment (numerator) and the acquisition of net financial activity (denominator) (cf. Chart 4). The higher is this ratio, the less firms go into debt to acquire financial titles. At the same time they amplify their ability to auto-finance their own acquisition of titles; an operation, this latter is in competition with another characteristic usage of internal financing: namely, physical investment. A negative ratio implies that the net increase of passivity is higher than the net acquisition of titles. A part of the supplementary debt is due to physical investments that cash flow cannot cover in full. A positive ratio—lower than 1—indicates that the positive increase in debt is inferior to the net increase of the financial activities. A part of the cash flow is then utilized to the net acquisition of titles.

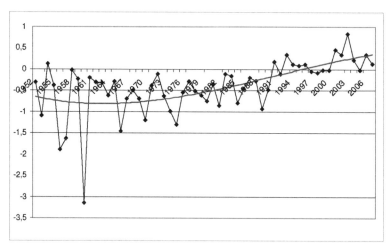

Chart 4: Net financial investment / Total net acquisition of financial activities. Source: Flow of funds of the United States, 6 December 2007. Table F.102 Nonfarm Nonfinancial Corporate Business. Annual sums, 4th trimester values.

Over the long-term, we have observed a tendency to increase in the ratio. If the size is judged via the polynomial curve, this trend emerges from the beginning of the 1970s onwards. The ratio, nearly always negative until 1993, becomes positive from 1993 to 1996 and from 2001 to 2007 (except for 2005, in which it turned slightly negative). Although the tendency is remote, both the passage to positive values and the maintenance in these zones in the first years after 2001, certainly constitute recent signals. However, we should be prudent in interpreting this recent evolution. Does it represent the development of financial investments or the extension of the subscriptions of participation or the Merger & Acquisitions operations?

c) Self-financing—The relation between auto-financing and physical capital, tied to the previous ratio, oscillates, over the long-term, around an average of 0.97% (cf. Chart 5). After 1979, very often this value is over, rather than under, such an average. Its extreme values have been reached in the early 1980s. The higher value recently reached occurred in 2000 (at 0.77%). The average of the 2000–2007 period is the highest of all the ten-year series between 1952 and 2007.

Sub-period Relation Average	
1952–1960	1.02
1961–1970	0.99
1971–1980	0.87
1981–1990	0.98
1991–2000	0.96
2001–2007	1.03

d) Net Action Emissions from Businesses—Another phenomenon directly tied to business financing is that the net action emissions from non-agricultural and non-financial companies turned out to be negative from 1994 to 2007 (cf. Chart 6). Although the phenomenon was already observed between 1963 and 1968, it is clear that from 1979 onwards, it becomes the rule rather than the exception: in the 1978–2007 period, 24 out of 30 years are "in the red." From this point of view, a historical change can indeed be observed. Nevertheless, this phenomenon is not truly recent; it become worthy of noticing in 1984 (at the same level as 1997). Yet in 1998 and, above all, between 2005–2007 reached a certain amplitude.

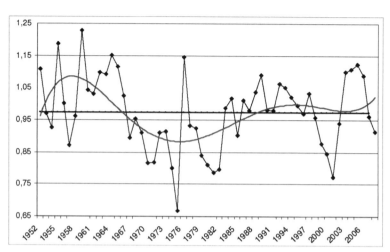

Chart 5. Ratio of auto-financing of material investment. Source: Flow of funds of the United States, 6 December 2007. Table F.102 Nonfarm Nonfinancial Corporate Business. Annual sums, 4th trimester average values. Ratio = [Total (US and foreign) internal funds + IVA]/Capital expenditures. (IVA = Inventory valuation adjustment).

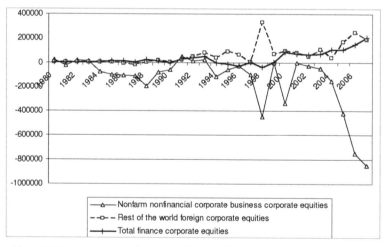

Chart 6. The net emission of stocks in the United States, 1980–2007.
Source: Flow of funds of the United States, 6 December 2007. Table F.213 Corporate Equities. Annual sums, 4th trimester values.

This evolution probably reflects the implementation of black-mailing strategies revealing the preoccupation attached to shareholder value. At any rate, financial markets are not limited to shareholder markets. Taking a step back, it is relevant to observe a general debt reduction as the global flow of business financing (stock emissions + obligatory emissions + credit variations) is negative in 1991, 2002 and in the two-year period between 2005–2007 (cf. Chart 7 and Chart 8). It is an essentially localized phenomenon after the shock in 2000. As a result, we assist to a large-scale restructuring of company liabilities.

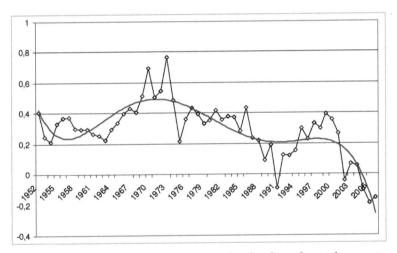

Chart 7. Evolution in net financing non-agricultural and non-financial companies in the United States, in respect to cash flow, 1952–2007. Source: Flow of funds of the United States, 6 December 2007. Table F. 213 Corporate Equities. Annual sums, 4th trimester values. 5th degree tendential polynomial curve.

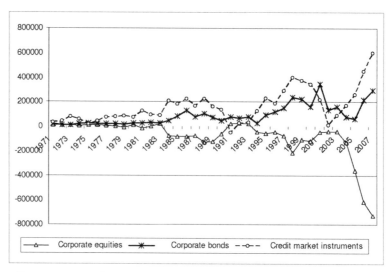

Chart 8. Financing for material goods in companies in the United States 1971–2007 (in millions of dollars). Source: Flow of funds of the United States, 6 December 2007. Table F.102 Nonfarm Nonfinancial Corporate Business. 4th trimester average.

e) Financial Accumulation and "Real" Accumulation in Business— Another approach to financialization consists in comparing the roles of "real" and financial accumulation. In order to justify the preeminence of financial accumulation, a number of authors have pointed out the disadvantaged position of productive investment if compared to the relevance of financial investment. In this way, these authors explain such a condition as the manifestation of shareholder power whose dividends increase at the cost of auto-financed investment. We must then examine dividend evolution too.

From the mid-1970s onwards, in the United States (cf. Chart 9), we can observe an increase (in nominal value) of firms' investment costs. Between 2000 and 2003, firms showed a net loss but a steady recovery began immediately after. On a macroeconomic level, investment doesn't seem to be supported by the evolution of profits. If we examine the most recent period (2005–2007), profits resuscitate, matching the level of physical investments. This realigning, the fact that profits can be gained once again after 2003 and reach the 7-year mobile average in 2006, can be interpreted as the consequence of relatively low values of investment.

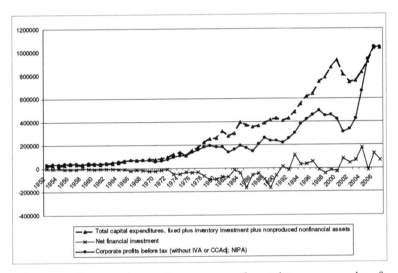

Chart 9. Evolution in business investment, net financial investment and profit before taxes (in millions of dollars). Source: Flow of funds of the United States, 6 December 2007. Table F. 102 Nonfarm Nonfinancial Corporate Business. Annual sums, 4 Trimester average value.

With regard to financial investments, if compared to physical investment, their relative value grows (cf. Chart 10). The values of the ratio (expenditures in capital/expenditures in financial activity) are not, except for a few cases, higher than in the past. The highest post-war value is in 1981 (at 12). The highest recent value is in 2003 (9), after 1992 (4.8). The historical tendency is regressive after 2003, namely, the financial activity grows *vis-a-vis* expenditures in capital. The long-term average (1952–2007) is 3.02. It is rather higher than the average until 1970 (with a downward tendency) and it has remained under that average up until today.

At the beginning of this long-term period, non-agricultural and non-financial businesses invested $4.4 in fixed capital for every dollar of financial activity. From then on, except in a few cases (notably in the 2000–2004 period), the ratio will be inferior to the long-term average with less than $3 of fixed capital invested for every dollar invested in financial activities. The average for the whole 1970–2007 period is 2.43.

The (linear) tendency between 1970 and 2007 is upward; in other words, the part of expenditures in fixed capital would tend to (slightly) recuperate over a very long-term period. We can observe that between 1997 and 2007, 6 points out of 11 are under the

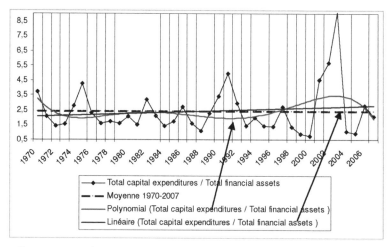

Chart 10. Expenditures in physical capital/Total financial activity acquisitions relation in the United States, 1970–2007. Source: Flow of funds of the United States 6 December 2007. Table F.102 Nonfarm Non-financial Corporate Business. Annual sums, Average 4 trimesters value. Ratio = [Total capital expenditures, fixed + inventory investment + nonproduced nonfinancial assets]/GDP.

long-term average of 2.4 (1970–2007). However, the 1997–2007 average reaches its stability at 2.9, and 7 points out of 11 are clearly under this value. Hence, we can observe the relative growth of financial titles. Beyond a precise interpretation, whether or not this is a very recent trend, that emerges in 2003, remains to be seen. Although it is difficult to suggest an abrupt rupture and a fundamental change on these bases only, the analysis can be further refined.

f) Evolution of Business Investment—Business investment expenditures with respect to the GNP (cf. Chart 11) fluctuate from 6% to 10%. In the long-term, from 1956 to 2006 a slightly increasing (linear) trend of investment expenditures against the GNP can be observed. But if

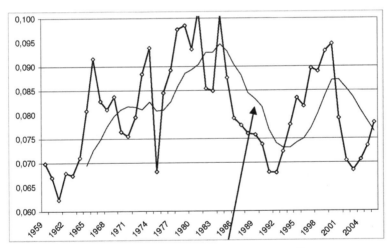

Chart 11. Non-agricultural and Non-financial Business Ratio [Investment expenditures (including stock variations)/GNP] in the United States. Source: Flow of funds of the United States, 6 December 2007. Table F.102 Nonfarm Nonfinancial Corporate Business. Annual sums, 4 trimester average values. Ratio = [Total capital expenditures, fixed+inventory investment+nonproduced nonfinancial assets]/GDP monthly mobile over 7 years.

the tendency is expressed by a polynomial relation, after the year 2000, becomes rather downward (value: 9.5%, a relative maximum after the mid–1980s). Also in the 2002–2003 period with quotes of 7% and 6.8% these last values never occurred after 1975 and between 1991–1992. The tendency of the investment rate to go down over the mid- to long-term, beginning during the 1980s, can be equally underlined.

g) Dividend Evolution—The issue of dividends is also important. At least partially, it clarifies the relationship between businesses and shareholders. We have calculated the ratio [Net dividends/Cash flow] for the non-agricultural and non-financial businesses (cf. Chart 12).

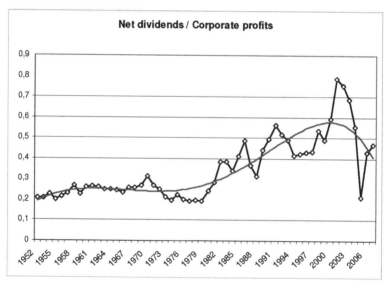

Chart 12. Relation [Net dividends/Corporate profit] in the United States, 1959–2007. Source: Flow of funds of the United States, 6 December 2007. Table F.102 Nonfarm Non-financial Corporate Business. Annual sums, 4 trimester average value. Ratio = [Net dividends/Corporate profits before tax]. The tendency curve is a 5th degree polynomial curve.

We see that the 1952–2007 period can be broken down into 3 phases: the period spanning from 1952 to 1979 characterized by relative stability (19%), followed by a phase lasting until 2001 characterized by a sustained growth (78%). The last phase, from 2001 to 2005, was characterized by a brutal downward turn (21%) that ends with an increase. Considered as one of the signals of financialization, the tendency to increase dividends is both intertwined with the Fordist crisis and shocked by the crisis in the new economy.

The information on the relative importance of dividends can be fully understood relativizing it through other information that concerns the number of businesses that distribute dividends (cf. Chart 13). After 1980, we can observe that the tendency of this series is downward. Between 1980 and 1997, it goes down slightly, then between 1997 and 2001–2002, it sharply goes down. It seems to pick back up after the *Jobs and Growth Act*.[13]

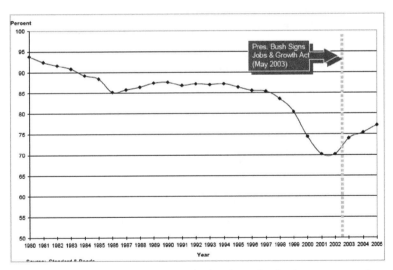

Chart 13. Percent of businesses which distribute dividends as represented in Standard & Poor's index. Source: Standard & Poor's.

Partial Conclusion

We have illustrated some of the difficulties and ambiguities relative to the empiric identification of financialization. We have not reached the end of the investigation that would consist in proposing a systematic list of interpretations and testing their validity or their empiric profile.

At this stage, we hope that the reader could agree with the following points: (i) the absence or, at least, the scarcity of phenomenon that point to an evident rupture and (ii) the interest in a long-term point of view able to show the historical continuity at least of a part of these phenomenons.

The analyticity relative to this second point consists in the fact that the process of financialization could be traced back to a remote epoch, to the extent that the Fordist crisis can be included in it. Often those who maintain the thesis of the emergence of financial capitalism seem to suggest that the key elements of this configuration would have emerged in the 1990s and, particularly, during the boom of the New Economy. Now less than a marginal part of the phenomenon considered as meaningful or illustrative of the emergence of this capitalism are in fact written in the extension of relatively old evolutions and, notably, in the liberalization of financial markets. Other more recent and meaningful evolutions can be observed. Sometimes following the pronunciation of the theses on financial capitalism or financialization.

Four Questions on the Role of Finance in Cognitive Capitalism

a) The Question of Financialization—What does the notion of financialization mean? We shall suggest a definition that is more qualitative than quantitive: financialization materialized itsef when the financial logic prevails over the economic one; in other words, when (market) actors' behaviors are focused less on the value of economic flows and more on the evolution of the state of the patrimonial balance. Financialization is translated into a "patrimonialization" of behaviors. This confirms what has been observed: namely, financialization of wage relations and businesses.[14] At the macroeconomic level, financialization is a diffused phenomenon that is translated into the emergence of an asset economy. This way of presenting the problem recuperates the approach proposed by K. Boulding at the end of the 1940s and therefore is not really new.

b) Financial Markets, a New Form of Governance—Let's go back to the concept of biopolitics that qualifies the way in which power approaches the issue of government. This concept is central for some proponents of the thesis of cognitive capitalism.[15]

According to Foucault,[16] biopolitics rests upon the principles that specify the way in which capitalism governs technologies. Biopolitics manifests itself via the managing of education, health care, alimentation, sexuality, etc.. Biopolitics rests upon the vital aspects that are the objects of Welfare politics. During the Fordist era, this latter was responsible for what B. Théret calls "the capital of life"[17] at the roots of a principle of solidarity, i.e. the virtuous alliance between Fordism and the welfare state. On the contrary, as a result of the implementation of remuneration policies constructed on individual bases and the trend of privatization of social security systems, the subsequent period is characterized by the crisis of the Welfare State. Financialization is stimulated by public debt.

Privatization and individualization can be accounted for in terms of governance in the following way: the biopolitics enforced by the State during the Fordist period have been replaced by commercial financial governance, all individuals are increasingly dependent upon the financial system. Through credit and the possible investment in complementary retirement funds, insurance policies, and the possible redirection of wage savings towards financial markets, we enter into a financial logic embodied by the limits that bear on individual lives and a variety of patrimonial strategies. Although these strategies assure one's present and future solvability, they deeply undermine one's creative and productive capacities. At the same time, they throw the world of wage laborers into a schizophrenic situation.

c) Finance, New Exodus of Capital and New Antagonistic Figures— Financial destabilization did not come about as a result of the Fordist crisis, rather it is part of this crisis. The empiric analysis presented above suggests that the evolutions that are tangible and that might be structurally significant in recent times have distant origins and courses.

The historic development of this long period can be traced using the analysis proposed by Antonio Negri. In the historical transition toward post-Fordism, a new subjectivity and laborer behavior might be said to hold a prominent position. These aspects, in fact, would constitute a major factor leading to the crisis of Fordism (becoming less manageable) and the creating act that triggered a process of reconfiguration. The decision taken by the Federal Reserve in 1979 can be considered as a political response "from capital," then fading toward the "disorders" of Fordism.[18] Thus, the Fed's decision would come second in the events that lead the inauguration of the post-Fordist period.

What is important here is the way in which we interpret the analysis of the statute of financial capitalism in post-Fordism: finance can be understood as the exodus of capital. Capital is no longer used in the same ways and at the same levels within industry, in the sense that it no longer assumes a long-term prospective. It plays the same game as the financial markets and acquires with considerable mobility and plasticity, thus avoiding a prolonged immobilization. Through finance, while capital reaches the appropriation of an important part of profit, the usual rules of production and competition are radically transformed. Capital has assumed a position that is quite far from being "real"; thus it has reached a form of scission. The antagonism between capital and labor assumes a new form whose structure depends on the long and complex paths of financing.

d) Finance and Evaluating the Common—Finance has many functions, among which there is that of being a representation of the decisions about the future. In post-Fordism, finance evaluates the capacity of production that, being cognitive, is shared and cooperative, i.e. common and projected toward the future. Keeping in mind capital's freedom of movement in financial markets, a production that is globalized, directly or indirectly, often in complex ways, corresponds to a system of evaluation which is also globalized.

Radical uncertainty has lead to the creation of new risk-management tools; among the most noted are the "derivatives" products. The efficiency of the socialization of market risk is posed in the measurement of the clarity and the comprehension of information communicated on the basis of these products. It should be noticed that the supplementary risk endogenously produced by those same financial markets is, today, high.

Financial market works starting from the evaluations depending on decisional criteria, opinions or beliefs.[19] By vocation, they cannot produce true representations. The financial sphere essentially produces judgments and justifications that reflect nothing else other than the values anchored to the "real"; on the one hand, because evolutions partially represent future performances and, on the other, because we are in the presence of a crisis in value measurement. This is explained by the creativity and the difficulty of identifying the factors of productivity, which is to say the difficult traceability of the sources of productivity upon which it depends. Only global judgments can be made and expressed.

Thus, any discourse on financing assumes a political character. On the one hand, it involves the authorities, experts, and finance managers, all of which are "authorized" figures. On the other, it aims at creating trust and spreading opinions. It affects human behaviors. Financial markets are opinion markets that do not work democratically because intermediaries and professionals monopolize their control mechanisms and their media space. These are the principle actors in the new technostructure. They are the ones that assure the prescriptive function.

If, as a language, finance is common, then it should be made clear that it has become a source of exploitation. Counting extra-financial values in market evaluations[20] plays a relevant role in the way in which control is maintained.

General Conclusion

Here we have developed a Keynesian analysis of the role of finance in contemporary capitalism. This analysis represents the compliment of a more institutional analysis centered around the study of the functioning conditions of business governance and that privileges power relations. Cognitive capitalism is not an alternative hypothesis to the coming of financial capitalism: financialization finds a justification and a development opportunity in the context of cognitive capitalism. Cognitive capitalism does not penalize an approach that goes back to the study of power relations and institutional roles: financial power must be re-collocated to a more global prospective that goes beyond the institutional level of business.

Karl Heinz Roth

Global Crisis—Global Proletarianization—

Counter-perspectives

Introduction

We are entering a world historical situation where all track switches of social-economic and political life are newly aligned. It will be the second epochal change for my generation after the period of 1967–1973. All the main facts and indicators of the last weeks point to the start of a world economic crisis which already now exceeds the extent of the 1973 crisis and of the intervening crises of 1982 and 1987. The current crisis is approaching the dimensions of the world-wide crisis and subsequent depression of 1929–1938.

How should we react to such a gigantic challenge? This has become the decisive question; this is why I have just completely rewritten a tract which is currently in the works and which was intended as a reply to the criticism of my hypotheses about the "condition of the world," published in 2005. I am presenting the thoughts and research results that I have worked out so far in the unfinished state of a synopsis because they will have to be checked, corrected and expanded in a continuous dialogue before the publication of the book; the first outcomes of the discussion at an event on the 27th November at the *Schorndorf Manufaktur* have already been included, as well as results from a *Wildcat* collective internet debate, those from a seminar of the Interventionistische Linke[1] on the 13th of December and those from dialogues with individual friends. In this way many weak points, unclear issues and short-comings were overcome, but due to lack of time I will be able to deal with some important objections only in the book manuscript, and I hope for your understanding. I hope my theses will still suf-fice to make clear the basis of the analytic approach and of my conceptual proposals. Thanks to everyone who joined the debate, not only for helping me through criticism but also for greatly encouraging me; I have not experienced such a wide and construc-tive dialogue, in such solidarity, for years.

1. The New World Economic Crisis

a) Development So Far—The first world economic crisis of the 21st century started during 2006 as a structural crisis and one of over-capacity in the car industry and as a real-estate crisis in the US, Great Britain, Ireland, and Spain. It was the end to an incomparable 6-year global boom which had led to a further expansion of the capital rela-tion, with all its classical and also some new speculative side effects; a development which had hardly been thought of as possible anymore. The inflated prices of houses, flats and business properties rapidly fell and this fall in value increasingly compromised the mortgages and mortgage derivatives secured on these properties. Additionally, the three US and some European and Japanese car companies experi-enced distinct sales slumps: this signaled the start of a worldwide crisis for the most capital-intensive sector of industrial production.

The crisis started to encroach on the financial sector at the turn of 2006 to 2007. The fall in private and commercial property prices expanded into a worldwide mortgage crisis. Local mortgage banks went into the red through massive writedowns and in June 2007 the American investment bank Bear Stearns had to liquidate two of its hedge funds, in the first incident of this kind. Because these suffering American mortgage credits had largely been packed into non-transparent credit derivatives (Collateralized Debt Obligations = CDO) which were sold on into the whole world, the drop in their price and the connected massive increase in risk premiums led to a global chain reaction which overlapped with the mortgage crises in Great Britain, Ireland and Spain. The subprime crisis reached its first peak in the summer of 2007. Its global character became immediately clear when the first action in support of banks threatened with collapse was taken at the periphery of events, while all the banks' troubles originated in the Anglo-Saxon crisis centers, as in the case of the illiquidity of Düsseldorf Internationale Kreditbank (IKB) or Sächsische Landesbank (SachsenLB), but also in that of the massive writedowns and trading losses of the Swiss "universal bank" [i.e. a single institution incorporating both investment and retail banking businesses] UBS.[2]

In five to six shock-waves since summer 2007, the mortgage crisis has become a world-wide financial crisis. It had encroached on the entire banking system by September 2008. The US investment bank Bear Stearns and the British mortgage lender Northern Rock collapsed in March 2008. Subsequently, after the initial German rescue missions of the previous year, the UK and the US also undertook state intervention on a massive scale for the first time: Northern Rock received a comprehensive guarantee of state support, while Bear Stearns was taken over by the "universal bank" JP Morgan Chase, and the Federal Reserve Bank (Fed), the US Central Bank, organized the break-up and refinancing of troubled securities.

A further shock followed in September: at the beginning of the month the two largest US mortgage institutions, Fannie Mae and Freddie Mac, were (saved from collapse and recapitalized by means of extensive state support. This was followed by the failure of the investment bank Lehman Brothers in the middle of the month, while the investment bank Merrill Lynch was saved in an emergency sale to the "universal bank" Bank of America. But over the next few months it was not only investment banks that suffered lethal blows and disappeared from the scene by transforming themselves into or merging with commercial banks. Leading insurance firms were also threatened, as was made clear by the effective ruin of the largest US insurance company, American International Group (AIG), one week later. It was mostly specific credit derivatives (Credit Default Swaps = CDS) that had started defaulting. CDS are used by buyers of bonds worldwide to insure themselves in off-market bilateral contracts against the issuers' risk of default. As there is no central counterparty and the CDS contracts are not subject to traditional reinsurance regulation, they are associated with high risk. CDS worth at least US$60 trillion have so far been distributed worldwide and could lead to a fatal chain reaction if one of their main pillars, such as AIG, should fail. In fact, AIG was supported by a series of government rescue packages, adding up to $153 billion so far. But irrespective of this, in September 2008 the effect of the mortgage crisis on a key element of the global derivatives market, whose volume is estimated to amount to at least $600 and at most $1000 trillion, showed that the financial sector—the decisive driving force of the previous cycle of expansion—was heading for the abyss. The entire international financial system was shaking in September 2008, with commercial banks and investment funds which had come into being in the 70s (hedge funds, private equity funds and pension funds) affected to the same extent.

But the shock waves still continue unabated, as is evident in the massive writedowns and operating losses of practically all globally acting banks. Government guarantees for increasingly outsourced toxic assets, public injections of capital to refill equity as well as an increasing number of state shareholdings in financial sector capital are rescue measures which have been launched in practically all metropolitan countries and which will most likely continue to be part of government agendas. Since summer 2007 governments have been trying to keep the money and capital markets going by means of coordinated interest rate cuts by Central Banks, along with supply of liquidity to the collapsed interbank markets and the absorption of troubled securities and debt instruments into the regulated public sphere. As the most recent data show, it has not yet been possible to halt the worldwide drying up of credit and the flight of asset owners from financial funds to the "safe havens" of "hard" currencies and state bonds. The reason for this is simple: the losses on mortgage paper and credit derivatives are followed by increasingly foul credit card, leasing, and department store credit debts, whose extent is as yet largely unknown but which has already led to the de facto breakdown of Citigroup, once the largest US commercial bank. An end to the global financial and credit crisis is not in sight, and this occurs in a situation where it worsens the structural and industrial sector crisis which started parallel to it, spreading like slow fire to affect all parts of the world economic system.

Following the spread of tighter credit conditions and moves towards capital flight, the events of the "black" quarter of September–November 2008 also reached the financial markets all over the world, i.e. those sectors of capital reproduction where long-term capital credits are traded as company shares, bond issues and equity derivatives (options and futures). The fall in securities initially dragged with it the market prices of structurally weak companies, especially in the car industry, before spreading structurally and geographically to all stock market-listed capital. Since the beginning of the year [2008], US, European and Japanese stock market indices have fallen by 35% to 40% on average; the turbulence of September and October increasingly evoked memories of the last century's world economic crises. During the autumn months the stock markets of the emerging nations began to feel the full effect, and capital losses there have increased so rapidly as not only to do away with any speculative overvaluations but also to initiate a phase of a massive destruction of financial assets. The stock markets in the so-called BRIC states (Brazil, Russia, India and China) are reporting year-on-year falls of between 60% and 70%.

A third decisive factor in the descent into the world economic crisis was the worldwide collapse in primary commodity prices, which began in July 2008 after another huge increase in food and energy prices and almost classically marked the turn from speculative bubble to crisis-type crash. By now the price of crude oil has fallen from its highest price of $147 a barrel to below $40, while prices of industrial metals and raw materials used in the agricultural industry (cotton etc) have halved, and the prices for basic foods (rice, corn, grain) have come down by about a third. Precious metals still manage to hold their ground on the commodity futures markets, but even the price of gold has been showing a tendential decline.

With these developments in mind, it comes as no surprise that transport costs have also fallen drastically, as in many cases they are an important element of primary commodity prices. Most notably, maritime transport, as the main carrier of the global transport chain, has suffered deflationary tendencies, with prices falling far below costs in some sectors and even exceeding the extent and speed of decline seen in comparable data of last century's world economic crisis. Rotterdam-Taiwan Lines cargo rates have dropped from $2,500 per container at the beginning of the year to $400 by October, and by November charter rates for the largest ship types for bulk cargoes had declined to an 11th of their highest price during the boom in 2007. This not only causes commodity prices to fall further, but also has significant further consequences. Up until this summer, the maritime port and logistics chain had been geared towards a massive expansion of capacity and infrastructure; now it is shaken to its core, and during the last weeks at least 80% of shipbuilding contracts of the leading shipyards in China, South Korea, Japan and Vietnam have been cancelled.

In a parallel development, the structural and overcapacity crises of the automotive, building, and real-estate sectors have deepened. Two of the US car industry's "big three"—General Motors and Chrysler—are about to go bankrupt. But in the week before Christmas, by granting them emergency credit, the Bush administration gave them a reprieve until March 2009; at the same time the historical attainments of the US car industry workers are now being wiped out. But the sector's crisis has by now reached all companies in the car industry. Even for "model" companies whose production is highly labor-intensive and technologically innovative, with low-emission products, worldwide turnover has fallen by about 20% to 30%. In most cases, temporary and contract workers etc have already disappeared from the factories, while regular staff have been sent on extended Christmas breaks with a view to a longer period of short time working to come. Such temporary solutions are not apparent on the lower levels of the car industry and news is piling up of sudden factory closures amongst the small and mid-sized suppliers.

All these tendencies are in a mutually intensifying and universalizing relation to the worldwide increase in credit costs. Since the third quarter of 2008 the "triad" regions of North America, Europe and Japan are in recession. Mass unemployment has risen dramatically in the USA, the UK and Spain and is by now extending its reach from the transatlantic region to all developed national economies. Its economic counterparts are drastically falling interest and profit rates which, together with the increasing cost of credit and the rapid decline in orders, have led to a drastic drop in investment projects. This on the other hand leads to a brisk contraction in exports and the most export-intensive countries of the triad—Japan, Germany and Switzerland—react to the loss of their export business with a disproportionate reduction of imports, thus initiating a self-exacerbating spiral of world economic decline.

Because of these massive import restrictions, the triad's crisis, which by this stage was fully developed, encroached onto the newly emerging and developing economies with full force from October 2008. They are hit by this development at a time when their economic development depends primarily on exports to the triad regions, with the associated economic imbalances compensated for (up to this point) by accumulation of large foreign exchange reserves. Now this unstable state of affairs ended abruptly. Tightening credit throughout the world economy, collapsing share prices and declining primary commodity prices, together with the losses of the export sector, added up to an explosive mix, which was balanced temporarily by a recourse to currency reserves and an increase in national debt.

But the BRIC states are not the USA, and even less so are the newly emerging "economies" of the second series, such as Mexico, South Korea, Indonesia, Hungary or Ukraine. The USA with its still-unchallenged world currency of reference can afford a gigantic balance of payment deficits and debt mountains without being called to account by its creditors. International investors took their capital away as soon as the emerging nations' currency reserves dwindled, their balance of payments worsened and budget deficits increased. Huge currency devaluations have followed, provoking explosive turbulence on the international currency markets. Additionally, and mainly in the South East Asian, South American and Central/Eastern European economies, the structural deficits and manifold constellations of over-indebtedness are becoming visible. Since late autumn they have led to the first de facto national bankruptcies, affecting Hungary, Pakistan, Latvia and Ukraine, as well as the North Atlantic island republic of Iceland. In those countries the social consequences are dramatically intensifying, but also in the US entire city neighborhoods are being "shut down" by the forced eviction of families from their owned houses and rented flats. In California, a recapitalization program to avert impending insolvency has just failed.

From a global viewpoint, a dramatic crash of gross domestic product has so far been averted by means of massive political provision of financial support by the countries and power blocs of the capitalist center (to the tune of an estimated minimum of $7 trillion) and the widespread introduction of anti-cyclical programs (China, EU, USA and Japan). Currency turbulence has also been fairly well controlled, with the dollar remaining surprisingly stable up to now (although this could change very quickly). This is the precondition for the continued functioning of the strategic debtor-creditor-axis of the world system, China and the US. Nevertheless the crisis has already exceeded the scale of the 1973 crisis and will introduce a new cycle of exploitation and a new era in the capitalist world system, even if it is successfully contained within the next few months. But stabilization in the short-term is rather unlikely. The first phase of politically-driven financial bail-out measures was attached to monetarist thought and has failed, as it tied much too closely to the conclusions of Milton Friedman, the mastermind of the economic counterrevolution: he had blamed the spread of the world economic crisis of 1929 almost exclusively on the Fed's mistaken monetary policies. The escalating credit and investment strike by asset owners and the business, bank and fund managers under their control cannot be stopped by a policy of cheap money and the flooding of credit and capital markets with interest-free liquidity. It is just as uncertain whether the economic stimulus plans, which are Keynesian in parts, will have an effect: they have not been globally adjusted and would need to be pushed speedily and on a grand scale most of all by the strongest creditor and exporting countries (Japan, China, euro-zone states). Investors are also not impressed by the public budget's more or less complete incorporation of "toxic" credit and private debts, as long as this means the now obvious failures and strategic mistakes of funds and bank managers are not followed up but pushed under the carpet. Moreover, this only delays the mechanism of crisis but does not stop it. For asset owners have long perceived the Fed as a huge hedge fund which is supplied with means by the US Treasury, acting as gigantic investment broker. Thus it is only a question of time until they rate "Uncle Sam" as no longer credit-worthy. But where can they invest then? Right now there is no new strategic economic sector in sight and the hope that the newly emerging economies could put an end to the trouble in the tow of their precursor, the strategic US creditor China, has long since evaporated.

b) Essential Attributes of the Crisis—We have put a lot of effort into showing how the various crisis factors in the newest cycle of the crisis are slowly becoming synchronized. But what were the main causes for the slow fire which started two years ago on some of the roofs of the world economic building complex, and which has now reached all sectors and territories of the global economic circuit? A brief glance at the conjunctions within this process shows that they can be traced back to three main characteristics. First, it is a crisis of a worldwide over-accumulation of capital in all its appearances and metamorphoses: productive industries are over-accumulated by an average of 25% (much more in the car industry), the global transport chains by 30–35%, and the banking and financial sector by at least 50%. Secondly, this over-accumulation goes hand in hand with a massive global under-consumption, due to capital's huge reduction of mass incomes in the centers in the course of the last cycle, its above average growth rates on the basis of the lowest wages in the emerging markets and its policy of leaving mass poverty in the South (slum cities, shadow economy) in a state of imminent genocide by hunger. Although the lower classes of those developed regions where the crisis started had managed to compensate for their income losses by means of diverse techniques of indebting themselves, their lowest segments were excluded from this on a constant basis. Compared with the large increase in the productive force of social labor, the difference between the development of productive forces and income continued to grow wider to the huge disadvantage of the class of workers, even in the US, Great Britain and Spain. Thirdly, a finance policy of cheap money and cheap credit nonetheless compensated for the interplay of over-capacity and under-consumption in the developed centers of the world, but this could only delay the outbreak of crisis by a few years. As the low-pay sector expanded and the precarization of employment conditions increasingly reached the middle classes, several million people worldwide indebted themselves to the tune of at least $12 trillion (mortgage debt without own means, credit card debt, hire purchase and leasing debt, student loans etc). This mechanism worked for such a long time because the credit debt pumped from the lower classes was diversified worldwide. But it reached its outer limit in the course of 2006 and dragged the entire financial system all the more abruptly into the abyss. Thus the mechanism enforced the already existing structural distortions and over-capacity in the key economic sectors (the construction and car industries and their supplier sectors, but also information technology and the steel industry), and, together with falling primary commodity prices, in the circulation sector, and on the stock markets, as well as with the escalating credit restrictions, it caused the new world economic crisis. A worldwide investment strike by asset owners was the consequence, which by now has affected all the main capital spheres because their interest and profit rates have dropped one after the other in the course of only a few months.

2. The Previous Cycle (1973–2006)

For a clearer idea of the inner dynamics, development perspectives and likely consequences of the current world economic crisis we need to look back briefly at the main characteristics of the previous global cycle spanning the years of 1973–2006. Initially we will have to limit ourselves to working out the main characteristics of the economic cycle of 1973–2006.

a) Characteristics of a Typical Long Wave (Kondratieff)—The cycle started in 1973 with the world economic crisis, which led to a depression that lasted several years. This crisis had been caused by workers' and social revolts worldwide between the years of 1967 and 1973, along with a world currency crisis (decoupling of the dollar from gold, transition to flexible exchange rates) and the 1973 oil shock (Yom Kippur war). During the following years, it turned into so-called stagflation, due to the prevalent use of inflationary policies against the wage rigidity of the working classes. Over the next 35 years, several five year-long boom cycles followed one after another, interrupted by partial crises of which some were serious: 1982 (second oil crisis), 1987 (USA), 1992–93 (Japan crisis), 1997–98 (East Asia- and Russia crisis), and 2000–2001 (collapse of the "New Economy"). There was a decisive break between 1989 and 1991 with the implosion of the Soviet empire and the start of the rise of China. Without the sudden and powerful expansionary push resulting from these events, the last long wave would have ended much earlier. Additionally, the credit expansion concentrated mostly in the last boom period of 2001–2006 was superimposed on the interplay of over-accumulation and shrunken mass income, delaying the onset of the crisis by several years.

b) From Crisis Attack to Over-exploitation of the Global Class of Workers—Attack by capital in the form of "crisis" forced the working class worldwide into retreat until the end of the '70s. Despite fierce class struggles continuing during the '80s, the working class was subjected to pronounced processes of (re-)proletarianization in the peripheries, in the newly emerging economies and in the developed centers. I will go into more detail on this later on in the text. Of interest here are the economic consequences: mass incomes dropped in relative and absolute terms in relation to capital and capital accumulation, and this process was kept going by a systematic strategy of under-employment until the end of the cycle. Capital's centers of activity managed to reap large profits and high interest during the cyclical booms, despite all temporary and regional slumps and despite some fierce struggles in which a new industrial working class in some newly emerging economies (particularly in South Korea and some South American countries) constituted itself. The suppression and disproportionate exploitation of the class of workers and the pauperization of some of its most important segments, pushing them into "working poverty," was a major feature of the previous long wave, despite all counteracting tendencies. But this feature was also the cause of this wave's collapse—a collapse which was only delayed by the credit boom of the "crazy" first decade of the millennium.

c) New Technologies—The reinforcement of capital's technological command was a further decisive endogenous factor. The "Kondratieff wave" of the 1973–2006 cycle helped capital increase its rate of profit through massive technical innovations by lowering the organic composition of capital in strategic areas (with a continuous drop in relative pay rates): transformation and standardization of the transport chain by means of the container, change of communication structures by means of computer science and information technology, micro-miniaturization and robotization of production facilities, and conversion of machinery into assemblages of individually enumerated and monitored components. There are no reliable data yet about the rise in the rate of exploitation achieved during the previous cycle by means of the further compression of labor processes, the introduction of new technological instruments of real subsumption, the commissioning and utilizing of the subjective creativity of the exploited, or the totalization of managerial command through the organization of work ("total productive management" etc). But we can be certain that the total productivity of the "social worker" has at least doubled over the previous cycle with annual growth rates of between 2.5 and 3 per cent, with no corresponding gain for the workers concerned.

d) Renewed Expansion of the World Market and the Worldwide Division of Labor—As indicated above, the expansion of capital asset spheres and markets was another important exogenous factor: it reached its peak at the beginning of the 90s. During those years, a scrap dealer's son from Calcutta was able to build up a steel empire from the investment ruins of Eastern Europe and the special economic zones of the periphery; this is only one of many examples. The decisive factor was the conjunction between this geographical process of expansion with new forms of an international division of labor: new forms made possible by a miniaturization of fixed capital, by the new information technology and by the massive lowering of transport costs. It became possible to establish global network companies whose chains of value creation are managed by development, design and marketing centers located mainly in the metropolis: segmented labor processes can be distributed over those world regions with the lowest rates of exploitation and then be connected to each other.

e) The New World Economic Axis: Washington—Beijing—The fact that the new forms of international division of labor were indeed the decisive strategic axis of the previous cycle becomes immediately clear if we look at the two most important national economies, which entered a silent symbiosis with far-reaching consequences at the beginning of the 1990s: the USA and China. This symbiosis consisted and consists of the following: one partner saves and works hard, whilst the other spends the resulting products and revenues wildly. Of course this is a very blurred image, but it does reflect the decisive facts. In the process of China's catching up with capitalist development, its state despotism chained the peasant-workers and migrant workers to the world's extended work bench, exported their products into the developed centers (especially the USA) at dumping prices, and was contented with payment promises (government bonds); this in turn made it possible for the USA to conceal the pauperization processes resulting from its own low-wage strategy through credit expansion, which itself was re-routed back out into the world. In this way, the extended work bench has advanced to the point that it also becomes the principal bank of the US, and it is chained to it for better or for worse, as a sharp fall of the dollar would ruin both partners at once. This is because the Chinese Central Bank has been holding the largest part of its currency reserves in US dollars ($2 trillion) for some time and it has taken up Treasury bonds amounting to almost $1 trillion: if there was an uncontrolled slump in the US dollar, China's creditor position would be dramatically weakened, while the US would go into national bankruptcy because of the resulting flight of international capital. Even short of such a horror scenario, a perverse debtor-creditor relation of this kind on such an enormous scale seems an intractable problem. Yet a solution of some kind has become unavoidable. A simple calculation shows how hard it will be to balance out the decline in relative US over-consumption, which is already under way and goes hand in hand with a reversion of the population to its earlier common savings ratio of 5% of GDP, through a comparable increase in Chinese mass consumption which would overcome the two-way distortion in the balance of payments: in order for this to work, Chinese mass consumption, which is currently very low, would have to be promptly raised by 40%. This seems almost impossible but it highlights the fact, that the lever for a world-wide anti-cyclical (and system-reinforcing) resolution of the crisis lies with China in the first place, and that further development of the crisis and the debt-depression likely to ensue will be decided primarily by the ongoing development of the "Chimerica"-project, should no revolutionary transformation alternative intervene.

f) Worldwide Expansion of Financial and Credit Markets—The restructuring and internationalization of the chains of exploitation and value creation would not have been possible without the international expansion of the financial system. The flexibilization of the foreign exchange rates led to the establishing of transnational currency markets (eurodollar market, petrodollar market, asiadollar market) with continuing supremacy of the dollar. Starting from these, new money and credit instruments were developed to hedge against risks associated with foreign exchange rates, constantly fluctuating commodity prices and stock market volatility. The "moderate"credit relation which had existed thus far between banks and industrial concerns had relied on mid-term profitability; it was now increasingly replaced by the autocracy of a growing layer of capital asset owners set on maximum short-term gains. They launched a new sphere of investment funds to put the short leash of maximum equity and debt yields on management of all economic and trade sectors. This led to the "financialization" of the entire economic system and of all stages of capital metamorphosis, increasing average capital yields to ratios of between 20 to 25%, but with a corresponding increase in risk and instability. At the same time, the expanding financial sector pushed credit into the lower and middle classes, who had to accept it as it made it possible to maintain living standards to some degree despite the increasing precarization of labor and income conditions.) Additionally, a new dimension of capital expansion into the inner workings of social reproduction began to develop, led by the new financial sector. I would like to call this "fee capitalism": publicly owned, largely communal resources were expropriated in order to transform everyday human reproduction needs (from drinking water to energy supply to health care and protection against all other risks associated with living) into commodities and to generate capital gains.

g) Increasing Destruction of the Material Basis of the Production and Reproduction of Capitalist Society—A last important exogenous factor of the previous cycle was the increasing destruction of the economic system's natural basis. This was not only a consequence of the immense qualitative and quantitative expansion of the immediate production processes and their network of transport chains, but also of the parallel marginalization of mass poverty in the South, which was increasingly pushed into the niches of still-intact ecosystems while, conversely, the new regimes and middle classes of the emerging economies began to copy the environmental sins of the metropolis. In the same way as the previous cycle had used the world-wide resources of labor power remorselessly, so the exploitation of ecosystems was now carried relentlessly to extremes. Without doubt there have by now been considerable efforts to start "ecologizing" capital reproduction but they don't yet amount to more than a drop in the ocean. Nevertheless these small-scale efforts, brought about by an increasing environmental awareness, have sufficed to bring about a serious structural crisis in industrial sectors, such as the car industry, which followed this trend either too late or not at all.

3. Differences From and Similarities To Earlier World Economic Crises

It is essential to think about the main endogenous and exogenous factors of previous cycles in order properly to understand the current crisis process. But the crisis phenomenon as they appear do not give us the means to think about its further development and its possible outcome, if such speculation is even possible at all. A supplementary glance at the largest previous world economic crises during the development of capitalist society in its industrial stage, i.e. during the last 150 years, will be of use. I want to work comparatively through the differences and similarities between the current and earlier world economic crises; this is a decisive way to maintain the thread of thought when dealing with the complex structures and manifestations of the present.

a) The World Economic Crisis of 1857–58—The 1857–58 world economic crisis was the first to take hold of capitalism (as developed thus far) in a synchronous way. It started in the US, where speculation on an immense scale in railroads, then the leading sector of capitalist development, caused a severe crisis. Soon it leaped to Britain and the Northern German trading cities, as well as Scandinavia, France and South-eastern Europe. The crisis was worsened by the initial and enormous pro-cyclical activities of Britain, went on largely to ruin world trade, and eventually also to penetrate what at the time were the centers of industry and infrastructure (Sheffield, Birmingham, Manchester, the Ruhr area, Northern France, world-wide railway construction projects etc). In the preceding years, capitalism had completed an enormous expansion of trade, following from the Crimean war (1853–56), and had also gone through a huge geographical enlargement push (colonialization of California, Mexico and Australia, deepening of British rule over India, enforced opening of China). Thus Karl Marx anticipated a transatlantic workers' revolution in 1857–58. But he was soon to find out that he had been wrong. The consequences of the crisis were mostly overcome in the course of 1858 and a new period of expansion and prosperity started and continued until 1870–71. People living at the time emphasized the far-reaching effects of the crisis process but in relation to later world economic crises it was rather embryonic.

b) The Great Depression of 1873–1895—The great depression started with the "founders' crashes" [Gründerkräche], which got underway simultaneously in several centers which were catching up in terms of capital accumulation, starting in particular in the newly founded imperial Germany and the Habsburg monarchy before encroaching on Britain and especially on the US. It lasted until 1879 and turned into a long depression that only ended in 1895. The world systems' national economies overcame its effects in very different ways. In the US the colonialization of the West was brutally completed, and mammoth enterprises ("Trusts") became established, taking a leading part in the advance of the new high-technology sectors such as the chemical and electrical industries. Imperial Germany also completed an analogous, science-intensive second wave of industrialization, after the effects of the "Gründerkrach" had been weathered. Thus the basis for a wide ranging reconstruction of the industrial exploitation and accumulation process was established, most of all in Germany and the US. The artisanal skills of the working class were dispensed with, with the class as "mass workers" subjected to the despotism of machine rhythms and processing plants. In this sense it was the first world economic crisis to accelerate greatly the recomposition of the industrial exploitation process in technological and labor-organization terms. The relation between labor and capital was placed on a whole new basis, and this was countered by the world working class in 1905 with its first global revolt and the development of revolutionary syndicalism (Industrial Workers of the World). Britain and France meanwhile realigned their colonial empires. Victorian Britain in particular destroyed the subsistence economy of what was then the periphery, to the extent that a hunger catastrophe followed, costing millions of lives and bringing about the "Third World."

c) The World Economic Crisis of 1929–1932 and the Depression of 1939–1940—There are still many enigmas surrounding last century's world economic crisis, even though it has been extensively researched for decades. We can take as certain that its massiveness was mostly due to the strangely proceeding growth cycle from 1896: the 1st World War was unleashed just when a global downturn was looming. Thus the cycle was lengthened by a global war boom and, after the defeat of the international workers' revolution of 1916–21 and the overcoming of a massive hyperinflation period, the cycle rose in the "golden" twenties which were very similar to the crazy' first decade of the 21st century: also were marked by excessive stock and credit speculation, low mass incomes and over-accumulation in the industrialized segments of agriculture and the streamlined industrial capital sectors. The crisis started as an international agricultural crisis with the decline of the most important agricultural commodity prices, then encroached on the US stock markets in October 1929 and led to the breakdown of world trade from 1930 onwards, after the US had unleashed a global wave of protectionism with a protective tariff law that covered practically all parts of the economy. After that, the crisis encroached on most industrial sectors; it was worsened from 1931–32 by a banking crisis which had originated in Europe and which was followed by a race to devalue the major currencies, leading to the halving of GDP and to unemployment of between 25% and 35% in all industrial countries. All attempts to overcome the following depression failed, even the American "New Deal." The situation reached the point of a global economic war, radicalized by the armament and expansion policy of the centers of the fascist axis: Germany, Italy and Japan. This big crisis was only overcome from 1938 onwards with the international arms race and the armament industries of the 2nd world war, starting in Europe and reaching the US from 1940 onwards. Such a catastrophic outcome of the crisis was by no means inevitable. Thus it should help us, as we debate the currently expanding crisis, to realize that it is our task to propose and push through ways to overcome the crisis which obstruct the path into a new world economic war and which can be used as levers for a socialist transformation of the world system.

4. Global Proletarianization

Before focusing on this question, we should ask who could be able to force a way out of the crisis, a way which does not lead into capitalist barbarism once more, but instead widens into a prospect of socialist transformation. It can be only those classes and layers which have to sell or divest their labor power to the capitalist machinery of accumulation and regulation in order to survive: all those of this world who own nothing and who form the constantly changing multiverse of the global working class.

a) Historical and Methodical Premises—This approach is anything but self-evident, so I would like to illustrate it further. It is based on a conception of global working class derived from the critique of the "national" and "eurocentric" perspectives of labor historiography, and from advances in the Marxist understanding of labor and class.

i) Processes of global proletarianization and de-proletarianization— Global labor history is a very young branch of labor history, but it has nevertheless delivered some important results. It is now understood that from its earliest beginnings, the formation of the working class took place in global contexts. The process began in the second half of the 18th century in the course of the transoceanic and transcontinental social revolts, which were fought by pressganged mariners of the merchant marine and navy together with slave laborers (Caribbean), the self-employed migrant workers of the colonies (small peasants and artisans) and the workshop and factory proletarians. These uprisings of the commoners in 1775–76 not only initiated the North American revolutionary war against colonial dependency on the British mother country, but also had enormous repercussions on the formation of the local working class. The recognition of all this has made it possible finally to overcome labor history's previous limitations of eurocentrism and fixation on the trans-Atlantic perspective, to which even the best scholars in the field, eg. E.P. Thompson, were prey. Since this first phase of formation in the late 18th century there have been specific phases of proletarianization and relative de-proletarianization of the subaltern classes of the world population. These phases partly anticipated the expansion of capital (intercontinental political and social migration) and partly followed in their wake. The last phase of relative de-proletarianization occurred during the cycle of welfare state-dominated accumulation of the 1950s and 1960s, which was accompanied by a temporary decolonization of the periphery. After 1973 it was replaced by a new wave of re-proletarianization, about which there will be a lot more to say, given that the internal composition of the global working class at the beginning of the crisis provides insights.

ii) The multiverse of the global working class—The global working class is not dominated by "doubly free" wage labor; rather, since the second half of the 18th century it has comprised a many-layered multiverse. Within this multiverse, wage labor in large-scale industry played an important and temporarily a politically dominant role, but there has never been a prospect that it would absorb the remaining segments of the proletariat and/or to turn them into a pure industrial reserve army. The global class of workers up to date constitutes itself in a pentagon of mass poverty and mass unemployment, subsistence farming among the small peasantry, self-employed labor (small peasants, artisans, small traders, formally self-employed science knowledge workers), industrial labor and un-free labor relations of all kinds (slavery, debt bondage, coolie or contract work, militarized or imprisoned forced labor, ranging up to the working poor in the metropolis who are deprived of their freedom of mobility, e.g. the Hartz 4 claimants in Germany).[3] In the various global regions these segments stand in very different quantitative relations to each other. Between these segments of the global working class there are fluid transitions and networks whose threads converge primarily in mass migration between proletarian/small peasant family units on one hand and transcontinental subcultures on the other. Referring to the young Marx, we assume that the propertyless class is the most agent in bringing about social, economical, sexual and ethnic equality. This is because only this class is able, by the general abolition of property, to overcome the double alienation of humankind from the practical processes of life and from objectified labor, which confronts it as an alien power: as capital. This is why the processes of homogenization and convergence within the proletarian multiverse are our main point of reference. Thus it is a matter not only of the abolition of wage labor, but also of all kinds of exploitation and oppression which result from the fact that most people have to divest their labor power in order to survive.

b) The Current State of the Global Class of Workers—So much for the conceptual premises. The question now is, what shape did the internal process of class formation and class fragmentation take in the course of the past cycle of strategic under-employment and intensified exploitation? What are the elementary life needs of the global class of workers and how will the class ensure that these can be met when confronted with the looming phase of mass unemployment and mass poverty? Will the class—or at least important parts of it—have the strength to go beyond this defensive position and to put social and egalitarian re-appropriation of social wealth on the agenda?

i) Subsistence farming families of the global South—Today subsistence farming families in the global South and in some important emerging economies still account for the majority of the global class of workers, comprising 2.8 billion people, of whom 700 million are in China alone. They reproduce themselves in family-based subsistence economies of the Caianov type.[4] These complex structures are interwoven with village communities and a system of patronage. They are increasingly endangered and are only able to survive through periodical or permanent labor income from non-agricultural sectors (continental and transcontinental migrant labor). Over the past cycle the basis of this group's existence was increasingly undermined by the transformation of the most fertile cultivated areas into mechanized large-scale farming enterprises, the consequences of climate change, and the expropriation of land.

ii) Mass migration and migrant labor—In the last decades hundreds of millions of people were on the move continentally or trans-continentally, in order either to get away from the mass poverty of the subsistence sector and the barbarism of civil war zones or in order to make a living for their subsistence-farming families left at home. Mass migration within China, mass migration from South-East and South Asia to the Gulf region, from Africa, passing through the Mediterranean region, to southern Europe, from Eastern to Western Europe, and from South and Central America to North America. Ten to twenty per cent of the underclasses of the metropolitan countries and of many emerging economies are migrants. Over time several waves of migration have overlapped and an everyday culture is in the making, which is cross-border, multilingual and highly intelligent. Within this culture tendencies towards multicultural identities and efforts for self-affirmation of ethnic identities also overlap. During the last decades these developments have shaped the process of proletarianization decisively, and today they constitute one of the most important reference points of global class composition.

iii) Mass poverty and the shadow-economy of the slum-cities—Not everyone who leaves the rural areas of subsistence and the regions of civil war manages to settle permanently or even temporarily in the emerging economies or metropolitan countries. Today this global surplus population lives in the slum cities which exist in peripheral zones and emerging economies. The impoverished mass of the slum cities survives within the shadow economy at the brink of starvation-genocide and mass epidemics; they are confronted with extreme forms of over-exploitation, which are dominated by unfree or formally "self-employed" labor relations. This is true of around a billion people who populate the huge urban agglomerations, eking out a miserable living alongside the transport routes and river courses of the metropolises of the global South. These poor are increasingly pushed out towards coastal and desert regions, which are threatened by natural disasters. The transitions between the rural subsistence economies and the communication channels of mass migration become increasingly precarious. There is justified fear that the current global economic crisis will further accelerate this gigantic process of slumification. And there are already indications that urban mass poverty—with its open and hidden homeless shelters and soup kitchens for the unemployed—is also starting to shape the cities of the global North.

iv) The new industrial working class of the emerging economies—In the past two decades the development of the new industrial working class in the emerging economies has changed the global class composition decisively. In the course of the last two economic cycles this class has passed quickly through intensive processes of acquisition of technical skills, while fighting for and winning considerable increases in income. During the 1980s and 1990s low-tech sectors were increasingly relocated from the old industrial centers to neighboring peripheral countries, and the working class of the "extended workbench" was relocated along with these sectors, particularly in the textile and consumer goods industries. Due to the leveling out of the technological divide between the former industrial centers and these emerging economies, together with the now nearly completed relocation of key sectors (shipyards, car industry, electronics industry, chemical industries, textile production), the poles of class composition between the emerging economies and the developed regions of the world system have moved towards each other. This is also true of the precarious segments of the working multiverse: while their numbers decrease in the emerging economies, they grow considerably in the metropolitan countries.

v) Relative de-industrialization and casualization of the working class in the former centers—In the past decades the industrial wage labor sector of the triad region (USA, Europe and Japan) has shrunken significantly. At the same time its technical composition has changed dramatically as a result of the technological innovation which seized and transformed all manufacturing and service sectors. In this way a lot of those sections of the working class which were resistant and particularly experienced in struggle have disappeared (printers, the classical manual dock worker) or their numbers have been reduced, even in the big national economies, to a few hundred thousand. In a parallel process, precarious and formally "self-employed" work has become an essential component of class composition in the metropolitan countries. In recent years the decrease in labor income has affected all segments, including the so-called core workforce of large-scale industry. A quarter of all people who are forced to engage in dependent wage labor are no longer able to maintain their living standard above the poverty line, despite extra-long working hours.

vi) Tendencies towards homogenization and fragmentation of the global working class—Overall, in the past cycle the tendencies of homogenization and fragmentation of the global working class have roughly balanced each other. In all regions of the world system the small peasant subsistence economies slumped into what may be a final crisis, triggering processes of mass migration and the formation of a global surplus population. These processes transformed the global class of workers, which is now generally characterized by a transcontinental and transcultural mentality. A process of homogenization which developed from the opposite direction was set in motion by the waged and industrial segments of the working class, mainly due to the now completed period of "peripheralization" of industrial mass production.

But there have also been significant tendencies of fragmentation. Although the working and living conditions have deteriorated on a world scale, regional differences in proletarian living standards have deepened considerably. The chances for survival at the fringe of open sewers and waste dumps of the slum cities differ enormously from those of the multicultural precarious workers in the metropolitan neighborhoods. In addition we can see elements of "negative" homogenization, such as the increasing fixation on religious promises for salvation and the subjugation to mafia-type patronage, which fortify the tendencies towards patriarchal and ethno-political regression worldwide. It is particularly important not to underestimate these tendencies, because they will impair our future scope of action considerably. It is a burdensome legacy: in 1979–1980 in Iran the social-revolutionary wing of Shiite Islam was eradicated by the archaic-theocratic Ayatollah faction; a few years later Islamist organizations massacred the remaining cadres of the political left in the Middle East and appeased the region's poor in patriarchal-reactionary structures of social policy; today the underclasses of the US rust belts are dominated by the evangelists; and in the slum cities the rudiments of social security and of a minimal education system are only maintained by Chiliastic churches with membership of over a hundred million. Even in Europe, the traditional labor movement has abandoned the working class, the results of which we can see in the case of Marseille, where after the exodus of the Socialist Party the second generation of labor migrants has increasingly turned towards the welfare office of the National Front. Undoubtedly, all of this has meant that the return of the left to the everyday reality of the working class has been made more difficult; a return which has become such a pressing issue with the emergence of the current crisis. But there is no alternative to it.

And this alternative does not seem forlorn to me. Before the onset of the crisis we could already notice a clear increase of struggles and revolts in which the protagonists relate to each other in solidarity, develop egalitarian ways of action and refuse more and more vigorously to bear the social cost of the crisis. Meanwhile we hear about mass revolts of entire business workforces in the Chinese Pearl River Delta, who violently resist the abrupt factory closures and the non-payment of the wages they are entitled to. In the rural provinces of western China things are heating up too, and the local and regional uprisings against arbitrary land expropriations and destruction of nature and livelihood are becoming more frequent. But also in the global north indications of a new dawn proliferate. In Chicago and Schleswig-Holstein (Germany), factory occupations after abrupt shutdowns of supplying companies in the automobile sector caught our attention. In France, Italy and Greece the youth fight back against the destruction of their chance for education, all the more so as along with the destruction comes a dramatic deterioration of the prospect for a professional life according to the qualifications achieved. During all these eruptions a growing consciousness of the crisis is being forged, which begins to homogenize under the slogan "we won't pay for your crisis." Will it be possible to extend this basic sentiment of solidarity to the workforce of the big factories and to break the hierarchical chain of dismissals—supported by works councils and unions—leading from the precarious workers to the "core work-force"? We should at least try it, under the slogan: "three day working week? Great!—but with full wages for everyone, regardless of job type, because we need two days a week for the takeover and self-management of the plant."

Altogether we can expect another global surge of proletarianization due to the crisis, following from the looming new wave of mass unemployment in the existing centers of crisis: USA, Europe and East Asia. Once more millions of people will tumble down the social abyss. How will they react? Once they have nothing left to lose, the proletarian families, the social groups surrounding them and the many-layered segments of the proletarian multiverse have different options at hand: they may revolt in order to secure their right to existence and impose an egalitarian society, but they could also take the path of individual, familial and social self-destruction, e.g. by restoring patriarchal violence or recharging ethnic conflicts in order to secure their survival at the expense of other proletarian groups. Thirdly, they could also choose the path of political regression by projecting their fears and frustration onto executive despotism and new leader figures who abuse the proletarians' social potential in order to secure the interests of non-proletarian classes. In contrast to these three possible courses of action it is of course also possible that the proletarians and proletarianized will be content to settle for a state-interventionist reform project to overcome the crisis. This reform project could found itself on the still enormous potential for renewal of the capitalist social formation and could thereby—in however limited a form—take the interests of proletarian survival into account. How can we foster the egalitarian tendencies of homogenization and emancipation under the conditions of global economic crisis?

5. Outline of a Program of Transition

a) Preliminary Thoughts—We should not hook up with those who, from a radical left perspective, pin their hopes on an acceleration and deepening of the dynamics of crisis, expecting an automatic process of revolutionary collectivization of all those with nothing left to lose. The conceptual automatism of crisis and revolution has been disproved at least since the outcome of the Great Depression in the last century. Furthermore we have learned from analyzing the processes of decolonization that the arm of criticism after its transformation into the criticism of arms from the position of a self-proclaimed vanguard does not necessarily lead to the longed-for liberation, but frequently brings forth a new governing class and discharges into bloody civil war, with the effect that the emancipatory aim is turned into its opposite and deprived of its material basis for decades. We want to prevent the transformation of the world economic crisis turning into a world economic war between the multi-polar superpowers, leading in turn to new large-scale wars. At the same time we want to keep clear of emotional, eschatological expectations for revolution focused on violence, because the proletarian demand for revolution can also drown in class conflict turned into civil war. There is no carte blanche for those confronted with the realities and dangers of social degradation. This view should not be mistaken for a plea for a Gandhian path of non-violent civil disobedience. Self-organized mass struggle to secure the material bases of existence and the appropriation of the means of production, housing and public goods are unthinkable without the use of proletarian violence. This aspect in particular should be reflected on and controlled collectively as much as any other component of the newly arising class conflict.

For all these reasons, the emancipatory perspective needs an analytically grounded vision of social transformation, linked to programs for immediate action. In order to keep the crisis from leading to a reformist renewal of capitalism or to the three possible variants of barbarism—internal self-destruction, civil war and capitalist world economic war bringing new large-scale wars—the perspective of proletarian self-emancipation should be distributed across two levels of action, with interlocking effects. First, a framework of action aiming at the radical sharpening of the anti-cyclical programs currently underway, and second, starting from there, a program to initiate a project of revolutionary transformation of capitalist society.

b) Imposition and Sharpening of Reformist Programs to Overcome the Crisis

i) Owners of capital must pay for the crisis—On the first level of action, we should reverse the direction of the government guarantees currently being provided for the financial system and the large-scale economic stimulus programs in China, the EU states, the US and Japan. The greater part of the $7 trillion now set in motion must be redirected to safeguard the existence of the world's poor, of small-scale subsistence farming in the South, the unemployed and precarious in the emerging economies and metropolitan countries and the industrial working class. This must be combined with a radical reduction of working time without wage cuts, accompanied by homogenization of working conditions. Social systems are either to be founded (in China and other emerging economies and developing countries) or to be upgraded again (raising unemployment benefits to three quarters of average income, restoring pensions and entitlements to pensions that have been cut, expanding of education, reconstructing the health sector according to mass needs). This transfer is not to be accomplished through further deficit spending, but through confiscating large capital assets (from $50 million upwards) as well as the progressive taxation of capital assets over $1 million and of all yearly income above $150,000.

This massive top-down redistribution of wealth does not at all aim at a general stabilization of the cycle of crisis, although it does draw on the Keynesian reformists' attempt to balance overaccumulation and underconsumption by raising mass income to overcome the crisis. There is an irreducible qualitative difference between the needs and wants of the working class and the economic category of "mass purchasing power," and this difference opens the opportunity for the propertyless class, as it gradually homogenizes, to push the anti-cyclical reform policy of the groups currently taking power beyond that policy's original intent. To achieve this, mass action coordinated on a global scale is needed, but equally necessary is a worldwide information campaign, which would have to avoid any institutional ties to the projects and parties advocating anti-cyclical crisis management within the bounds of the existing system.

ii) A new global currency and reintroduction of fixed exchange rates—At the same time we ought to support a new global currency, to be composed of a representative currency basket of national economies at all stages of wealth. From this starting point, fixed exchange rates could be re-established to balance under and overvaluation, standardize monetary reserves and reciprocally stabilize balances of payment. In this way, the overaccumulated world financial system largely vanishes. Furthermore the lethal dollar symbiosis between Washington and Beijing, which is increasingly sliding into the abyss, could also be overcome.

iii) Democratizing economic consolidation programs—Third, in connection to the developing global mass struggles, we should advocate the introduction of democratically elected workers' councils into the initial processes of resizing and restructuring the large branches of the world economy. These workers' councils would supersede the co-managers of bureaucratic workers' organizations (trade unions and works councils). In the coming weeks and months the restructuring of the automobile industry will be the top priority. Hence it seems urgent to create a worldwide car industry workers' association on the basis of the factory occupations which can be expected. This should combine struggles for a radical reduction of working hours and equalized working conditions (particularly the abolition of the gulf between core workforce and outsourced temp workers) with the demand for an accelerated development of pollution-free and "resocialized" means of transport. The degree of success of this initiative will largely decide the extent to which the working class is able to find a self-determined solution to the crisis, and also whether a protectionist process of deglobalization of the capital-intensive segment of the capitalist world system can be forestalled. At the same time, these moves by car industry workers would shape a matrix for the launch of mass initiatives in the neighboring sectors (energy, transport chain) and the coordination of the objectives of their action. All this would also mean the launch of mass learning processes, to be connected globally from the beginning and perhaps serving as preparation for collective self-government of social life and reproduction.

c) On a Local, International and Global Level: First Key Points for a Program of Revolutionary Transformation

i) Three basic preconditions—By pushing for and sharpening anticyclical reform programs, the way is to be cleared for a process of revolutionary transformation. This approach makes possible collective learning processes which should generate mass need for radical change towards emancipation and social autonomy. The transition to socialism only has a chance if it has grown into a mass need throughout the world.

This process needs time—several years for sure. But the transformation process itself will also stretch over decades until the point of no return is reached. By this stage the producers' direct self-management of the re-appropriated means of production will have created egalitarian and grass-roots democratic ["democratic" used in this sense henceforth] structures which will make the restoration of class rule impossible.

ii) Locally and regionally: social re-appropriation on a democratic foundation—A first fundamental precondition is the implementation of democratic structures (rearranging the trade unions to use principles of direct, revocable delegation (Vertrauensleutekörpermodell), debureaucratization and cutback of the co-manager salaries of leadership; democratic reorganization of municipal government and administration as a first step of a general dismantling of the state advancing to the top).

Second, tax revenue is to be redirected to local structures (as in Switzerland, where 60% of all taxes are poured into the municipalities). Once this is accomplished, the people's interest in the self-management of their payroll taxes will be aroused, and democratic learning processes will be coupled with legitimate self-interest.

Third, we should head for a radical reduction of working time and a simultaneous increase and homogenization of earned income, in order to create the disposable time and necessary resources for building up democratic self-government. The actors in this democratic self-government would not only push forward processes of socialization, but would also see off the "political class" in the process of abolishing power structures (the state) from below.

Starting from these three basic premises it should be possible to begin preliminary moves towards local or regional autonomy, to associate them with local or regional segments of the workforce, and to launch a first inquiry project about local and regional specificities of class composition.

If this is accomplished, what seems impossible today will turn into a mass need. The actors of the local democracies will begin to appropriate the means of production necessary for life in their region and adjust them to their needs: drinking and waste water systems in the slum cities, local socialization of land in favor of the landless and small peasants, but also socialization of housing and local enterprises. Concurrently they will embark on the local and regional socialization of public goods (social funds, transport, education, health sector, savings banks etc). On this basis of interdependent local and regional self-government of social life, structures of social autonomy will finally grow which abandon political and economic managerial elites and preclude the rise of a new caste of experts and bureaucrats. At the same time, local processes of socialization will link on a regional, subcontinental and continental level.

iii) Foundation of international workers' federations—Without the simultaneous construction of international interfaces, the local and regional transformation processes will not be viable in the long run. These interfaces could most likely emerge from the transnational trade unions suggested above, by incorporating the strategic segments of economy into their self-organization. From the start they would have the responsibility for linking the developing local and regional democracies on a global scale and for using general strikes to protect them from counterrevolutionary attacks.

During the transformation towards self-government, the transnational trade unions should concentrate on those branches of economy that operate worldwide and stretch beyond the regional systems of production and reproduction, while providing for the regional council democracies materially and establish the workers' countervailing power in the key industries of the world system, particularly in the international transport chain, but also the media, information technology etc. After the socialization of the car industry, the global transport chain could serve as a showcase, because it holds particularly rich experiences in organization and struggles (ITF—International Transport Workers' Federation, strikes of truck drivers and in the aviation and railroad industries). The ITF would only have to be democratized and extended to all segments of the transport chain.

iv) World federation of autonomy—As soon as the first council democracies and workers' federations are established, they could approach the foundation of a world federation of social autonomy which would serve as an interface between the council democracies and the international workers' federations. In this world federation the council-democratic and federated delegations of (sub-)continents would be represented with equal rights. It would build up a series of reconstruction and transformation institutions to overturn the geographical imbalance of the material basis of existence, i.e. provision of food and energy, income, education and health care. Other bodies would concentrate on bringing about worldwide disarmament, restoring the ecosystem and harmonizing material production as active life processes of humankind with natural processes. Moreover a special conflict institution could aim at overcoming power structures that have also evolved outside the capitalist system (patriarchal domination, ethnic conflicts, racism).

v) Global association for autonomy—After a great deal of hesitation I have finally made up my mind to suggest an organizational anticipation of this concept through a globally linked association that acts on all three levels at the same time. It is not supposed to be a cadre organization claiming to be the vanguard, but a free and democratic association of people who have criticized, corrected, revised, expanded and subsequently appropriated this concept to test its usefulness in dialogue with the proletarian multiverse. The resulting experience and learning processes will entail an ongoing correction of the model. As soon as the proletarian multiverse makes the transition into global autonomy irreversible the association will dissolve.

In this sense the first three simultaneous steps for the foundation of such an association are to be determined as follows: First, local or regional action groups and a common network of communication and publicity (internet, regional media) are to be established in all continents. Second, the association should participate in the constitution of the transnational workers' federation in the key industries. Third, it should initiate a global analysis, the form of global social reports, with particular attention to the social effects of the crisis. In parallel, a conceptual frame and the resulting options for action should be worked out and constantly revised.

6. Outlook

These suggestions seem exaggerated and utopian. But I regard concrete utopias as an appropriate answer to a historical situation of radical change, because this liberates us from the "tradition of all dead generations" that "weighs like a nightmare on the brains of the living" (Marx) and obstructs our view of suddenly emerging options for action. But who is supposed to put them into practice? How can we dare to suggest a new dialectic between the conceptual-organizational anticipation of a new "political" class composition and the social and cultural composition of the multiverse of the propertyless? Who gives us the right, after the decades of defeat and strategic mistakes which made us untrustworthy in the past cycle?

But let us also consider that we are moving into a world-historic situation, that the strategic window opens anew, so that the cards are being reshuffled. Just as our children, nieces and nephews ask us today what we did between 1967 and 1973, the coming generations will ask the younger ones among us how and where they were active in the years of crisis and depression from 2008 to 2012. Nothing is impossible. Who knows if the Chinese peasant-workers will not dispose next spring of the state despotism that has chained them with an iron grip since the 1990s to the central debt axis of the world economic engine? The dollar would hit rock bottom immediately, and we would be confronted with two facts: first, the abrupt deepening of the world economic crisis beyond the level of that in the 20th century, and second, the emergence of a new actor on the world-historical stage, one which has rather cowered in the first phase of the crisis: the global working class. It could just as well happen that the mass revolts on the horizon in China and elsewhere fail and are put down by counter-revolution, even more violently than in the events in Turkey 1970–71, in Chile 1973, in Argentina 1976 and in Italy 1979. That would clear the way for a scenario in which the sharpening world economic wars could not be resolved without the opening of a new era of large-scale global wars. Maybe such escalations will not happen, maybe the Washington-Beijing axis will succeed in managing the crisis and introducing a new phase of state interventionist class compromise. But in this case new options of action would also arise, because a new cycle of the antagonism between labor and capital would commence. We should prepare convincing arguments for this "mild" variant of crisis outcome, arguments which are inseparable from the project of social equality and social progress.

Nothing Will Ever Be the Same

Ten theses on the financial crisis

1. The Current Financial Crisis Is a Crisis of the Whole Capitalistic System

The current financial crisis is a systemic crisis. It is the crisis of the whole capitalistic system as it has been developing since the 1990s until today. This depends on the fact that the financial markets today are the pulsing heart of cognitive capitalism. They finance the activity of accumulation: the liquidity attracted to the financial markets rewards the restructuring of production aimed at exploiting knowledges and the control of spaces external to traditional business.

Furthermore, thanks to the distribution of capital gain, financial markets play the same role in the economic system that the Keynesian multiplier (activated by deficit spending) did in the context of Fordism. However—unlike the classic Keynesian multiplier—this leads to a distorted redistribution of revenue. So that such multiplier is operative (> 1) it is necessary that the financial base (i.e. the extension of financial markets) constantly grows and that the matured capital gain is on average higher than the average wage depreciation (that, since 1975, has been about 20%). On the other hand, revenue polarization increases the risk of debt insolvency

which is at the base of the growth of that same financial foundation and lowers the median wage. Here is a first contradiction
whose effects are visible today.

Thirdly, financial markets forcefully redirecting growing parts
of labor revenues (like severance pay and social security, other than
revenues that, through the social state, are translated into state
health programs and institutions of public education) substitute
the state as the main provider of social securities and welfare.
From this point of view, they represent the privatization of the
reproductive sphere of life. They therefore exercise *biopower*.

The financial crisis is consequently a crisis of the structure of
the current capitalistic biopower.

Lastly, the financial markets are the place where capitalist valorization is fixed today, which is to say the exploitation of social
cooperation and the rent from general intellect (cf. Thesis 2).

On the basis of these considerations, it is necessary to understand the difficulty in separating the real sphere from the financial
one. Proof of this is the effective impossibility of distinguishing
the profits from financial rent (cf. Thesis 8).

2. The Current Financial Crisis Is a Crisis of the Measurement of Capitalistic Valorization

With the advent of cognitive capitalism, the process of valorization loses all quantitative measuring units connected with
material production. Such measurements were in some way
defined by the content of labor necessary for the production of
merchandise, measurable based on the tangibility of production
and on the time necessary for production. With the advent of

cognitive capitalism, valorization tends to be triggered in different forms of labor that cut the effectively certified work hours to increasingly coincide with the overall time of life. Today, the value of labor is at the base of capitalistic accumulation and is also the value of knowledge, affects and relationships, of the imaginary and the symbolic. The result of these biopolitical transformations is the crisis of the traditional measurement of labor-value and with it the crisis of the *profit-form*. A possible "capitalistic" solution was measuring the exploitation of social cooperation and general intellect through the dynamics of market values. In this way, profit is transformed into rent and the financial markets became the place where labor-value was determined, transformed into a *financial-value* which is nothing other than the subjective expression of the expectations for future profits generated by financial markets that, in this way, lay claim to rent. The current financial crisis marks the end of the illusion that financing can constitute a unit of measurement for labor, at least in contemporary capitalism's current failure in cognitive governance. Consequently, the financial crisis is also a crisis of capitalistic valorization.

3. The Crisis Is the Horizon of Development for Cognitive Capitalism

Traditionally, the phenomenon of crisis in the world of capitalistic production were classified in two main categories: crises that are derived from the exhaustion of a historical phase which represented the conditions to open a potential perspective of change, and crises that come about as the consequence of a change in the historical phase of the new socioeconomic paradigm that arduously tries to impose itself. The first case has been called "crisis of saturation," while the second "crisis of growth."

Following this model, the current crisis could be defined, unlike the one in the '70s and in the same way as the one in 1929, as a "crisis of growth." It finds its harbingers at the beginning of the '90s, when the characteristics of cognitive capitalism began to configure themselves and the last phase of the crisis in the Fordist-Taylorist paradigm (or "post-Fordism") was brought to an end.

In fact, ever since the second half of the '70s, the irreversible crisis of the Fordist-Taylorist paradigm, founded on the productive model of the large company and Keynesian policies born from the 1929 crisis and the Second World War, has been developing.

During the '80s, in the so-called post-Fordist period, there were different social and productive models that preluded the surmounting of Fordism without, however, being able to establish a dominant and hegemonic paradigm.

At the beginning of the '90s, after the financial crack in 1987 and the 1991–1992 economic recession (alternating with the fall of the Berlin Wall and the first Gulf War), the new paradigm of cognitive capitalism began to unravel itself with all its contemporary force and instability. The role of financial markets, together with the transformations in production and labor, were redefined in this context, while the role of the nation-state and Keynesian welfare were structurally modified; this meant the decline of forms of public intervention as we had known them in the precedent historical stage.

Today's financial crisis, which follows other crises that have taken place in the last fifteen years, systematically and structurally highlights the inconsistency of the regulatory mechanism of accumulation and distribution that, up until now, cognitive capitalism has tried to give itself.

Let it be clear, however, that talking about the current crisis in terms of "crisis of growth" does not in any way mean advocating the "automatic" triumph of the present phase in a positive and socially satisfying way. At the moment, in fact, not only is it still not possible to recognize an exit strategy for such crisis, but it is the nature of crisis itself that is changing. It is no longer limited, if it ever was, to a descendent phase of the economic cycle in linear relation to the development that preceded it and the struggles that follow it. In the case of 1929, the crisis was overcome with the Fordist regulation paradigm thanks to the New Deal and the Second World War. Today (cf. Thesis 9), such a perspective cannot be given. Where capitalistic accumulation is reproduced in the subsumption of the common, the crisis becomes, in fact, a permanent process. In this framework, the very category of economic cycle should be radically rethought, in the light of the transformations in labor, the impossibility for capital to organize the productive cycle *a priori* and the shifts of the spatial-temporal coordinates determined by globalization. The occurrence of economic-financial crises in such a brief time span (from the East-Asian crisis of '97, to the fall of the Nasdaq in 2000, up to the crisis of the debt system and subprime loans, to name only a few), making the reconstruction of the cyclic dynamics—even if only *ex-post*—impossible, demonstrates this fact. This means that many roads are open. It is up to the will of transformation and social movements' political action to choose the right one.

4. The Financial Crisis Is a Crisis of Biopolitical Control—A Crisis of Governance That Demonstrates a Systemic Structural Instability

The current financial crisis demonstrates that an institutional governance of the processes of accumulation and distribution founded on finance is not possible. The (*ex-post*) attempts at governance that have been launched in the last few months are hardly able to affect the crisis underway. It couldn't be otherwise if one considers that the BIS (Bank for International Settlements) estimates the value of derivatives in circulation at about $556 trillion (equal to 11 times the world GDP). Over the course of last year, this value was reduced by over 40%, destroying more than $200 trillion in liquidity. Once more, toxic assets circulate according to a "viral" modality, and it is literally impossible to know where they are nesting.

Now, the monetary interventions of the injection of new liquidity carried out worldwide until today don't amount to more than $5 trillion: a mere drop in the ocean of value, a sum structurally insufficient to compensate for the losses and invert the tendency to decline. What follows is that the only possible political governance is to attempt to modify the climate of trust, or rather, act on languages and conventions, in full respect of those institutions, real and/or virtual organizations that are able to dynamically influence the so-called "public opinion." Nevertheless, against an "excess" of the effective weight of the crisis, which is not quantifiable even for the operators most intimate to financial market dynamics, thinking to stigmatize fraudulent behaviors or to inject doses of trust seems completely inadequate and impracticable.

Hence the crisis of governance is not only a "technical" crisis but it is also, and most importantly, a "political" crisis. We have already seen (in Thesis 1) that the condition for financial markets to be able to support phases of expansion and real growth is a constant increase of the financial base. In other words, it is necessary that the share of global wealth redirected toward financial markets continually grows. This implies a continuous increase in the relations between debt and credit, either through the increase of the number of people in debt (the degree of financial market extension) or through the construction of new financial instruments that feed on pre-existing financial exchanges (the degree of intensity of the financial markets). Derivative products are a classic example of this second modality of expansion of the same financial markets. Whatever the factors taken into consideration, the expansion of financial markets is necessarily accompanied both by the increase of debt and by the speculative activities of the risk associated with them. It is an intrinsic dynamic in the role of financial markets as a founding element of cognitive capitalism. Speaking of an excess of speculation due to manager or bank greed has absolutely no sense and can only serve to deviate the attention from the true structural causes of this crisis. Necessarily, the final result is the unsustainability of an ever-growing debt, above all when high-risk sectors of the population begin to be too far in debt: the social strata that, following the process of labor precariousness, find themselves in the condition of not benefiting from the *wealth effect* that participation in the stock earnings permitted to the more well-to-do social classes. The insolvency crisis in real-estate mortgages thus finds its origin in one of the contradictions of contemporary cognitive capitalism: the irreconcilability of an unequal revenue distribution with the necessity of widening the financial base to continue to develop the process of accumulation. This contradictory node is nothing other than the coming to light of an irreducibility (an excess) of life of a large part of social components (be they singular fragments or definable as class segments) to capitalist subsumption. An excess that today is expressed in a multiplicity of behaviors (from forms of infidelity to company hierarchies, to the presence of communities that oppose territorial governance, from individual and group exodus from the dictates of life imposed by the dominant social conventions, all the way to the development of self-organizational forms in the work world and open revolt against the old and new forms of exploitation in the slums and the megalopolis of the global South, in Western metropolises and in the most recently industrialized areas of South-East Asia and South America). An excess that declares in unison, from the four corners of the globe, that it will not pay for this crisis. The irremediable instability of contemporary capitalism is also a result of this excess.

5. The Financial Crisis Is a Crisis of Unilateralism and a Moment of Geopolitical Re-equilibrium

The current crisis puts the financial hegemony of the United States and the centrality of Anglo-Saxon stock markets in the process of financialization into question. The exit from this crisis will necessarily mark a shift in the financial barycenter towards the East and, partially, South (i.e. South America). Already on the level of productivity and control of commercial exchanges, which is to say on a real level, the processes of globalization have always highlighted a shift of the productive center towards the Orient and the global South. From this point of view, the current financial crisis puts an end to a sort of anomaly that had characterized the first phase of the diffusion of cognitive capitalism: the movement of technological centrality and cognitive labor to India and China while maintaining financial hegemony in the West. As long as the development of Eastern countries (China and India), Brazil and South America was pulled along by the processes of externalization and delocalization set by the large Western corporations, it was not possible to identify a spatial dystonia between cognitive capitalism's two main variables of command: the control of currency-finance on the one hand, and the control of technology on the other hand. It is beginning with the end of the '90s that the newly industrialized countries begin to put the Western and Japanese technological leadership into crisis, through the passage from a productive model based on imitative capacity and knowledge distribution to a productive model able to favor processes of generation, appropriation and amassing of knowledges, already starting with the formation of "human capital." The 1997 financial crisis, that, beginning with the devaluation of the Thai *bat*, particularly hit the Asian and South American stocks (other than the Asian countries of the ex-USSR), enabled Anglo-Saxon financial markets to reassert their supremacy on a global scale, but in any case didn't impede the shift of techno-productive leadership Eastwards. So, a first contradiction within the global geoeconomic equilibrium came to pass: Western supremacy in finance, Eastern supremacy in the "real" economy and in international exchange. This is an unstable equilibrium that, for the first five years of the new millennium was stalled *de facto* by the permanent war in Afghanistan and Iraq, and that is essentially at the base of the failure of the various international commerce summits—from Doha (in November 2001) to Cancun (in September 2003) up to Hong-Kong (in December 2005).

Nevertheless, the growing American debt (both domestic and international) and the necessity of widening the extension of financial markets with further relations of debt and credit increasingly at risk made it so that this equilibrium, already unstable, couldn't last long. The current financial crisis put an end to this spatial dystonia. Technological and financial supremacy are tending to rejoin one another on a geoeconomic level. As a result, cognitive capitalism as a paradigm of bioeconomic accumulation is becoming hegemonic even in China, India and in the global South. This doesn't mean, let it be clearly stated, that the sometimes radical differences between different spaces and times through which capitalistic processes of valorization and through which the composition of work commanded and exploited by capital is continually re-articulated have ceased to operate. Nor it is possible to forge a series of skeleton-key concepts, indistinctly applicable to Nairobi, New York and Shanghai. The point is rather that the very sense of the radical differences between places, regions and continents must be re-compressed within the heterogeneous interlacing of the productive systems, temporalities and subjective labor experiences that constitute cognitive capitalism.

6. The Financial Crisis Demonstrates the Difficulties of the Construction Process of the Economic European Union

One of the goals of the construction of the monetary European Union was the protection of the Euro area countries from the speculative turbulence of currency markets with the objective of building a strong currency able to form a shield against possible financial crises. In effect, during the 1996–97 and 2000 crisis, the presence of the Euro impeded international speculation from uniting in an anti-European function. However, such argumentation fell when the financial crisis, starting from the heart of American hegemony, not only brought the main Western investment companies to their knees but also began to have effects on the "real" economy as well.

The answer of half the world's monetary authorities and the main governments hit by the crisis was to supply the most liquidity possible to plug the holes opened in the credit and real-estate sectors. However, such interventions—that have mobilized huge quantities of public money—were done in a random order in the European context, with the level of coordination nearly exclusively technical and never political. The result is that every European state, in concrete terms, moved autonomously and with differentiated modalities. In reality, they pay for having exclusively focused on the monetary union without worrying about creating the premises for a European fiscal policy with a budget independent from the influence of the single member States. Today the tools for a coordinated fiscal intervention able to attribute a real counterattack to the financial crisis are missing. This is an ulterior symptom of the failure to economically and socially (not to mention politically) construct Europe.

7. The Financial Crisis Marks the Crisis of Neoliberal Theory

The current financial crisis shows how the capitalistic system is structurally unstable and how the free market theory is not able to affront such instability. In the dominant vulgate of neoliberal thought, the free functioning of the market should guarantee not only an efficient accumulation process but also a correct and balanced distribution of income, according to each individual's contribution and commitment. The existence of social differentiation is the *ex-post* result of the economic agents' choices based on freely expressed preferences.

Such orientation is based on two assumed principles.

The first regards the idea that economic process is exclusively exercised in the activity of exchange (allocation), where the consumer (economic demand) determines the offer, all in a context where production capacity, being founded on natural and not artificial resources, is by definition limited and therefore subject to scarcity.

The supremacy of the allocative process over production implies that the market becomes the place where economic activity is exclusively determined, thanks to the principle of *consumer sovereignty*. This principle is linearly translated into "*individual sovereignty*," according to which every individual is the sole judge of himself/herself (the principle of free will) and social variations must be solely founded on the evaluations expressed by single individuals (the supremacy of individualism). Consumer sovereignty, however, reduces individual sovereignty to the act of consumption. This famous free will is thus exclusively articulated in free consumption, but which is not absolute liberty anyway, being confined by an individual's particular spending capability and on market availability. Consequently, those that don't have monetary resources (like, for example, many migrants) that allow them to create demand for goods or services in the market don't exist from an economic point of view. What actually counts is not demand—understood as a whole of goods and services that each individual desires to have to satisfy their needs—but *solvent* demand, expressed with cash in hand. Desires that can't be satisfied in markets because of a lack of money, don't exist *de facto*. Since the sums available for consumption (which are limited by income) depend, for most human beings, on labor wages, one could conclude (although it is denied) that *working conditions determine the effective degree of individual liberty*.

The second point, closely tied to the first, affirms the preeminence of property individualism as the result of the crisis of industrial-Fordist capitalism and of its transformation into bioeconomic capitalism. Every economic agent is considered the sole actor responsible for the choices of consumption and investment. On the financial side, this is translated into a reduction of national debt into individual debt; on a political and economic level this theoretical approach serves to sustain the banishment of conjectural finance and a legitimation of private consumption based on individual debt. Starting from the ascertainment that the capitalistic system is, as economic accumulation, always a monetary economy that is based on debt, and after the 1929 economic crisis the state has assumed the role of last resort loaner, taking on the responsibility to manage public debt (the Keynesian policies of deficit-spending). Instead, the passage from Fordism to cognitive capitalism, in the name of property individualism, marked the transformation from public debt to individual debt through financial "privatization" of the social rights won after the World War II.

The neoliberal ideological crisis rests in the failure of the free market as an efficient mechanism of resource production and allocation and of the role of financial markets as mechanism of income redistribution. In the first case, we have witnessed a process of financial and technological concentration like never before in the history of capitalism, with all due respect to free competition. In the second case, the redistributive governance of the financial markets has revealed itself to be a complete failure.

8. The Financial Crisis Highlights Two Internal Contradictory Principles of Cognitive Capitalism: The Insufficiency of the Traditional Forms of Labor Remuneration and the Vileness of the Proprietary Structure

In the framework of the structural instability of present-day cognitive capitalism, translated in the current financial crisis, it becomes necessary to rethink the definition of the redistributive variables in a way that they can refer to value production in contemporary cognitive capitalism.

As far as the sphere of labor is concerned, it is necessary to acknowledge that in cognitive capitalism labor remuneration should be translated into life remuneration: consequently, the conflict *in fieri* that is opened is not merely a constantly necessary struggle for high wages (to say it in Keynesian terms), but rather the struggle for a continuity of income regardless of the labor activity certified by any type of contract. After the crisis of the Fordist-Taylorist paradigm, the division between life and labor time is not easily distinguishable. The most exploited people in the work world are those whose whole lives are put to work. This happens, in the first place, through the lengthening of work hours in the service sector and, above all, in the migrant workforce: a large part of the labor time spent in the third sector activities doesn't actually happen on the job. Wages are the remuneration of certified labor acknowledged as productive, while individual income is the sum of all the returns that are derived from living and relationships in a territory (work, family, subsidies, possible rent, etc.) that determine the standard of living. As long as the separation between work and life exists, a conceptual separation will exist between wages and individual income, but when life time is put to work it tends to blur the difference between income and wage.

Thus it isn't about opposing wage struggles and income struggles, resigning the former to sectorial resistance and the latter to a simply ideological preposition. The political node is rather rethinking a virtuous combination, starting from the productive transformations and from the subjective materiality of labor's new composition.

De facto, the tendential overlapping between work and life and consequently between wages and income is not yet considered within the limits of institutional regulation. From different points of view, it is sustained that basic income can represent an element of institutional regulation suitable for the new tendencies of capitalism. What most interests us, however, is not slipping toward a theory of social justice, or complaining about the missing acknowledgment of productive rationality or, least of all, about the absence of regulatory devices that allow capitalism to overcome its own crisis. Income is, first and foremost, the identification of a battleground within the changes of contemporary capitalism, which is to say an element for a political program inside the constitutive processes of antagonist subjectivity. From this point of view, basic income can be seen as a directly *distributive*, and not redistributive, variable.

As far as the sphere of production is concerned, a second aspect to take into consideration is the role played by intellectual property rights. They represent one of the tools that allow capital to appropriate social cooperation as well as general intellect. Since knowledge is a common good, produced by social cooperation, the surplus value that springs from its use in terms of innovative activity and increases in labor productivity is not simply the fruit of an investment in a physical or individual capital stock (which is to say ascribed to a capitalist defined as a single entity, be it a person or business organization) but rather depends on the use of social patrimony (or "social human capital" as some economists say) that is sedimented over the territory and that is independent from the initiative of single entrepreneurs. The rate of profit that springs forth is therefore not the simple ratio between the investment level and stock capital that defines the value of a business, but rather "something" that the business, with the existent "social" capital, depends on. In other words, as long as profit is born in measures increasingly consistent from the exploitation and expropriation of a common good like knowledge for private purposes, it can be partially assimilated to a *rent*: a rent from the territory and from learning, which is to say a rent that comes from the exercising of intellectual property rights and knowledge ownership.

Now, to paraphrase Keynes in the last chapter of his *General Theory*, one could maintain that, "The owner of *knowledge* can obtain *profit* because *knowledge* is scarce, just as the owner of land can obtain rent because land is scarce. But whilst there may be intrinsic reasons for the scarcity of land, there are no intrinsic reasons for the scarcity of *knowledge*."[1]

Even so, at the same time, over the last few years various liberal theoreticians have maintained the necessity of reducing or even eliminating copyright licensing that, in the long run, risks blocking innovative process. Cognitive capitalism should become, they say, a sort of "propertyless capitalism," a model that is supposedly prefigured by the web 2.0 and exemplified by the clash between Google and Microsoft. Where capital toils to organize social cooperation *a priori*, it is forced to chase it and capture it afterwards: accumulation and surplus value consequently pass primarily through a process of financialization. This is what circles close to financial capitalism have defined as "the communism of capital." Still, admitting that it can do without property, capitalism certainly cannot give up control, even if this means continually blocking the potential of cognitive labor. Here the classic contradiction between productive forces and production relations is re-qualified in completely new terms.

The mingling of profit and rent is derived from the fact that, in cognitive capitalism, the process of accumulation has extended the very base of accumulation, co-opting the activities of human pursuits that did not produce surplus value in industrial Fordist capitalism, nor were they translated into abstract labor.

From this point of view, the political economic indications proposed by Keynes right after the paradigmatic 1929 crisis could be rewritten taking into account the new elements inborn to cognitive capitalism.

The measure of a basic income substitutes the political policy of high wages, while the euthanasia of Keynes' *rentier* could be articulated in the euthanasia of the positions of rent derived from intellectual property rights (or cognitive *rentier*), accompanied by fiscal politics able to redefine the assessable base while keeping in mind the role played by spatial valorization, knowledge and financial flows. This doesn't paint an ideal picture, but at least defines an area of tension in which to rethink the forms of conflict and the possible conditions to organize new *institutions of the common*.

Regarding Keynes' proposal to socialize investments, cognitive capitalism is characterized by a socialization of production facing an ever higher concentration of technological and financial flows: in other words, levers that today allow the control and command of a flexible and outsourced production. Any political program that intersects such concentration, which is at the base of investment flows, therefore directly affects the proprietary structure and undermines the very capitalistic relation of production at its roots.

The possible "reformist" proposals that could define a social pact in cognitive capitalism are therefore limited to the introduction of a new wage regulation based on basic income and on a reduced intellectual property right weight, which could possibly lead to the euthanasia of intellectual property rent.

9. The Current Financial Crisis Cannot Be Resolved With Reformist Politics That Define a Renovated New Deal

In the current situation there are not any economic or political premises sufficient for a new social pact (or New Deal). It is therefore a mere illusion.

The Fordist New Deal was the result of an institutional assemblage (Big Government) that was based on the existence of three assumptions: 1) a nation state able to develop national economic policies independent, even if coordinated, from other states; 2) the possibility of measuring productivity earnings and therefore see to their redistribution between profits and wages; 3) industrial relations between social components that were reciprocally recognized and were legitimized on an institutional level, able to sufficiently and unequivocally represent (not excluding margins of arbitrariness) entrepreneurial interests and those of the working class.

None of these three assumptions are present in today's cognitive capitalism.

The existence of the nation-state is put into crisis by the processes of productive internationalization and financial globalization, that represent, in their declinations in terms of the technological control of knowledge, information and war apparatuses, the bases for the definition of supranational imperial power.

In cognitive capitalism it is at least possible to imagine—as a reference unit for the economic and social policy—a supranational geographic spatial entity (and not by chance the countries that are protagonists on a global level today, like the United States, Brazil, India and China, are continental spaces quite different from the classic European nation-state). The European community could represent, from this point of view, a new definition of a public socioeconomic space in which to implement a New Deal. However, in the current condition, European construction proceeds along fiscal and monetary political lines that represent the negation of the possibility of creating a public space and an autonomous and independent space, not conditioned by the dynamics of the financial markets (cf. Thesis n. 6).

The dynamics of production tend to depend on immaterial production and the involvement of cognitive human faculty, difficult to measure with traditional criteria. The current difficulty of measuring social productivity doesn't allow for a wage regulation based on the relation between wages and productivity.

The proposal of basic income meets opposition and diffidence from various figures. Entrepreneurs consider it, in the first place, a subversive proposal to the extent that it is able to reduce the blackmail of need and dependence on labor coercion. In second place, if basic income is correctly understood as direct remuneration of precedent productive activity (as it should be), without being subject to any condition whatsoever, it risks not being controlled by the hierarchical structure even though being financed through the general taxation system. Instead, a reform proposal of social security cushions would be differently accepted from a hierarchical point of view, even if geared toward expansion (hopefully including "precarious" workers too, in accordance with *flexsecurity*). They would in fact be a "redistributive" measure and not directly distributive (like a basic income would be): in other words, social security cushions transfer rent once a direct distribution of rent is sanctioned and therefore extensively reforming them wouldn't put a dent in the remunerative dynamics of labor. In the second place, being subject to restrictions and exact allocative conditions, social security cushions not only become an element of differentiation and segmentation of the workforce, but are also wholly congruent with social policy with a "workfare" orientation.

Instead, for labor unions, basic income contradicts the work ethic that they continue to base their existence on.

Lastly, but no less importantly, we are witnessing a crisis of the forms of social representation both in the entrepreneurial area as well as in the labor unions. Lacking a single organizational model induces the fragmentation both of capital and labor. The first is split between the interests of small businesses, often tied to relations of hierarchical sub-supply, the interests of large multinational corporations and the speculative activities of currency and financial markets, the appropriation of profit and rent from monopolies in distribution, transportation, energy, military contracts and research and development. In particular, the contradiction between industrial capital, commercial capital and financial capital in terms of strategies and diversified temporal horizons, and that between national capital and supranational capital in terms of geoeconomic and geopolitical influence, makes a level of the capitalistic class' homogeneity of intent and the definition of shared goals very problematic. The element that most joins capital's interests is the pursuit of short-term profits (that have origins in different ways), and this makes the formulation of progressive political reforms practically impossible, unlike the era of Fordist capitalism.

Conversely, the work world seems ever more fragmented not only from a juridic point of view but above all from a "qualitative" point of view. The figure of the salaried industrial worker is emergent in many parts of the globe but is in decline in Western countries, favoring a variegated multitude of atypical precarious, migrant, para-subordinate and autonomous figures, whose organizational and representational capacity is increasingly limited by the prevalence of individual negotiation and the incapacity of the union structures formed during Fordism to adapt.

The overall result is that in cognitive capitalism there isn't space for an institutional political reform able to reduce the instability that characterizes it. No innovative New Deal is possible, if not one that is pushed by social movements and by the practices of autonomous institutionality through the re-appropriation of a welfare system ravaged by private interests and frozen in public policy. Some of the measures that we have identified, from wage regulation based on the proposal of a basic income to production based on the free circulation of knowledges, are not necessarily incompatible with the systems of accumulation and subsumption of capital, as various neoliberal theoreticians have suggested. In any case, new campaigns of social conflict and re-appropriation of common wealth can be started and through which to undermine the very base of the capitalistic productive system, that is the coercion of labor, income as a tool of blackmail and domination of one class over another and the principle of private property of the means of production (yesterday the machines, today knowledge too).

In other words, we can assert that in cognitive capitalism a possible social compromise of Keynesian origin but adapted to the characteristic of the new process of accumulation is only *a theoretical illusion*, and it is unfeasible from a political point of view.

A full-fledged reformist policy (which tends to identify a form of mediation between capital and labor that is satisfactory for both), able to guarantee a stable structural paradigm of cognitive capitalism, cannot be delineated today.

So, we are in a historic context in which social dynamics don't allow space for the development of reformist practices and, above all, reformist "theories."

What follows is that, since it is praxis that guides theory, only conflict and the capacity to create multitudinary movements can permit—as always—the social progress of humanity.

Only the revival of strong social conflict on a supranational level can create the conditions to overcome the current state of crisis. We are facing an apparent paradox: to make new reformist perspectives and the relative stability of the capitalistic system possible, it is necessary for a joint action of the revolutionary sort, able to modify the axes on which the very structure of capitalist command is based.

We must then start to imagine a post-capitalist society, or better yet, re-elaborate the battle for welfare in the crisis as an immediate organization of the institutions of the common. This doesn't definitively eliminate the functions of political mediation but does definitively take them away from representative structures and absorbs them in the constituent power of autonomous practices.

10. The Current Financial Crisis Opens New Scenarios of Social Conflict

Socialism has traditionally offered itself to save capitalism from its cyclical crises, dialectically overcoming endemic instability through a superior rationality of development. In other terms, taking on the responsibility to actuate the promises of progress that capitalism has not structurally been able to maintain. Today, the era in which socialism and capitalism have mirrored one another in an assumed objectivity in the hierarchy of labor, technology and production, is happily over.

Once again, only our behaviors can smash the unjust social system that we are forced to live in and develop the material basis for equal life chances and freedom. The situation of economic crisis is palpable. Once again, it is the level of resistance that continually puts the forms of command under stress. There are those who, not able to pay the mortgage, after an initial moment of panic realize that they have at least three years before being evicted, and think. There are those who never believed in the chimera of the stock market and decided to not deposit their severance pay in investment funds, despite the massive media and labor union campaigns that promised lavish earnings in the financial markets.

Such behaviors—together with many others that expressed resistance and insubordination—acquire a particular importance because they represent cracks in the impalpable social control that the rhetoric of proprietary individualism was able to build with the help of a pseudo-imaginary social cohesion, founded on merit and loyalty behaviors.

An important signal was sent in Italy by the "Anomalous Wave" movement.[2] The fact that this movement made a break-through on the themes of income and welfare of the common is hugely important. It wasn't limited to a mere theoretical elaboration or an avant-garde political position: the problem of income became common sense in the emergency of social composition molded by conflicts over knowledge production and against class de-classification and precariousness. In this way it was de-ideologized, identifying itself in concrete goals (for example the demand for money, or wages, for the free labor provided to support the *corporatization* of the university, from internships to vocational training programs, to didactic responsibilities held by precarious researchers). In the Anomalous Wave, the topic of income has therefore become a political program within the crisis, giving concrete meaning to the slogan "we will not pay for the crisis."

The critique of knowledge as a commercial product, the acknowledgment that the difference between the moment of education and the moment of production tends to blur (which is where the need to remunerate educational periods comes from), the demand to access material and immaterial services that constitute the environment of social cooperation and general intellect, the production of the common as a new narrative, a new horizon of social relations and cooperation, finally goes beyond the "public-private" dichotomy: these are, in synthesis, a few programmatic elements that are extremely useful in delineating a political process able to overturn the systemic crisis into a space of possibility for action and proposal.

If we look simply at the European panorama, there are numerous insurgent signals that in the last few months have sprung up: other than the Greek revolt and the social movements that swept across the educational sector in Spain, France and Germany, we can also point to the conflictual tensions that, dealing with different social strata, were manifested in Copenhagen, Malmö, Riga and in other European metropolises.

We are dealing with overturning the "communism of capital" into the "communism of general intellect," as a living force of contemporary society, able to develop a structure of *commonfare* and establish itself as an effective and real condition of human choice for freedom and equality. Between the "communism of capital" and the institutions of the common there is no speculation or linear relation of necessity: it is, in other terms, about collectively re-appropriating produced social wealth and destroying the devices of subsumption and capitalistic command in the permanent crisis.

In such a process, the autonomous role played by social movements is increasingly important, not only as a political program and action but also, and above all, as a reference point for those subjectivities, singularities or segments of class that are hit hardest and defrauded by the crisis.

The capacity of real subsumption of life into work and production processes, the diffusion of pervasive cultural and symbolic imagery from elements of individualism (beginning with "proprietary" individualism) and "security" measures construct the main hinges of the process of social and cognitive control of worker and proletariat behavior. The achievement and the organization of an autonomous subjectivity, that already lives in the practices of resistance and production of a new class composition, are necessary conditions for triggering conflictual processes that are able to modify the current socioeconomic hierarchies. From this point of view, all of the excesses and the insurgencies that nomadic subjectivities are capable of achieving and animating are welcome. It is only in this way, like a thousand drops that meet to form a river or a thousand bees that form a swarm, does it become possible to put into motion forms of re-appropriation of wealth and knowledges, inverting the redistributive dynamics, forcing those who caused the crisis to pay for it, rethinking a new structure of social and common welfare, imagining new possibilities of self-organization and production compatible with the respect of the environment and of the dignity of the men and women who inhabit this planet.

The king has no clothes. The path before us is arduous but, really, we have already started down it.

Antonio Negri

Postface: A Reflection on Rent in

the "Great Crisis" of 2007 and Beyond

We all know what rent is. We all know what a *rentier* is. Each of us has looked him directly in the eyes, at least once, when we pay the rent for our apartment. We can have envied him or hated him, but anyway we consider him—at least in our case—someone who earns without working. The laws of rent governed the *ancien regime*. Reactionaries praised it through Burke and Hegel, considering it natural; the revolutionary disciples of Rousseau, the Enlightenment reformist and the founders of Human Rights hated it. English liberalists and Kantian philosophers thought that liberty could not grow from and be based on the exploitation of inherited wealth: that a "worthy" wealth must instead be founded on work. And for the theorists of the "wealth of nations," the inventors of the political economy? They were ambiguous on the subject: on one hand, in fact, they thought that capitalist wealth should be built *against* rent (and the truth of economic theory consisted in identifying this); on the other hand, they didn't hide the fact (even though often hiding it from their readers) that capitalistic development could not have ever had the possibility of being constructed and implemented with such great force if not for a violent, original appropriation. That is what happened historically—the appropriation of the common, of lands and labor—in the age of the

Enclosures. This is what, therefore, "absolute rent" is: an original violent, but necessary, accumulation—but it had to be hidden because it was heinous—enslaving, perverse, atrocious in its ways... Certainly, absolute rent survived in the ordinary, daily processes of consumption, but it was so subordinated to the other forms of the generation of wealth (economists said this, or at least they hoped it, but certainly they suffered from ambiguity in their analyses) that in the end it became relevant only when it was represented as the prize of a contest between property owners (of land and/or money). "Relative rent" thus became one of the figures in which surplus value produced by labor was found, emerging though the difference in the productivity of worked land just as it did in commercial funds. Through "relative rent" economists tried, on one hand, to appeal to the reformists, while trying to find some plausibility for their reasoning; in reality, and not very secretly, together with capitalist development they legitimized the violence of original appropriation, of primitive accumulation. When, at the halfway point that brought the founders of the political economy to our times, Keynes (nearly a century ago) continued to curse rent, wishing for "the euthanasia of *rentier*"; who would have ever thought that the beginning of the twenty-first century would be characterized by the debate over rent once again? And by the political effects of its enforcement? And by the reactionary ideological glorification of its worst outcomes?

When we study democratic constituent power in the founding processes of the modern legal order, we cannot help but note that it always touches—or better yet strikes—the proprietary structure of the capitalistic order (from a critical point of view it attacks pre-constituted proprietary relations; from a reformist and/or revolutionary point of view, it expresses the desire for a new social order of property). Given the intensity of this intention of constituent power, it isn't surprising that the fact that bourgeois legal theory has, throughout modernity, tried to isolate the concept, ripping it from the materiality of social relationships where it hides—social relationships of property, first of all; and later, relationships of capitalist appropriation. Constituent power stops where law begins. The Thermidor was the moment when constituent power was realized to then be immediately negated, erased. Nevertheless, constitutional theory knew that this neutralization was in vain. Even when constituent power is formally isolated, immediately afterwards the jurist and the politician are forced to fully assume, for the orientation of their work, the analysis of the "material constitution" (which is to say the study of the social relationships that are, in their complexity and their possible antagonism, at the base of the legal or "formal constitution"). A strange situation was thus articulated. Property relations accounted for the problem that was at the base of the insurgencies of constituent power; instead constituted power held property relations as sacred and immutable. In the formalist hypocrisy of contemporary jurisprudence, constituent power, when it was reassumed, could only be read as "power of exception," lacking all content that wasn't the intensity of the decision. Against this, every time it was presented in its materiality and made the topic of property arise again, constituent power was spread over constitutional time and therein—proposing itself as an element of today's legal innovation and social emancipation—opened toward the possibility of democratic institutions. Constituent power thus clashed with "absolute rent," construing itself—as a democratic function—over the long-term of the material constitution, and fought inside the legal forms of "relative rent."

Today, democracy is no longer faced merely with (and against) landed rent (land and real-estate)—but above all faced with financial rent, the capital that money mobilizes, globally, as a fundamental instrument for the governance of the multitudes. Financialization is the current form of capitalistic command. It is clearly still interlaced with rent, and it repeats both the violent intentionality as well as the ambiguity and contradictions of every figure of capitalistic exploitation. It would therefore be silly to think that financial capital did not contain, within itself, an antagonistic relationship: it always includes labor power as one of its necessary elements, both the producer of capital and conflict. The form in which financial capital contains this antagonism is defined according to wholly determining specificities: a strong abstraction of the bodily quality of work and citizenship, the capitalistic construction of a world masked by distorted needs, and a monstrous community of exploitation. Regarding the exploitation of the common: when labor power has become multitude and labor has become cognitive and cooperative, capital no longer exploits the single laborer, it essentially exploits the whole of labor in as much as it is cooperative, it expropriates the common that this labor produces. *The exploitation of the common is therefore financial rent.*

Absolute or relative rent? Rent founded on a gesture of radical appropriation, of expropriation or a generalized exploitation articulated on the entirety of produced value and common valorization? In all probability, the contemporary economist, postindustrial in nature, will answer without hesitation to our query, saying: "we live in a world of relative rent." But then, when profit itself is presented as rent (since on the global market it is immediately translated into this form of the existence of capital), financial rent and financial flows—in the world of rent—are immediately touched and conditioned by multitude struggles. Nevertheless, when the world of relative rent is brought to us again, what enormous *difference* is demonstrated by the same relative rent! The world of rent confronts the common, it emerges inside the common, inside a generality of exploitation. There are countries (China for example) where these processes are presented in such a "pure" way that the social relationships between the political centralization of command and the dimension of welfare, of social wage and the distribution of wealth in general, are all immediately revealed as a relationship of struggle: even wages have reached the generality of financial rent. Looking at countries where the complex articulation of rent and profit comes in an "impure" form, like the United States and Europe (or in all of the ex-third world countries where income "oligarchs" persist), even here it has to be noted how intense the struggle for income re-appropriation is in the formation of relations of social reproduction. However, resistance against rent is fierce everywhere. Everywhere, on the other hand, the defense of rent reaches the point of re-proposing the synthesis between absolute rent and the state of exception that we have seen throughout its genealogy. It is here, then, that this kind of rent reappears, violently opposing democratic processes. This is the moment when absolute rent is vindicated, overturning the historic development of capitalism in order to guarantee profit.

Is it possible, where rent has absorbed or at least integrated the dynamics of profit, to define a struggle over "relative wages"? Is it possible to describe apparatuses of conflict directed against rent? What is a struggle over rent? What is a "rent wage"? Every answer to these questions must first of all reintroduce a subject: between whom does the struggle take place when rent mystifies the common of social production? A subject, we said: an antagonistic, multitudinary force, that has the capacity to demolish the rigid biopower exercised in the name of absolute rent. But how is this subject constructed? It can only be constructed imposing a terrain of struggle based and structured on, and oriented toward, relative rent. How to succeed in doing this? It can only be done through the construction of a struggling subject. *Rent is transformed from absolute to relative when it is subjugated to democracy by social struggles.* Hence struggles that lead to the construction of this subject will need to be conducted. Uniting precarious workers and those who are socially excluded, recomposing material and immaterial labor: the former inside the complexity of its factory and metropolitan articulations, the latter on the same space and in the same complexity of its articulations (from call centers to universities, from industrial production to communication, from research centers to social, sanitary and educational services). This is the multitude that can compose a political subject that actively penetrates the territory of rent commanded by finance and can introduce (with the same force that the battle for wages had for the workers in the Fordist factories) a struggle for income. A "rent wage" can and must be configured on this dimension.

Attention: this is not to say that the quantity of wages torn from rent (first absolute, then relative) can in some way determine a crisis in capitalistic command. The struggles around rent (in particular for a basic income) are first and foremost a means—a means for the construction of a political subject, of a political force. A means without an end? Yes, because its scope is not, nor can it yet be, the conquest of power, nor a lasting transformation of the mechanisms of reproduction of the capitalist society: in the struggle only the reality and the acknowledgement of a force that knows how to efficiently move on the terrain of rent can be built.

It is beginning with this passage, from this constituent use of struggle for the definition and the acknowledgement of a political subject—only arising from this passage will it be possible to open a new struggle not limited to the negotiation of basic citizen income, but aimed at the re-appropriation of the common and its democratic management.

Class struggle doesn't happen without space. Today this space is the metropolis. Once it was the factory; it still is today, but saying factory today means something different from what it once did. Today's factory is the metropolis—with its productive relationships, research companies, the sites of direct production and communication, transportation, separations and confines, crises of production and circulation, diverse forms of employment, etc. The metropolis: an ultramodern factory as only the prevalence of cognitive labor in the processes of valorization can determine; yet it is also an ancient factory in which slaves, migrants and women, precarious workers and the socially excluded are put to work and exploitation invades every aspect and moment of life. The metropolis: a pre-industrial factory that plays on cultural and social differences with different degrees of exploitation, like gender and race differences used as class differences; and yet a postindustrial factory where these differences constitute the common of the metropolitan encounter, continual and creative hybridization, the meeting of diverse cultures and lives. A common that can be recognized and brought to light in the metropolis. Rent clothes this common: it accumulates it in the highest floors of skyscrapers, rent dominates the common in stock markets, rent reveals itself to those that hide the common from its producers. Against this, an absolute democracy of struggles for transparency, for *Glasnost*, can indicate a way to emancipate the common to us. Attacking all of rent flows, from real-estate (*through* the financial articulations of profit) to the rent of copyright and digital production. The struggles that we have here indicated in parentheses constitute the heart of capital today. Democracy can and must destroy absolute rent to reach the power and intensity that is necessary to develop struggles against relative rent. Absolute rent, after having been the initial and violent figure of the capitalist period of take-off is now the figure of capitalistic exploitation that lives at the highest level of development: it is the figure of the *exploitation of the common.* The path to go down is intensifying the relationship between command and the common until that contradiction explodes, knowing full well that there is no dialectic that can resolve this problem. Only democracy, when it becomes absolute, can do this; when the acknowledgement that every person is necessary to the others because all are equal in the common...

The great crisis has begun within the metropolis. The new proletariat—created by the capitalistic production of subjectivity as proprietary individuals, then pushed toward a patrimonial condition in the neoliberal conversion of the welfare state (but at the same time reduced to the fatigue of a precarious life while the last century of worker struggle had improved living conditions and re-qualified labor into cognitive labor)—well, this new proletariat has rebelled. They have impeded capital from the faculty of social income, they have stolen its homes, they have demonstrated again how capitalistic rent could not compromise, even when facing the urgency of the equilibrium of its own command. Resisting, rebelling... Here is the new production of subjectivity that is put to play by the proletariat.

Closing the seminar from which this book is born, I believe that all the conditions that determine this radical overturning of the processes of production of subjectivity are put forth in conclusive terms here. What remains is to begin to understand how to re-appropriate what capital has turned into rent for the common subjectivity. It is not inappropriate to pose this question in an era when passion, intelligence, and "revolutionary" practices are coming back to liven up the scene. On a global level. The analyses of the crisis and the consequent political thoughts that are contained in this volume not only describe and criticize the current historical phase of capitalism but also open new horizons of desire.

— February 2009

Notes

Introduction

1. The materials can be found in Bascetta M, Tarì M, *Guerra e democrazia*, Manifestolibri, Rome 2005.

2. *Workerism* is a name given to different trends in left-wing political discourse, especially anarchism and Marxism. In one sense, it describes a political position concerning the political importance and centrality of the working class. Because this was of particular significance in the Italian left, it is often known by its Italian translation, *Operaismo* [translator's note].

3. See the presentation of the UniNomade project by Marco Bascetta and Sandro Mezzadra, "Il sapere come passione" in "Il Manifesto," 1 April 2005 (the article is available in Italian online at http://www.globalproject.info/art-4255.html).

4. "Social center" is an approximate translation of the Italian *centro sociale*, referring to self-managed squatted or occupied structures as a re-appropraition of abandoned urban spaces. See N. Klein, *Fences and Windows: Dispatches from the Front Lines of the Globalization Debate*, Picador, London 2002 [translator's note].

5. Cf. G. Arrighi, *The Long Twentieth Century: Money, Power, and the Origins of Our Times*, Verso, London, New York 1994.

6. Ibid. Rich in innovative ideas from this point of view is the recent and important work G. Arrighi, *Adam Smith in Beijing: Lineages of Twenty-first Century*, Verso, London, New York 2007.

7. R. Hilferding, T.B. Bottomore, *Financial Capital: A Study of the Latest Phase of Capitalist Development*, Routledge & Kegan Paul, London 1981.

8. On the concept of "articulation" in reference to global capital, see Chapter 6 of S. Mezzadra, *La condizione postcoloniale: storia e politica nel presente globale*, Ombre corte, Verona 2008.

9. See K.H. Roth, *Der Zustand der Welt: Gegen-Perspektiven*, VSA-Verlag, Hamburg 2005, where many of the theses presented in his contribution in this volume have already been amply argued, also online at http://www.wildcat-www.de.

10. In this sense, see M.V.D. Linden, "Normalarbeit—das Ende einer Fiktion. Wie "der Proletar" vershwand und wieder zurückkehrte," in *Fantomas* 6 (Winter 2004–2005).

11. See the work of M.V.D. Linden, *Transnational Labor History: Explorations*, Ashgate, Aldershot, Hants, Burlington 2003. See also, M.V.D. Linden, *Workers of the World: Essays Toward a Global Labor History*, Brill, Leiden, Boston 2008. But keep in mind the extraordinary book P. Linebaugh, M.B. Rediker, *The Many-headed Hydra: Sailors, Slaves, Commoners, and the Hidden History of the Revolutionary Atlantic*, Becon Press, Boston 2000.

12. Again, see Chapter 6 of S. Mezzadra, *La condizione postcoloniale*, op. cit.

13. W. Benjamin, *Paris capitale del XIX secolo*, Einaudi, Turin, 1986, (X, 11a, p.3).

14. Cf. John Maynard Keynes, *General Theory of Employment, Interest and Money*. Palgrave Macmillan, New York 1936. Keynes also writes: "A conventional valuation which is established as the outcome of the mass psychology of a large number of ignorant individuals is liable to change violently as the result of a sudden fluctuation of opinion due to factors which do not really make much difference to the prospective yield" (http://www.marxists.org/reference/subject/economics/keynes/general-theory/ch12.htm). Already forty years before, Max Weber—in the framework of an analysis of stock markets as "regulation and organization devices" now unavoidable in the industrial capitalist economy—underlined how vitally important "the formation and fixing of prices (of 'courses') in the markets were [to be realized] in a solid and correct way." M. Weber, *Gesammelte aufsätze zur soziologie und sozialpolitik, Mohrm Tübingen*, p. 278, [our translation]. And had then called attention to the effects of perturbation that the intervention, difficulty "calculable," of the "public" (das Publikum) could determine (Ibid. pp. 308, 313 and 316).

15. The crisis' repercussions on migrant labor, in a situation where mobility is a key element in the definition of the composition of living labor on a global level, are a fundamental theme of analysis and political intervention, here only briefly touched on. Without being silent about the fact that, at the beginning of December of last year, Vladimir Putin practically announced his intention on live television to expel a few million migrants for the most part from the ex-Soviet republics. We will limit ourselves to two other examples, both from recent events and refer to the internal migrations that represent one of the essential shuttlecocks of the Chinese economic development of the last few years and to the Indian migrants in the Gulf states: Simon Rabinovitch, "Economic crisis reverses flood of migrants in China," in "International Herald Tribune," 30 December 2008 (http://www.iht.com/articles/2008/12/30/business/col31.php) and N. Raghuraman, "Indians Flee Dubai as

Dreams Crash—Fall out of Economic Crisis," in "Daijiworld.com," 14 January 2009, (http://www.daijiworld.com/news/news_disp.asp?n_id=55704&n_tit=Indians).

The Violence of Financial Capitalism

An extended version of this text can be found in Christian Marazzi, *The Violence of Financial Capitalism*, Semiotext(e), Los Angeles, 2010. This version was edited and revised by Jason Francis Mc Gimsey.

1. Martin Wolf, *Financial Times*, 7 January 2009.

2. Stephen Roach, "US Not Certain of Avoiding Japan-Style 'Lost Decade,'" *Financial Times*, 14 January 2009.

3. Carmen Reinhart and Kenneth Rogoff, "The Aftermath of Financial Crises," December 2008, http://www.economics.harvard.edu/faculty/rogofff/files/After math.pdf.

4. "Emerging Markets: Stumble or Fall?" *The Economist*, 10 January 2009.

5. Michael Aglietta, *La crise. Pourquoi en est-on arrivé là? Comment en sortir?*, Michalon, Parigi, 2008, p. 118.

6. Paul Krugman "Il piano Obama non basta," *La Reppublica*, 10 January 2009.

7. *Ibid.*

8. Joseph Stiglitz, "Do not Squander America's Stimulus on Tax Cut," *Financial Times*, 16 January, 2009.

9. Chris Giles, David Oakley, and Michael Mackenzie, "Onerous issuance," *Financial Times*, January 7, 2009.

10. Michael Husson, *Les enjeux de la crise*, in "La Brèche," November 2008.

11. Luciano Gallino, *L'impresa irresponsabile*, Einaudi, Torino, 2005.

12. Giovanni Arrighi, *Adam Smith a Pechino. Genealogie del ventunesimo secolo*, Feltrinelli, Milano, 2007, pp. 159–60.

13. See Carlo Vercellone, "Crisi della legge del valore e divenire rendita dei profitti," in this volume.

14. Jacques Sapir, *L'économie politique internationale de la crise et la question du "nouveau Bretton Woods": Leçons pour des temps de crise*, Mimeo, sapir@msh-paris.fr.

15. Augusto Illuminati, *Spinoza atlantico*, Edizioni Ghilbi, Milano, 2008, p. 15.

16. Sandro Mezzadra, *La "cosiddetta" accumulazione originaria*, in AA.VV., Lessico marxiano, minifestolibri, Roma, 2008.

17. Jeff Howe, *Crowdsourcing. Why the Power of the Crowd is Driving the Future of Business*, Crown Business, New York, 2008.

18. Vanni Codeluppi, *Il biocapitalismo. Verso lo sfruttamento integrali di corpi, cervelli ed emozioni*, Bollati Boringhieri, Torino, 2008.

19. The first effort in this sense is the work by Andrea Fumagalli, *Bioeconomia e capitalismo cognitivo*, Carocci, Roma, 2007.

20. Of the most recent works on the consumer-as-producer phenomenon, see Marie-Anne Dujarier, *Le travail du consommateur. De McDo à eBay: comment nous coproduisons ce que nous achetons*, La découverte, Paris, 2008.

21. *Op. cit.*

22. Christian Marazzi, *Capitalismo digitale e modello antropogenetico del lavoro. L'ammortamento del corpo macchina*, in J. L. Laville, C. Marazzi, ed. M. La Rosa, F. Chicchi, *Reinventare il lavoro*, Sapere 2000, Rome, 2005.

23. Codeluppi, *op. cit.*, p. 24.

24.Jeremy Rifkin, *L'era dell'accesso. La rivoluzione della new economy*, Mondadori, Milano, p. 57.

25. For an analysis of the deregulation of the banking system that began in the 1970s in the midst of the Fordist crisis, see Barry Eichengreen, "Anatomy of the Financial Crisis," Vox, http://www.voxeu.org/index.php?q=node/1684.

26. Aglietta, *La crise, op. cit*, pp. 33–37.

27. Sapir, *op. cit.*, p. 5.

28. Michel Aglietta and Laurent Berrebi, *Désordres dand le capitalisme mondial*, Odile Jacob, Paris, 2007.

29. Aglietta, *La crise, op. cit.*, p. 39.

30. To confirm this reconstruction of the post-Asian crisis, see "When a Flow Becomes a Flood," *The Economist*, 24 January 2009.

31. Eichengreen, *op. cit.*

32. See André Orléan, *La notion de valeur fondamentale est-elle indispensable à la théorie financière?, Regards croisés sur l'économie. Comprendre la finance contemporaine*, March 3, 2008.

33. Lucio Caracciolo, *L'impera senza credito*, Limes, 5, 2008.

34. "Asia's Suffering," *The Economist*, 31 January 2009.

35. David Brooks, *Herald Tribune*, 2 August 2008.

36. Sapir, *op. cit.*, p. 3.

37. Sapir, *op. cit.*, p. 32.

38. Martin Wolf, "Why President Obama Must Mend a Sick World Economy," *Financial Times*, 21 January 2009.

39. "Top 10 Business Battles," *Business Week*, 2 February 2009.

40. James C. Cooper, "Job One: Build a Flour Under Housing," *Business Week*, 9 March 2009.

41. Frédéric Lordon, Jusqu'à quand?, *Pour en finir avec les crises financières*, Raisons d'agir, Paris 2008.

The Global Economic Crisis and Socioeconomic Governance

I'd like to thank Stefano Lucarelli, Sandro Mezzadra and Cristina Morini for their comments on the first draft of this article, Sabrina Del Pico for editing the English translation, and the Grateful Dead and Jimi Hendrix for their psychedelic support.

1. See for example L. Bazzicalupo, *Il governo delle vite. Biopolitica ed economia*, Roma-Bari, La Terza, 2005, C. Vercellone (ed.), *Capitalismo cognitivo*, Manifestolibri, Rome, 2006, A.Fumagalli, *Bioeconomia e Capitalismo Cognitivo. Verso un nuovo poaradigma di accumulazione*, Carocci, Rome, 2007.

2. The Dow Jones reached its maximum on October 9, 2007, with a value of 14,164 points. At the end of January 2009, its value was 8,077. If we observe the main real-estate companies and financial institutions that managed the vast patrimony of investment funds and retirement pensions, we have even worse data. In the period between June 2007 and the end of January 2009, Morgan Stanley lost 67,3% of their social capital, Rbs 95,8%, Deutsche Bank 86,6%, Barclays Bank 92,3%, Crédit Agricole 74,6%, Unicredit 72,0%, Ubs 69,8%, Goldman Sachs 65%, J.P.Morgan 48,5%, Credit Suisse 64%.

3. Cf. M. Whitney, "Economic depression in America: evidence of a withering economy is everywhere," *GlobalResearch*, 2 June 2008.

4. Cf. http://www.nexusedizioni.it/apri/Argomenti/Economia/sta-per-scoppiare-la-bolla-dei-derivati-di-Maurizio-Blondet.

5. According to the *Financial Times*, the state interventions between Europe and the United States amount to around $2.2 trillion. Another $2.8 trillion were derived from the joint operations of the Federal Reserve, the ECB and the Bank of Japan.

6. Cf. A. Gorz, *L'immateriale*, Bollati Boringhieri, Torino, 2003. It is important to remember that since the mid nineties, intangible capital (human, cognitive, immaterial) exceeds physical capital in value.

7. P. Virno writes: "The metamorphosis of social systems in the West, during the eighties and nineties, can be properly synthesized with the expression: communism of capital [...]. If Fordism encompassed, and revised in its own way, some aspects of the socialist experience, post-Fordism has fundamentally dismissed both Keynesism and socialism. Post-Fordism, based as it is on general intellect and the multitudes, articulates in its own way instances typical of communism (the abolition of labor, the dissolution of the state, etc.). Post-Fordim is the communism of capital." Cf. P. Virno, *A Grammar of the Multitude*, Semiotext(e), Los Angeles, 2004, pp. 121–122.

8. Cf. "Nothing Will Ever Be the Same," in particular Thesis 2, in this volume.

9. Cf. A. Negri, "J.M. Keynes e la teoria capitalistica dello Stato" in AA.VV., *Operai e Stato*, Feltrinelli, Milan, 1972, p. 7 [our translation].

10. For further information on this aspect, see the contribution of C. Marazzi in this volume.

11. Cf. F. Saccomanni, "Nuove regole e mercati finanziari," Speech at the Scuola Superiore della Pubblica Amministrazione, Rome, 19 January 2009, http://www.bancaditalia.it/interventi/intaltri_mdir/saccomanni_190109/sacco manni_190109.pdf. Saccomanni is the General Manager of the Bank of Italy.

12. Cf. F. Saccomanni, cit.

13. Regarding this fact, it is important to remember the liquidity injections deriving from the "criminal" economy that is tied to arms and drug trafficking. On January 26th 2009, the United Nations Office for drug control and crime prevention, directed by the Italian Antonio Maria Costa, with headquarters in Vienna, stated that the money from the drug trade is inserted in the circuit of the legal economy to such a point that "there are indications whereby some banks have been saved thanks to this aspect of the global financial crisis." The profits from drug trafficking, that amount to around $90 million, are the only liquid capital available to buy, for example, real-estate. Now, such injections of liquidity cannot be attributable to public spending in the strict meaning of the term, even though often some state apparatuses are strongly attached to it. It is important to note that, while abroad the UN denouncement raised quite a fuss, in Italy it was not reported by any newspaper. Cf. http://www.wikio.it/webinfo?id=88781387.

14. Cf. P. Krugman, editorial in the *New York Times*, 9 January 2009.

15. This means that every state could have enough reserve currency and gold able to blunt possible speculative attacks.

16. The equivalent relation dollar-gold was fixed at $35.00 per ounce of gold.

17. Cf. V. Comito, "Sindrome cinese per il piano Obama," 3 February 2009, http://www.sbilanciamoci.info/Sezioni/globi/Sindrome-cinese-per-il-piano-Obama.

18. Cf., *ibid.* At the moment of writing, it seems that such protectionist measures are partially sweetened up however.

19. A clamorous example of this emerged in Great Britain regarding the hiring of Italian workers in English building yards.

20. See C. Marazzi, "The Violence of Financial Capitalism" in this volume.

21. Regarding the Italian situation, in the course of 2008 the distinct management of retirement and insurance funds saw an average real loss of 6% (cf. F.M. Pizzuti, "Se la bolla scoppia sulle pensioni," 27 January 2009, http://www.sbilanciamoci.info/Sezioni/italie/Se-la-bolla-scoppia-sulle-pensioni) causing family debt to grow by more than 30% (according to the Bank of Italy).

22. Cf. "Nothing Will Ever Be the Same" in this volume; in particular Theses 8 and 9.

23. See, A. Fumagalli, *Bioeconomia e capitalismo cognitivo. Verso un nuovo paradigma di accumulazione*, Carocci, Rome, 2007, especially chap. 9: 201–228, and A. Fumagalli, "Trasformazione del lavoro e trasformazioni del welfare: precarietà e welfare del comune (*commonfare*) in Europa" in P. Leon, R. Realfonso, (eds.), *L'Economia della precarietà*, Manifestolibri, Rome, 2008: 159–174.

24. In *Capital*, Marx ironized about the freedom of the worker to sell his labor, writing: "Its owner is not only free to sell it, but finds himself obliged to do it. Why? To live." Quotation from C. Vercellone, "Il prezzo giusto della vita," *Il Manifesto*, 24 November 2006: http://multitudes.samizdat.net/Il-giusto-prezzo-di-una-vita.

The Crisis of the Law of Value and the Becoming-Rent of Profit

This text is in large part the transcription of a speech at the UniNomade seminar held in Rome on January 30th and 1st February 2009. The provisional character of the formulation of these hypotheses is to be taken for granted: I promise to go further into depth in the near future. I'd like to thank Hervé Baron that has contributed in improving this article referencing the Italian bibliographic citations of the various authors.

1. It's enough to remember that in France, before the crisis, the returns on the funds of CAC 40 non-financial businesses was around 15–20%, while those for financial companies, in particular for business banks, could be more than 50%. Another extremely significative fact, regarding the United States: in the 1970s, the profits of the financial sector represented around 10% of the profits of American businesses. This percentage represented 40% in 2006 (!) and it would be much higher if the financial profits made by non-financial business was taken into account too.

2. For an analysis of the NASDAQ speculative bubble and the crisis of the Net Economy, see R. Boyer, *La croissance, début du siècle. De l'octet au gène*. Albin Michel, 2002.

3. André Gorz, *L'immatériel*, Galilée, Paris, 2003, p. 84.

4. For a more detailed analysis in the theoretic and historical sense of the law of value and its crisis, see: Antonio Negri, "Valeur-travail: crise et problèmes de reconstruction dans le postmoderne," *Futur Antérieur* 10, 1992, pp 30–36; Carlo Vercellone, "Lavoro, distribuzione del reddito e valore nel capitalismo cognitivo, una prospettiva storica e teorica," 2008, http://www.posseweb.net/spip.php?article242; Carlo Vercellone, *L'analyse "gorzienne" de l'évolution du capitalisme*, in Christophe Fourel (ed.), *André Gorz, un penseur pour le XXIème siècle*, La Découverte, Paris, 2009, pp. 77–98.

5. See Karl Polanyi , *La grande trasformazione*, Einaudi, Torino, 1974, particularly: Parte Seconda, ch. VI, pp. 88–98.

6. Claudio Napoleoni, *Dizionario di economia politica*, Edizioni di Comunità, *1956*.

7. Karl Marx, *Capital*, Progress Publishers, Moscow 1887; [online at: http://www.marxists.org/archive/marx/works/cw/index.htm], (vol. III, http://www.marxists.org/archive/marx/works/1894-c3/ch49.htm).

8. In fact, even Keynes in his observation on the nature of capital, in Chapter 16 of General Theory (cf. John Maynard Keynes, *General Theory of Employment, Interest and Money*, Polygraphic Company of America, New York 1935, Online at: http://www.marxists.org/reference/subject/economics/keynes/general-theory/) will give a strong and original answer to this question: he will consider that remuneration of capital as such depends on scarcity; it is therefore a figure of rent and Keynes will articulate this affirmation to the adhesion to the classic theory of labor value.

9. On this point, cf. Karl Marx, *Capital, op. cit.*, vol I, 4th section, http://www.marxists.org/archive/marx/works/1867-c1/ch01.htm#S4.

10. Karl Marx, *Storia dell'economia politica. Teorie sul plusvalore*, Editori Riuniti, Rome, 1993, vol. II, p 35 [our translation].

11. John Maynard Keynes, *General Theory of Employment, Interest and Money, op. cit.* chap. 24.

12. *Ibid.*

13. *Ibid.*

14. Karl Marx, *Capital, op. cit.*, vol III, footnote 7, http://www.marxists.org/archive/marx/works/1894-c3/ch23.htm#n7.

15. *Ibid.*

16. The "Hot Autumn" (*autunno caldo* in Italian) of 1969–1970 was a massive series of strikes in the factories and industrial centers of northern Italy, during which workers demanded better pay and better conditions. Between 1969 and 1970 there were over 440 million hours of strikes alone [translator's note].

17. Jean-Marie Chevalier, *L'économie industrielle en question*, Calmann-Levy, 1977 [our translation].

18. The putting-out system was a means of subcontracting work, also known as the workshop system. In putting-out, work was contracted by a central agent to subcontractors who completed the work in their own facility, usually their own home. It was used in the English textile industry, in small farms, and lock making trades as late as the 19th century [translator's note].

19. Today, the average wage for an American citizen is less than it was in 1979, and much less for 20% of the poorest workers. The tendency is analogous in Europe. For example, in France, buying power of market index increased by 120% in 20 years (which the current crisis makes relative) while full-time wages only 15%, without considering that wage growth rate would be much lower considering the different forms of precarious work that today concerns about 20% of the labor force (intern-workers, limited contracts, part-time contracts, etc.).

20. Cited in D. Boutillier and S. Uzundis, *L'entrepreneur. Une analyse socio-économique*, Economica, 1995, p. 41.

21. Mouhoud El Mouhoib and Dominique Plihon, *Finance et économie de la connaissance: des relations équivoques*, from the seminar hétérodoxies de Matisse, Paris, Novembre 2005, http://matisse.univ-paris1.fr/.

22. Laurent Cordonnier, *Le profit sans l'accumulation : la recette du capitalisme gouverné par la finance*, in *Innovations*, 2006/1—n° 23, pp. 79–108.

23. A. Gorz, *op. cit.*, p 55.

24. It also demonstrates the way numerous mainstream economists alarmingly signal the way that the multiplication of the number of copyrights goes hand in hand with a flagrant deterioration of their quality and acknowledgement as the real source of innovation is increasingly found in noncommercial networks of common production.

25. For the relation between cognitive capitalism and bioeconomy, see Andrea Fumagalli, *Bioeconomia e capitalismo cognitivo*, Carocci, 2007.

26. For a detailed description of these macroeconomic mechanisms, see Michel Aglietta *La crise. Pourquoi en est-on arrivé là? Comment en sortir?*, Michalon, Parigi, 2008.

27. Antonio Gramsci, *Quaderno 3*, p. 311 [our translation].

28. For a more detailed analysis of these points, see: Jean-Marie Monnier and Carlo Vercellone, *Travail, genre et protection sociale dans la transition vers le capitalisme cognitif*, in *European Journal of Economic and Social Systems*, volume 20—n° 1/2007, pp. 15–35.

29. The French *Revenu Minimum d'Insertion*, or "Minimum Insertion Income" is a form of social welfare. It is aimed at people without any income who are of working

age but don't have any other rights to unemployment benefit (e.g. contributions based unemployment benefit). It was created in 1988 by Jean-Michel Belorgey by the government of Michel Rocard (Socialist Party, PS) and aimed at helping the people who had the most problems with finding work [translator's note].

Financialization as Biopower

This text is an edited and expanded version of the speech presented at the UniNomade seminar in Bologna on September 12th and 13th, 2008. I would like to thank all of the seminar participants. I would also like to thank the conference organizers of the conference on the financial crisis held at C.S.A. Barattolo in Pavia on November 20th, 2008 that gave me the opportunity to return to these themes again. I am also grateful to Adelino Zanini and Hervé Baron who contributed to improving the previous version of this text. Obviously, I am the only one responsible for the theses that I present here.

1. It is a crisis that cannot be simply reduced to the classic scheme described by Galbraith, that is, however, necessary to make clear: "A handmade article or evolutionary process, apparently new and desirable—tulips in Holland, gold in Louisiana, lands in Florida, the ambitious economic plans of Ronald Reagan—attract the financial mind [...] The price of the speculation object rises. Titles, land, art objects and other properties, if bought today, tomorrow will be more valuable. This increase and that forecast attract new buyers [...] Inherent to such situation is the final crash [...] and because both groups of participants in the speculative situation [who have full faith in the rise of the market and those who believe they feel the speculative atmosphere of the moment] are programmed for sudden instances of escape" (John Kenneth Galbraith, *A Short History of Financial Euphoria*, Penguin, London 1994, pp. 11–19).

2. According to Robert Boyer, these regularities principally regard: the type of evolution of the organization of production and wage relations; the temporal horizon of valorization of capital on the basis of which managerial criteria are established; the criteria of the division of value produced necessary for the reproduction of time in social groups that participate in production; a composition of social demand compatible with the tendential evolution of productive capacity; lastly, the modality of articulation between the sphere of capitalist production and the non-capitalist areas. The Regulationists in fact acknowledge that the non-capitalistic forms are relevant in the evolution and the very formation of the different socioeconomic assets ascribable to the capitalist mode of production. Cf. Robert Boyer, *Regulation Theory: The State of the Art*, Routledge, Kentucky, 2002. The main contribution to the Regulation Approach in the UK has come from Bob Jessop, cf. Bob Jessop, *State Theory*, Polity, Cambridge, 1990, p. 308: "The key concepts initially offered by the Parisian regulationists were 'regime of accumulation' and 'mode of regulation.' An accumulation regime is defined as a particular combination of production and consumption which can be reproduced over time

despite conflictual tendencies; and a mode of regulation comprises an institutional ensemble and complex of norms which can secure capitalist reproduction *pro tempore* despite the antagonistic character of capitalist social relations."

3. In the reflections that are here presented, I have constantly consulted with Renata Brandimarte, Patricia Chiantera-Stutte, Pierangelo Di Vittorio, Ottavio Marzocca, Onofrio Romano, Andrea Russo, Anna Simone (eds.), *Lessico di Biopolitica*, Manifestolibri, Rome 2006. I have particularly adopted Dario Melossi's interpretation, "Controllo Sociale," applying it in a totally personal way to financialization.

4. The choice of referring to Foucaultian categories depends first of all on the desire to re-elaborate one of the directions traced by the "Primo Maggio" workgroup on money. In particular, see Christian Marazzi, *Alcune proposte per un lavoro su 'denaro e composizione di classe,'* in "Quaderno n. 2 di Primo Maggio," Supplement to n. 12 of "Primo Maggio," pp. 75–80. See also, Christian Marazzi, *Commento a Convenevole*, in "Primo Maggio," 11, winter 1977/78. Marazzi, commenting, maybe in an excessively critical way, on an important study conducted in the attempt to build a new distribution statistic of incomes in a monetary economy of production, stressed how the critique of the political economy was behind in respect to the critique of power developed by Foucault: "In fact it is simpler to see the simultaneousness of the knowledge-power relation than the exchange-wealth relation" [our translation]. The workerist journal Primo Maggio opens in 1973 and ends in 1986. Its founders Sergio Bologna, Lapo Berti, Franco Gori, Andrea Battinelli, Guido de Masi were interested in innovating in the areas of the methodology of history, sociology, economics and political science; "its main focus was on placing itself within a network of initiatives of self organisation at the level of political culture and formation 'at the service of the movement.' Primo Moroni's bookshop Calusca in Milan was the most original and important of these initiatives. If Primo Maggio had not joined this network, it would have never exercised the influence that is only today being recognised. [...] Primo Maggio was also able to produce interesting, new and forward looking material in the analyses of financial capital, the welfare state, history and class composition because its editorial board was comprised of comrades who differed in age and experience from 'classical operaismo,' such as Cesare Bermani, Bruno Cartosio, Marco Revelli, Christian Marazzi and Marcello Messori." Cf. Sergio Bologna, Steve Wright's Storming Heaven. Class composition and struggle in Italian Autonomist Marxism, http://www.generation-online.org/t/stormingheaven.htm. About the "Primo Maggio" workgroup on money, the English reader can refer to Steve Wright, "Revolution from above? Money and Class composition in Italian *operaismo*," presented at the 5th annual Historical Materialism Conference, School of Oriental and African Studies, London, 7–9 November 2008, steven.wright@infotech.monash.edu.au.

5. Carlo Vercellone has maintained in various contributions how the new technological paradigm (that he has defined together with other scholars of cognitive

capitalism) is rooted in three processes: the contestation of the scientific organization of labor; the expansion of the guarantees of collective welfare services; the constitution of a diffused intellectuality as a result of the democratization of learning. Cf. Didier Lebert and Carlo Vercellone, "Il ruolo della conoscenza nella dinamica di lungo periodo del capitalismo: l'ipotesi del capitalismo cognitivo" in Carlo Vercellone (ed.), *Capitalismo cognitivo. Conoscenza e finanza nell'epoca post-Fordista*, Manifestolibri, Rome 2006. However, it is evident that at least one of the above cited three processes (the diffused intellectuality tied to the democratization of learning) is put into crisis by the command devices on which the new form of capitalism is structured: reform processes of public education that are pushing down both traditional knowledges and students' critical sense are being seen; in a parallel manner, a rhetoric of permanent formation is being spread to support business restructuring, that rarely reinforces the innovative capacity of the economic system. In other terms, "the investment that assures the reproduction of fixed human capital is actually reduced consequent to the dismantling of the social state and the increase of educational costs." The paradoxical result is "the increasingly strategic importance of cognitive social labor and the simultaneous worsening of the living conditions of those same knowledge workers." Cf. Christian Marazzi, "L'ammortamento del corpo," in *Posse. La classe a venire*, November 2007, http://www.posseweb.net [our translation]. It becomes legitimate to ask: up to what point can this constant exploitation of qualified knowledges that have consolidated thanks to specific institutional factors (the democratization of learning) last? Or, under what conditions can knowledge continue to represent a fundamental valorization element in contemporary capitalism? On the hypothesis of a cognitive capitalism, see Carlo Vercellone, "From Formal Subsumption to General Intellect: Elements for a Marxist Reading of the Thesis of Cognitive Capitalism," in *Historical Materialism*, Vol. 15, 1 2007, pp. 13–36.

6. In other words, as Zanini maintained in a previous UniNomade seminar: "The 'phase' that has lasted for at least 15 years is characterized by 'downward' regulatory politics of the value of the workforce. Above all in powerful countries, knowledge production and innovation through precarious labor is the distinct sign of this new phase." Cf. Adelino Zanini, "New Deal e democrazia conflittuale," in AA.VV., *Guerra e democrazia*, Manifestolibri, Rome 2005.

7. Beyond the contributions of Andrea Fumagalli and Christian Marazzi in this volume, cf. André Orléan, "Beyond Transparency," 18 December 2008, http://www.eurozine.com; Dmitri B. Papadimitriou and Randy Wray, "Time to Bail Out: Alternatives to the Bush-Paulson Plan," in "Policy Note of The Levy Economics Institute of Bard College," 6 November 2008; Pavlina R. Tcherneva, "Obama's job creation promise: a modest proposal to guarantee that he meets and exceeds expectations," in "Policy Note of The Levy Economics Institute of Bard College," 1 January 2009, http://www.levy.org; Martin Wolf, "Why Obama's plan is still inadequate and incomplete," in *Financial Times*, 13 January 2009; Martin Wolf, "Why President Obama must mend a sick world economy," in *Financial Times*, 21 January 2009.

8. See the conference "Les mailles de pouvoir" held by Michel Foucault in 1981; the paraphrased passages in the text are cited in Adelino Zanini, "Invarianza neoliberale," in Sandro Chignola (ed.), "Governare la vita. Un seminario sui Corsi di Michel Foucault al Collège de France (1977–1979)," Ombre corte, Verona 2006, p. 122.

9. *Ibid.*, p. 124.

10. Micheal Foucault, *Security, Territory, Population. Lectures at the Collège de France*, Eng. trans., Picador, New York 2009, p. 258.

11. *Ibid.*, p. 88.

12. Massimo Amato, *Il bivio della moneta. Problemi monetari e pensiero del denaro nel Settecento italiano, Egea*, Milano 1999, p. 20 [our translation].

13. Christian Marazzi, La monnaie et la finance globale, in "Multitudes," 32, March 2008, pp. 115–127. In reality, the definition of the word "financialization" is problematic in itself, see Bernard Paulré's contribution in this volume.

14. Cf. Michel Aglietta, *Into a New Growth Regime*, in "New Left Review," n. 54, November–December 2008, p. 69: "After all, the radical change in monetary policy in the late 1970s and early 1980s triggered financial liberalization. Not only was there a shift from intermediate to market financing that redistributed risk-taking from banks to institutional investors; there was also a dramatic change in the ownership structure of corporations, that has shifted business strategy from 'insider productivity-sharing' to 'shareholder value-optimizing.' The norm of profitability has changed altogether. Market-value accounting has replaced reproduction-cost accounting as the yardstick of corporate performance. Furthermore, achieving shareholder value in practice means extracting a rent on behalf of shareholders. This rent is the positive difference between the actual rate of return on equity and the equilibrium stock-market rate of return of the corporation, given by the capital asset pricing model (capm), multiplied by the capital of the firm. Combined with the long ascending wave in the stock market, the imperative of shareholder value gave rise to a much higher required rate of return than in the heyday of postwar growth. Most business strategies—downsizing, spin-offs and the like, but also external growth via mergers and acquisitions and share buybacks—were driven by the lucrative adjustment of corporate executives to the principle of shareholder value. The US adopted shareholder value on a large scale in the early 1990s, at a time when Europe was crippled by extravagantly high real interest rates. Shareholder value does not hamper innovative investment spurred by private-equity funds, especially venture-capital funds; it has had a large impact on productivity growth—the revolution was largely financed by such investment funds." The doctrine of shareholder sovereignty does not consider that, being dispersed, shareholders do not have the real means to exercise their sovereign control. But external and internal controls compensate for the shareholders' inability: externally auditors, financial analysts and rating agencies are responsible for accounting

information for investors; internally, the board of directors assumes the task of re-establishing shareholders' real rights Cf. Michel Aglietta and Antoine Rebérioux, "Regulating finance-driven capitalism," *Issues in Regulation Theory*, n. 51, January 2005, pp. 1–5.

15. For wealth-effect, usually the modification of aggregated demand caused by variations in the real value of wealth that happens following changes in prices is intended. When this refers to a shareholder, it has a positive wealth-effect if the movements in the prices of the shares are associated with a movement in interest rates: a fall in interest rates augments the valuation of the representative capital titles and therefore the perceived wealth as a whole. Neoclassic economists during the Great Crisis amply used the wealth-effect to support the existence of automatic mechanisms able to guarantee full employment over a long-term. The fact that I refer to this concept absolutely does not mean that I am assuming a neoclassical point of view. Instead, I believe that the American model is based on the wealth-effect, first tied to technological titles, then to real-estate, in a low interest rate context and this practice of social control is split by the ambition of a full employment political program.

16. Andrea Fumagalli and Stefano Lucarelli, A model of cognitive capitalism: a preliminary analysis, in "European Journal of Economic and Social Systems," XX, 1, 2007, pp. 117–133. The cited result was obtained in the macroeconomic model that I studied together with Andrea Fumagalli. In more rigorous terms: in a model where economic scale dynamics directly influence productivity, there is a positive correlation between the dynamic of demand and the dynamic of productivity if and only if the sum of the propensity to invest and the propensity to consume depending on allocation of financial surplus value, is higher than the tendency to consume deriving from wages.

17. The positive expression is from Michel Aglietta, "Le capitalisme de bulle en bulle," in "Le Monde," 5 September 2007. Aglietta writes that we pass from one bubble to the next because the system is not equipped with any internal brakes. Even when prices have totally lost any relation with fundamental value, short-term logic prevails. Fund managers, intermediaries and business managers have built a mechanism of remuneration and incentives that answers to this logic. Thus it is the same financial organization that causes the next bubble!

18. John Maynard Keynes, *General Theory of Employment, Interest and Money, Polygraphic Company of America*, New York 1935, online at:
http://www.marxists.org/reference/subject/economics/keynes/general-theory/, chap. 12, http://www.marxists.org/reference/subject/economics/keynes/general-theory/ch12.htm.

19. Following Keynes, André Orlean proposed a definition of "collective belief" that is essential for studying financial markets: an individual *i* believes that the group *G* believes the proposition *Q* if he believes that, in the majority, the members

of the group believe that the group *G* believes *Q*. The definition is "self-referential," it does not involve any reference to the "primary beliefs" of individuals, but only refers to beliefs that bear directly on what the group *G* believes. The self-referential hypothesis therefore reconciles the *ex ante* existence of a heterogeneous set of individual fundamentalist estimates and the *ex post* emergence of a unique representation that gives the price its significance. A convention determines more than just the definition of a "scenario of reference": "We must go further, and also consider the battery of specific criteria it constructs to serve as a basis for the concrete valuation of companies. Thus, in the case of the 'New Economy convention,' faced with the difficulty of accounting for stock market prices solely on the criterion of profits, as most 'dot.com' businesses were loss-making, a new basis for making estimates appeared, in the form of 'value per user.' So the potential number of subscribers, visitors or customers was adopted as the strategic variable, supposed to enable the level of value creation to be assessed." Cf. André Orlean, "Knowledge in Finance: Objective Value versus Convention," in Richard Arena and Agnès Festré (eds.), *Handbook of Knowledge and Economics*, Edward Elgar, 2008; also cf. André Orlean, *Le pouvoir de la finance*, Odile Jacob, Paris 1999.

20. About "Primo Maggio" see footnote iv. English readers can refer to Christian Marazzi, *Money in the World Crises*, in "Zerowork," n. 2, autumn 1977, pp. 91–111, http://libcom.org/library/money-world-crisis-christian-marazzi-zerowork: "First, the international monetary system has more and more grown dependent on the national currencies that have acted as means of payment for world accumulation. Second, both domestic and international credit have been increasingly transformed into credit ex nihilo, into artificially created money which is no longer based on accumulated surplus value, but on no existing value. The requirement for 'artificial money' to act as a productive force beyond the value embodied in gold reserves is that it must become money as capital, that is, it must become credit which commands alien labor: money must become command. But precisely because this form of money as capital makes for both an extension and intensification of the basis of accumulation, gold comes to function increasingly marginally as the measure of value, which in turn comes to depend less and less on socially necessary labor time and increasingly on imperial command. In other words, if money becomes increasingly less convertible in terms of gold, it has to become ever more convertible in terms of command of capital over labor-power. The problem for capital is that while international credit-the World Bank, the International Monetary Fund, etc.-has increasingly functioned as the lever of capitalist socialization on a world scale, the command function upon which money now rests is not solid-precisely because of the new era of international working class struggle."

21. Marcello De Cecco wrote this on May 13th in "Affari e finanza" in an article now published in Marcello De Cecco, *Gli anni dell'incertezza*, Laterza, Rome-Bari 2007, [our translation]. On the "New Consensus," see chap. 3 in Marc Lavoie, *Introduction to Post-Keynesian Economics*, Palgrave-Macmillan, 2006.

22. In other words, we are referring to the forms of appropriation of use-values.

23. The disinvestment in fiscal capital that freed up liquidity from productive processes should be taken into account. This liquidity was used to increase the market value of capital: "If in addition to the increase in liquidity, consequent to the reduction of investments in fixed capital, the increase of business debt to the banking system is added, we can understand why the financialization of the economy (payment of dividends, interest, Merger & Acquisitions, the buyback of already exposed stocks) was an extraordinary transfer of wealth to the class of stock investors and the managers who were responsible for financialization processes." Cf. Marazzi, *L'ammortamento del corpo macchina*, cit. [our translation].

24. According to the definition proposed by Robert Boyer.

25. Christian Marazzi, "Research Finance. The privatization of 'General Intellect,'" http://www.ssrc.org/blogs/knowledgerules/2008/02/19/the-privatization-of-the-general-intellect/.

26. Joseph E. Stiglitz, *The Roaring Nineties: A New History of the World's Most Prosperous Decade*, W. W. Norton & Co., New York 2004, p. 4.

27. Christian Marazzi, "Dietro la sindrome cinese," in *Il manifesto*, 1 July 2004.

28. Joseph Stiglitz, America's Day of Reckoning, http://www.project-syndicate.org/commentary/stiglitz90, August 2007, our emphasis.

29. Robert Boyer, Mario Dehove and Dominique Plihon, "Contemporary financial crises: between newness and repetition," in "Issues in Regulation Theory," April 2005. As Marazzi notes in his contribution to this volume, the bigger crisis that we are experiencing is partially triggered by the declassification of the titles emitted on credit by rating agencies in August 2007, a year after the inversion of the business cycle!

30. For example, see Allen Sinai, chief economist of Decision Economics of New York, interviewed by Eugenia Occorso in "La Repubblica," 21 August 2008, p. 21.

31. Toni Negri has posed a question that I think is necessary to pose here: is the financialization that we are dealing with today, the technical instrument that aims at negating every possibility to accumulate the revolutionary power of cognitive labor and/or autonomous experimentation of the common capability of management? Cf. Antonio Negri, *The Porcelain Workshop: For a New Grammar of Politics*, Semiotext(e), Los Angeles 2008.

32. However, it should be considered that the wealth-effect is a complex phenomenon: the irrationality that supports financial booms, in as much as answers to a convention that is given in the technological paradigm of cognitive capital, gathers in itself the desire of an anthropogenetic model in which the productive power of diffused intellectuality is recognized outside of a logic of exploitation. On the

anthropogenetic model, see chap. 8 in Robert Boyer, *The Future of Economic Growth: As New Becomes Old*, Edward Elgar, Cheltenham 2004.

33. Judith Revel, "Biopolitica: politica della vita vivente," in "Posse, La classe a venire," November 2007, http://www.posseweb.net, [our translation]. The modalities of construction of biopolitics are all open to invention, yet cannot exclude the definition of forms of monetary creation that open democratic spaces and spaces of non-capitalistic valorization of living labor. In that sense, it seems to me that there is an urgent re-elaboration of the theme of basic income, but starting from an attentive confrontation with the scholars of complementary monetary systems. Cf. Luca Fantacci, *La moneta. Storia di un'istituzione mancata*, Marsilio, Padua 2005; cf. Massimo Amato, *Le radici di una fede. Per una storia del rapporto fra moneta e credito in Occidente*, Bruno Mondadori, Milano 2008. The Anglophone reader can refer to Luca Fantacci, "Complementary Currencies: a Prospect on Money from a Retrospect on Premodern Practices," *Financial History Review*, 12, 1, 2005.

On the Threshold of Capital, At the Thresholds of the Common

1. Jean-François Lyotard associated the theme of decadence to capitalism in this sense: "[…] capital doesn't recognize a crisis, in itself it isn't in decadence, but its functioning assumes and brings on decadence, or if you prefer, crisis. Even better, crisis is a condition of its possibility to function" (Jean-François Lyotard, "Piccola messa in prospettiva della decadenza e di alcune lotte minoritarie da condurre," in AA.VV., *Politiche della filosofia*, Sellerio, Palermo 2003, p. 96) [our translation]. In line with these argumentations, even if developed within another interpretative perspective, are the reflections in Luc Boltanski and Eve Chiappello, *The New Spirit of Capitalism*, Verso, London 2007.

2. "In the measure in which the debt-credit relation is imprinted on an unstable dissymmetry—facing the creditor's effectively dominant position, its potential weakness always exists too, due to the risk, fundamentally unforeseeable in itself, of a structural insolvency of the debt holders as a 'class,' and therefore their 'last instance' force of pressure –, it puts into play trust relations which cannot be simply the fruit of a convenient economic calculation, but must be previously put to work, and, in this precise sense, instituted. Since, in its dissymmetry, the debtor-creditor relation is fundamentally uncertain, and therefore risky, various procedures, literally rites, must be put into act; these procedures aimed at stabilizing a system of trust in which only such relations can have an ordinary functioning" (Massimo Amato, *Le radici di una fede. Per una storia del rapporto fra moneta e credito in Occidente*, Bruno Mondatori, Milan 2008, p. 21) [our translation].

3. Michel Aglietta, "Regolazione e crisi del capitalismo," in Michel Aglietta and Giorgio Lunghini, *Sul capitalismo contemporaneo*, Bollati Boringhieri, Turin 2001, p. 16 [our translation].

4. *Ibid.* [our translation].

5. "It is at this level of crisis of the relation between capital and labor—of crisis in the classic separation between productive forces and relations of production and of the following crisis in the governability of civil society—that the financialization of capital comes into play" (Christian Marazzi, "Socialismo del capitale," in AA.VV., *Lessico Marxiano*, Manifestolibri, Rome, 2008, p. 164).

6. Cf. Federico Chicchi, *Lavoro e capitale simbolico. Una ricerca empirica sul lavoro operaio nella società post-fordista*, Franco Angeli, Milan 2003 [our translation].

7. Claudio Napoleoni, "L'enigma del valore," in *Dalla Scienza all'utopia*, Bollati Boringhieri, Turin 1992, p. 128 [our translation].

8. On this topic, other than Carlo Vercellone's most recent contributions on these themes, see Yann Moulier Boutang, "Financiarisation et capitalisme cognitif. Le sens et les problèmes d'une liaison," in Gabriel Colletis and Bernard Poulré (eds.), *Les nouveaux horizons du capitalisme: Pouvoirs, valeurs, temps*, Economica, Paris 2008, pp. 277–294.

9. Cf. Judith Revel, "Identità, natura, vita: tre decostruzioni biopolitiche," in Mario Galzigna (ed.), *Foucault oggi*, Feltrinelli, Milan 2008, pp. 134–149.

10. Christian Marazzi, "Il corpo del valore: bioeconomia e finanziarizzazione della vita," in Adalgiso Amendola, Laura Bazzicalupo, Federico Chicchi and Antonio Tucci (eds.), Biopolitica, *bioeconomia e processi di soggettivazione*, Quodlibet, Macerata 2008, p. 139.

11. Michel Foucault, *Discipline and Punish: The Birth of the Prison*, Vintage, New York 1995, p. 140.

12. Christian Marazzi, "Il corpo del valore," cit. p. 139 [our translation].

13. On the concept of bioeconomy, see: Laura Bazzicalupo, *Il governo delle vite. Biopolitica ed economia*, Laterza, Bari 2006; Andrea Fumagalli, *Bioeconomia e capitalismo cognitivo. Verso un nuovo paradigma di accumulazione*, Carocci, Rome 2007; Federico Chicchi, "Bioeconomia: ambienti e forme della mercificazione del vivente," in Adalgiso Amendola, Laura Bazzicalupo, Federico Chicchi and Antonio Tucci (eds.), *Biopolitica, bioeconomia e processi di soggettivazione*, cit.

14. For an in-depth analysis, see Federico Chicchi, "Capitalismo lavoro e forme di soggettività," in Jean-Louis Laville, Michele La Rosa, Christian Marazzi and Federico Chicchi, *Reinventare il lavoro*, Sapere 2000, Rome 2005, pp. 149–185.

15. Christian Marazzi, *Socialismo del capitale*, cit., p. 164.

16. Naturally, this opens, over time, the problem of the possible interruption of the reproductive processes of the resources of valorization. Maybe this is the densest intrinsic contradiction of post-Fordist capitalism.

17. Cf. Antonio Negri, *The Porcelain Workshop: For a New Grammar of Politics*, Semiotext(e), Los Angeles 2008., p. 68.

18. Carlo Vercellone, "Trinità del capitale," in AA.VV., *Lessico Marxiano*, cit., pp. 181–196.

19. Antonio Negri, "Poteri e sfruttamento: quale nuova articolazione in una prospettiva marxiana?," http://seminaire.samizdat.net/, 2005. This article is, in our opinion, extremely interesting.

20. Antonio Negri, *Dall'operaio massa all'operaio sociale. Intervista sull'operaismo*, ed. by Paolo Pozzi and Roberta Tomassini, ombre corte, Verona 2007, p. 11 [our translation].

21. On this topic, and particularly on the political relevance of the struggles in defense of Susa Valley (Italy), we would like to indicate the text of Emanuele Leonardi, "Il movimento No-Tav in Valle di Susa; dispositivo-grandi opere e fermento soggettivo," in Adalgiso Amendola, Laura Bazzicalupo, Federico Chicchi and Antonio Tucci (eds.), *Biopolitica, bioeconomia e processi di soggettivazione*, cit., pp. 415–424.

22. Judith Revel, "Identità, natura, vita," cit., p. 147 [our translation].

New Economy, Financialization and Social Production in the Web 2.0

1. Cf. John Cassidy, *Dot.con. The Greatest Story Ever Sold*, HarperCollins, New York, 2002.

2. Cf. Fred Turner, *From Counterculture to Cyberculture: Stewart Brand, the Whole Earth Network and the Rise of Digital Utopianism*, Chicago University Press, Chicago, 2008.

3. Douglas Coupland, *JPod*, Bloomsbury, London 2006.

4. Cf. Bill Lessard and Steve Baldwin, *Netslaves. True Tales of Working the Web*, McGraw Inc, New York, 1999; from the same authors, see the successive *Netslaves. Tales of "Surviving" the Great Tech Gold Rush*, Allworth Press, New York, 2003.

5. Cf. Andrew Ross, *No Collar: The Humane Workplace and Its Hidden Costs*, Basic Books, New York, 2004 and Rosalind Gill, *Technobohemians or the New Cybertariat? New media work in Amsterdam a decade after the web*, Institute of network cultures, Amsterdam, 2007.

6. Cf. Bifo, "Abbandonate le illusioni preparatevi alla lotta," 10 October 2002 (http://www.rekombinant.org/old/article.html.sid=1840).

7. Tim O' Reilly, "What Is Web 2.0. Design Patterns and Business Models for the Next Generation of Software," 30 September 2005 (http://www.oreillynet.com/pub/a/oreilly/tim/news/2005/09/30/what-is-web-20.html).

8. Cf. Tiziana Terranova, *Network Culture: Politics for the Information Age*, Pluto Press, London 2004.

9. On protocol control, see Alexander R. Galloway, *Protocol: How Control Exists after Decentralization*, The MIT Press, Cambridge, Mass. 2004.

10. For an ethnography on the externalization of the user as "co-creator" in an Australian dot.com that works in the videogame market, cf. John Banks, "The Labor of User Co-Creators: Emergent Social Network Markets?" in "Convergence: The International Journal of Research into New Media Technologies," vol. 14, n. 4, 401–418 (2008).

11. See the site http://www.tre.it/public/home.php. I'd like to thank Sandro Mezzadra for pointing out this Italian version of the web 2.0 as an externalization of user assistance services to the same user community.

12. For an analysis of participative internet culture and user relations with the media industry, see Henry Jenkins, *Convergence Culture: Where Old and New Media Collide*, NYU Press, New York 2006.

13. Cf. for example Henrik Ingo, Ethics, Freedom and Trust in "Re-public: re-imagining democracy" (http://www.re-public.gr/en/?p=275). On p2p as human evolution, see Michel Bauwens, "Peer to Peer and Human Evolution: Placing Peer to Peer Theory in an Integral Framework" (http://integralvisioning.org/article.php?story=p2ptheory1).

14. Cf. Tiziana Terranova, "Il potere della rete: Intervista a Michel Bauwens," in *il manifesto*, 5 November 2008.

15. Cf. Yochai Benkler, *The Wealth of Networks: How Social Production Transforms Markets and Freedom*, Yale University Press, New Haven 2007. For an effective criticism of the invisible hand as miraculous market harmonizer, see Maurizio Lazzarato, *Puissances de l'invention. La Psychologie économique de Gabriel Tarde contre l'économie politique*, Les empêcheurs de penser en rond, Paris, 2002.

16. Cf. Benkler, *The Wealth of Networks*, cit., for a taxonomy of different levels of participation in network social production.

17. Cf. "The First Disaster of the internet Age" in *Newsweek*, October 2008, http://www.newsweek.com/id/164588.

18. *Ibid.*

19. Cf. Geert Lovink, "Blogging, the nihilist impulse" (http://www.eurozine.com/articles/2007-01-02-lovink-en.html).

20. The "First Disaster of the internet Age," cit.

21. *Ibid.*

22. Cf. Karin Knorr Cetina, "The Market," in *Theory, Culture and Society*, 23 (2006), 2–3 (Problematizing Global Knowledge: Special Issue), pp. 551–556 and

Karin Knorr Cetina and Urs Bruegger, "The Market as an Object of Attachment: Exploring Postsocial Relations in Financial Markets," in "Canadian Journal of Sociology" 25 (2000), 2, pp. 141–168.

23. Karin Knorr Cetina "The Market," cit., p. 551.

24. "The First Disaster of the internet Age," cit.

25. On the chromatic alert system introduced by the Bush administration as a part of a new neoconservative governmentality, see cf. Brian Massumi, "Fear the Spectrum Said," in "Multitudes. Compléments bibliographiques," 23, 4, January 2006 (http://multitudes.samizdat.net/Fear-The-spectrum-said).

26. For an example of an empirical-mathematical study of the "herd" behavior of financial operators aimed at creating better models, see Fabrizio Lillo, Esteban Moro, Gabriella Vaglica and Rosario N. Mantenga, "Specialization and Herding Behaviour of Trading Firms in a Financial Market," in "New Journal of Physics," 10 (2008) (http://www.njp.org/).

27. Nassim Nicholas Taleb, *Fooled by Randomness: the Hidden Role of Chance in Life and Markets*, Penguin, London 2004.

28. For a history on the use of the Monte Carlo simulator in the nuclear physicist community, see cf. Peter Galison, *How Experiments End*, University of Chicago Press, Chicago 1987.

29. Cf Robert J. Shiller, *Irrational Exuberance*, Broadway Business, New York 2006; also Cf. Christian Marazzi, *E il denaro va. Esodo e rivoluzione dei mercati finanziari*, Bollati Borlinghieri, Turin 1998.

30. For a less anecdotal and more rigorously scientific exposition of the culture and sociality of financial operators, see cf. Caitlin Zaloom, *Out of the Pits: Traders and Technology from Chicago to London*, University of Chicago Press, Chicago 2006.

31. Cf. Amanda Gardner, "Testosterone Levels Among Financial Traders Affect Performance: British Study Found Those With More of the Male Hormone in the Morning Made More Money," in *USA News*, 14 April 2008 (http://health.usnews.com/usnews/health/healthday/080414/testosterone-levels-among-financial-traders-affect-performance.htm).

32. In October 2008, *USA Today* recorded a significant shift from the financial sector to the educational sector: cf. Greg Toppo, "Financial Sector's Loss Could Spell Gain for Teaching," in *USA Today*, 16 October 2008 (http://www.usatoday.com/news/education/2008-10-15-meltdown-teachers_N.htm). A similar tendency was seen in England by the *Times Educational Supplement*: cf. Kerra Madera, "Bust Causes Boom in 'Suit Recruits,'" in *Times Educational Supplement*, 23 January 2009 (http://www.tes. co.uk/article.aspx?storycode=6007515).

33. For an example of the first, see cf. John Arquilla and David Ronfeldt, "Networks and Netwars: The Future of Terror, Crime, and Militancy," National Defense Research Institute, 2001. On networks that battle networks, see Antonio Negri and Michael Hardt, *Multitude: War and Democracy in the Age of Empire*, Penguin, New York 2005.

34. Alexander R. Galloway and Eugene Thacker, *The Exploit: A Theory of Networks*, University of Minnesota Press, Minneapolis-London 2007, pp. 21–22.

35. *Ibid.*,p. 82.

36. *Ibid.*,p. 81.

37. http://www.theyesmen.org/. See also the documentary "The Yes Men: Changing the World One Prank at the Time" (2003) and the following "The Yes Men Fix the World" (2009), and the book *The Yes Men, The Yes Men: The True Story of the End of the World Trade Organization*, The Disinformation Company, New York, 2004.

38. Cf. "Cruel $12 Billion Hoax on Bhopal Victims and BBC," in "The Times," 4/12/2004 (http://www.timesonline.co.uk/tol/news/uk/article398896.ece).

39. Cf. Ubermorgen.com, Ludovico and Cirio, "Hack the Google self.referentialism" (http://gwei.org/pages/texts/theory.html).

40. *Ibid.*

41. *Ibid.*

42. *Ibid.*

43. *Ibid.*

44. Cf. their example of a biological and computer virus as examples of exploits in Galloway and Thacker, "The Exploit," cit., pp. 81–97.

Cognitive Capitalism and the Financialization of Economic Systems

The text presented here is a reduced version—as agreed with the author—of "Capitalsme cognitif et finanziarisation de économies," recently published in the volume *Les nouveaux Horizons du capitalisme*, edited by Gabriel Colletis and Bernard Paulré, Economica, Paris 2008. We'd like to thank the editor of Economica that authorized its partial translation from French to Italian by Stefano Lucarelli and its English translation by Jason Francis Mc Gimsey. Revisions by Cosma Orsi.

1. We've used the translation "intellectual activities" for the French expression "activités de l'esprit" knowing that the French version assumes tones that are lost in the English translation [translator's note].

2. Many empirical studies clearly show the increase of immaterial investments and practices of knowledge management over the course of the last twenty years. More than the quantitive importance of this phenomenon, it is its qualitative centrality that attracts our attention. Cf. Bernard Paulré, "Le capitalism cognitif. Une approche schumpéterienne des économies contemporaines," in *Les nouveaux Horizons du capitalisme*, edited by Gabriel Colletis and Bernard Paulré, Economica, Paris 2008.

3. The concept of "major crisis" is typical of the so-called French Regulation School. The anglophone reader can refer to Bob Jessop, *The Regulation Approach, Governance and Post-fordism, Economy and Society*. Blackwell Publishing, 1995; B. Milani, *Designing the Green Economy: The Postindustrial Alternative to Corporate Globalization*. Rowman and Littlefield, 2000.

4. What has just been said can appear to belong to the French Regulation School. Nevertheless, it seems to us that it rather corresponds to a fundamental methodological principle that doesn't necessarily imply a regulationist methodology.

5. An inflection point is a point where—in respect to a given trend—a change in curve or convexity is manifested [translator's note].

6. We are alluding to, among other things, the problem of dialectics and Hegel. Just as pertinent in respect to the point in question are a few typical topics in mathematics, like the "Catastrophe Theory," Stephen Jay Gould Gould's "Apunctuated Equilibria" or the analyses of Ilya Prigogine.

7. Cf. Gilbert Colletis, "Èvolution du rapport salarial, financiarisation et mondialisation," Cahiers du GRES, n. 15, 2004; Gilbert Colletis and alii, "La financiarisation des stratégies: transferts de risque, liquidité, propriété et contrôle," Cahiers du GRES, Paris 2007–09; Laurent Batsch, *Le capitalisme financier*, La Découverte, Paris 2002; Roland Pérez, *La gouvernance de l'entreprise*, La Découverte, Paris 2003.

8. Michel Aglietta, *Le capitalisme de demain*, Fondation Saint-Simon, Paris 1998.

9. Paulré, Bernard, "Le capital-risque aux Ètats-Unis," Rapport pour l'Institut CDC, 2001.

10. On this level of our argument, we share the restlessness typical of post-Keynesian and certain Marxist analyses that we are assuming in a wider version without limiting ourselves to simple governance.

11. Gerald A. Epstein (ed.), *Financialization and the World Economy*, Edward Elgar, 2005.

12. The French term used by the author to express speculative maneuvers in the market is *rotations*.

13. In 2003, George W. Bush proposed the suppression of the double taxation of business profit and decided to lower the taxation on earnings in capital and

dividends to 15% until 2008 (down from 20%). For lower incomes taxes passed from 10% to 5%.

14. Cf. Gilbert Colletis, "Èvolution du rapport salarial, financiarisation et mondialisation," cit. and Gilbert Colletis et alii, *La financiarisation des stratégies*, cit.

15. Cf. Antonio Negri, *The Porcelain Workshop: For a New Grammar of Politics*, Semiotext(e), Los Angeles 2008.

16. Michel Foucault, *The Birth of Biopolitics. Lectures at the Collége de France 1978–1979*, Eng. trans. Palgrave Macmillan, New York 2008.

17. Cf. Bruno Théret, "Ètat, Finance publiques et Régulation," in Robert Boyer and Yves Saillard (eds.), *Théorie de la régulation, l'état des savoirs*, La Découverte, Paris 1995.

18. Less than two months after his nomination to head of the Federal Reserve, Paul Volker sharply raised the tax on federal funds, to the point that real taxes became positive, nearly 3.5%.

19. Cf. André Orlean, *Le pouvoir de la finance*, Odile Jacob, Paris 1999.

20. We are referring to ethical considerations, of durative development, social responsibility, etc.

Global Crisis—Global Proletarianization—Counter-perspectives

As explained in the Introduction of this volume, this text originally appeared (21 December 2008) in the German webszine "Wildcat" (http://www.wildcat-www.de/). This version was revised and edited by Jason Francis Mc Gimsey to include the additions included in the Italian version.

1. Interventionistiche Linke (IL) is a network of collectives, individuals and social movement projects formed in Germany in 2005. IL (to which autonomous and/or "postautonomous" zines, antifascist groups and anti-imperialist collectives belong) was one of the promoters of the mobilizations against the G8 in Heiligendamm in June 2007. See, http://www.dazwischengehen.org/ [translator's note].

2. This is the only institution that deals with bank affairs of both investment and details [translator's note].

3. "Hartz-project" means the whole of reform proposals of the labor market from the "Modern Services for the Labor Market" Commission headed by Peter Hartz. The commission presented its report to the government headed by the social democrat Gerhard Schröder in August 2002. Divided into 4 parts, the Commission's proposals where largely translated into law between 2003 and 2005. The Hartz IV package, entering in vigor in January 2005, entirely reformed social security and unemployment subsidies [translator's note].

4. A reference to the Russian agrarian economist Aleksandr Cajanov (1888–1939), creator of agricultural cooperation and prolific writer [translator's note].

Nothing Will Ever Be the Same

The present text is the fruit of a collective discussion that began with the seminar on the financial crisis organized by UniNomade in Bologna on the 12th and 13th of September 2008 and that still continues today. Marco Bascetta, Federico Chicchi, Andrea Fumagalli, Stefano Lucarelli, Christian Marazzi, Sandro Mezzadra, Cristina Morini, Antonio Negri, Gigi Roggero, Carlo Vercellone all participated while Andrea Fumagalli drafted the text. Translated by Jason Francis Mc Gimsey and revised by Sabrina Del Pico.

1. Here we have taken the citation of Keynes from the last chapter of *General Theory of Employment, Interest and Money*. Palgrave Macmillan, New York 1936, http://www.marxists.org/reference/subject/economics/keynes/general-theory/ch24.htm, "The owner of capital can obtain interest because capital is scarce, just as the owner of land can obtain rent because land is scarce. But whilst there may be intrinsic reasons for the scarcity of land, there are no intrinsic reasons for the scarcity of capital" and we have substituted the term "capital" with the term "knowledge" and the term "interest" with "profit."

2. The Anomalous Wave, or "Onda anomala" in Italian, was a student movement that broke out in the fall of 2008 after a massive funding cut and organizational reform that threatens to privatize public universities. For resources in English see, http://edufactory.org [translator's note].

About the Authors

Federico Chicchi teaches "Sociology of Labor and Organization and Business" in the Department of Political Science at the University of Bologna. He is editor of the editorial series poiesis&praxis, pubished by Sapere2000 and member of the Palea Study Center (Permanent seminary of Psychoanalysis and Social Sciences). His most recent work available in English: "Empirical Analysis of the Risk of Social Exclusion of Long-term Unemployed Young People in Italy" in Thomas Kieselbach, *Living on the edge: an empirical analysis on long-term youth unemployment and social exclusion in Europe*, Leske + Budrich, Germany 2001.

Andrea Fumagalli is Professor of Macroeconomy and Business Theory in the Department of Political Economy and Quantitative Methods in the Department of Economics at the University of Pavia, and Political Economy for the Multimedia Communications course at the same university.

Stefano Lucarelli is Assistant Professor in Political Economy at the Department of Economics, University of Bergamo, Italy, where he teaches International Monetary Economics and Public Finance. He has published articles about the crisis of Welfare State, the basic income hypothesis and cognitive capitalism in "Review of Social Economy" and "European Journal of Economic and Social Systems." Recently, together with Andrea Fumagalli, he has edited the special issue of *European Journal of Economic and Social Systems*, titled "Money and Technology. The Role of Financing in the Process of Evolution."

Christian Marazzi is a professor at the Italian University School of Switzerland. Among his works available from Semiotext(e) are: *Autonomia: Post-Political Politics* in 2007; *Capital And Language: From the New Economy to the War Economy* in 2009 and *Sock's Place*, forthcoming.

Sandro Mezzadra teaches Colonial and Post Colonial Studies and The Frontier of Citizenship at the Department of Political Science at the University of Bologna. Among his most recent publications in English: "Border as Method, or, the Multiplication of Labor," *EIPCP Multilingual Webjournal*, 2008; "Citizen and Subject. A Postcolonial Constitution for the European Union?" in: *Globalization, migration, human rights: a new paradigm for research and citizenship*, Brussels, Bruylant, 2007; "'Property of the Self,' Individual Autonomy and the Modern European Discourse of Citizenship," in: *Autonomy. Beyond Kant and Hermeneutics*, New Delhi, Anthem Press, 2007.

Antonio Negri, ex-professor of Law at the University of Padua, has taught in numerous European universities. His rich theoretical production has been recognized in various international environments. Among his most recent work: *The Porcelain Workshop: For a New Grammar of Politics*, 2008 and, with Michael Hardt, *Commonwealth*, Belknap Press, Cambridge, 2009.

Bernard Paulré is a professor of Economy at the University of Paris 1 Panthéon-Sorbonne and director of the Matisse-ISYS Laboratory. He is the author of numerous papers on the theme of the industrial economy and cognitive capitalism.

Karl Heinz Roth, physician and historian, was one of the most prominent figures of the New Left and German Autonomous Workers in the 1970s. His 1974 book, *The other workers' movement and the development of the capitalistic repression from 1880 to the present*, Trikont publishing house, Munich 1976, is a classic in worker-oriented historiography. His most recent publications include: with Angelika Ebbinghaus (eds.): *Red chapels—Kreisauer of circles—black chapels. New aspects on the resistance against the LV dictatorship 1938–1945*, VSA publishing house 2004; *The Nazi Census: Identification and Control in the Third Reich*, Temple University Press, Philadelphia 2004; and *The condition of the world. Counter perspectives*. VSA publishing house 2005.

Tiziana Terranova teaches the Sociology of Media and Culture in the Department of Sociology at the University of Essex. She has published various pamphlets and essays on digital cultures, in Italian and English.

Carlo Vercellone is Maître de Conférences at the University of Paris 1 Sorbonne and member of the research laboratory Matisse-ISYS. He is the author of numerous papers on the themes of cognitive capitalism and basic income.

SEMIOTEXT(E) Post-Political Politics

AUTONOMIA
Post-Political Politics
Edited by Sylvère Lotringer and Christian Marazzi

Semiotext(e) has reissued in book form its legendary magazine issue *Autonomia: Post-Political Politics*, originally published in New York in 1980. Edited by Sylvère Lotringer and Christian Marazzi with the direct participation of the main leaders and theorists of the Autonomist movement (including Antonio Negri, Mario Tronti, Franco Piperno, Oreste Scalzone, Paolo Virno, Sergio Bologna, and Franco Berardi), this volume is the only first-hand document and contemporaneous analysis that exists of the most innovative post-'68 radical movement in the West.

7 x 10 • 340 pages • ISBN: 978-1-58435-053-8 • $25.95

CAPITAL AND LANGUAGE
From the New Economy to the War Economy
Christian Marazzi, translated by Gregory Conti
Introduction by Michael Hardt

Capital and Language takes as its starting point the fact that the extreme volatility of financial markets is generally attributed to the discrepancy between the "real economy" (that of material goods produced and sold) and the more speculative monetary-financial economy. But this distinction has long ceased to apply in the postfordist New Economy, in which both spheres are structurally affected by language and communication. Marazzi points to capitalism's fourth stage (after mercantilism, industrialism, and the postfordist culmination of the New Economy): the "War Economy" that is already upon us.

6 x 9 • 180 pages • ISBN: 978-1-58435-067-5 • $14.95

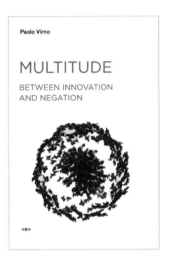

Paolo Virno

MULTITUDE

BETWEEN INNOVATION
AND NEGATION

<8>

MULTITUDE BETWEEN INNOVATION AND NEGATION

Paolo Virno, Translated by Isabella Bertoletti, James Cascaito, and Andrea Casson

Multitude between Innovation and Negation offers three essays that take the reader on a journey through the political philosophy of language.

"Wit and Innovative Action" explores the ambivalence inevitably arising when the semiotic and the semantic, grammar and experience, rule and regularity, and right and fact intersect. "Mirror Neurons, Linguistic Negation, and Mutual Recognition" examines the relationship of language and intersubjective empathy: without language, would human beings be able to recognize other members of their species? And finally, in "Multitude and Evil," Virno challenges the distinction between the state of nature and civil society and argues for a political institution that resembles language in its ability to be at once nature and history.

6 x 9 • 200 pages • ISBN: 978-1-58435-050-7 • $14.95

Antonio Negri

THE PORCELAIN
WORKSHOP

FOR A NEW GRAMMAR OF POLITICS

<8>

THE PORCELAIN WORKSHOP
For a New Grammar of Politics
Antonio Negri, Translated by Noura Wedell

In 2004 and 2005, Antonio Negri held ten workshops at the Collège International de Philosophie in Paris to formulate a new political grammar of the postmodern. Biopolitics, biopowers, control, the multitude, people, war, borders, dependency and interdependency, state, nation, the common, difference, resistance, subjective rights, revolution, freedom, democracy: these are just a few of the themes Negri addressed in these experimental laboratories.

Postmodernity, Negri suggests, can be described as a "porcelain workshop": a delicate and fragile construction that could be destroyed through one clumsy act. Looking across twentieth century history, Negri warns that our inability to anticipate future developments has already placed coming generations in serious jeopardy.

6 x 9 • 224 pages • ISBN: 978-1-58435-056-9 • $17.95